A New Science

A New Science

THE DISCOVERY OF RELIGION
IN THE AGE OF REASON

Guy G. Stroumsa

HARVARD UNIVERSITY PRESS

Cambridge, Massachusetts

London, England

2010

Library of Congress Cataloging-in-Publication Data
Stroumsa, Guy G.
  A new science : the discovery of religion in the Age of Reason / Guy G. Stroumsa.
    p. cm.
  Includes bibliographical references and index.
  ISBN 978-0-674-04860-7 (alk. paper)
  1. Religion—Study and teaching—Europe—History. 2. Enlightenment. I. Title.
BL41.S73   2010
200.71—dc22   2009044453

CONTENTS

The religious explosion of the present day, with the urgency of its immediate threats, has taken us by surprise. This explosion was quite unforeseen by the great minds of the twentieth century and has found us intellectually unprepared. Neither radical Islamism nor Christian fundamentalism in their various garbs nor similarly threatening violent trends among members of other religious communities, be they Jews, Hindus, Buddhists, or worshippers of Mother Earth, seem to have been adequately understood by contemporary students of religious phenomena. *Tantum religio potuit suadere malorum (so potent was religion in persuading to evil deeds):* Lucretius's *obiter dictum,* which Montaigne found, in his *Apology of Raymond Sebon,* to be painfully relevant in his day, remains no less true in our own time. The next generation of scholars and intellectuals should therefore strive to offer new interpretive patterns to help us better understand the dangerous world we live in. To find our way in still uncharted territory, a better understanding of the origins of the modern comparative study of religions may be of significance.

Until recently, the scholarly study of religions, variously called Comparative Religion, *histoire des religions,* or *Religionswissenschaft,* seemed to be a branch of scholarship that had passed its prime. After the naïve confidence of late-nineteenth-century historicism, which sought to reconstruct religious history beyond the affirmations of orthodoxies, the pretensions of religious phenomenology before and after the Second World War (from Gerardus vand der Leeuw to Mircea Eliade) claimed to identify a perennial *homo religiosus* beyond the various historical and cultural conditions. Intellectual discomfort with both the explicit vagueness and implicit dangers of this phenomenological inclusivism grew and seemed for a while to sound the dirge of ambitious comparative studies of religious phenomena, past and present. In our generation, historians of religions have increasingly become historians of, at most, one religion. Gone are the days of encompassing theories and of daring comparative studies. The more one invokes interdisciplinary studies, the less one seems to practice that dangerous sport. Safe scholarship, with clearly defined boundaries, not to be trespassed, and with no threat of unexpected results, has become the name of the game. But the new, or newly perceived, immediate challenges compel us to renounce this epistemological timidity. We must urgently find new tools to understand religion, if only to confront its current threats to our societies. A way to developing such new tools, I argue, can be found in the long-forgotten beginnings of the discipline.

It is in this context that the present book inscribes itself. Its main argument is that the modern science of religion was not born, as is usually thought, in the second half of the nineteenth century, when the first Chairs dedicated to the general and comparative study of religious phenomena were established in Western European universities (the first such Chair was established in Geneva in 1873). I shall argue that one must rather go back to the age of reason, broadly defined (the long Enlightenment, from 1600 to 1800), to witness the birth of the modern comparative study of religious phenomena. This birth followed nothing less than the early modern implosion of the very concept of religion. Although seventeenth- and eighteenth-century intellectual history is well-known territory, and although a great number of excellent studies and monographs have been written on almost all aspects of the phenomena analyzed in this book, its overall thesis does not seem to have yet been clearly stated. To be sure, any chronological boundaries must remain artificial, as the course of science and scholarship is a continuum. Important contributions to the study of religion, such as those of Vincenzo Cartari, Paolo Morigi, or Johannes Boemus, were made in the sixteenth century. And yet, some periods testify to a special fecundity and reflect the crystallization of new concepts, the blossoming of new questions. From Pinard de la Boullaye through Eric Sharpe to Hans-Georg Kippenberg, whose *Discovering Religious History in the Modern Age* originally appeared in German in 1997, scholars have usually argued that the second half of the nineteenth century saw the most dramatic development in the modern study of religion. My claim here, rather, is that the period between Renaissance and Romanticism is the crucial one in European intellectual history for the first emergence and early formation of the modern study of religion. It is then that a new paradigm of religion was constituted, a paradigm that permitted an intellectual revolution.

This book, devoted to a major yet somewhat understudied aspect of early modern intellectual history, should be seen as an epistemological reflection on the very roots of the modern study of religion. As far as I can remember, it finds its origin in a footnote. In *Les langues du paradis: Aryens et sémites: un couple providentiel* (*The Languages of Paradise: Race, religion, and philology in the nineteenth century*) (Paris: Seuil, 1984; English translation [Cambridge, Mass.: Harvard University Press, 1992]), Maurice Olender's reference to Richard Simon's French translation and publication of the work of the Venetian Rabbi Leone Modena caught my attention. Simon's appendix, in the second edition, from 1684, struck me as representing, perhaps, the first nonpolemical comparative study of Judaism and Christianity. My interest in Simon's and Modena's texts resulted in their new publication, which I prepared together with Jacques Le Brun, *Les juifs présentés aux chrétiens: textes de Léon de Modène et de Richard Simon* (Paris: Les Belles Lettres, 1998).

The research for this book, over the years, was conducted in a number of libraries in Israel, Europe, and the United States, mainly during summers and sabbaticals, and side by side with my "staple" work on religions of late antiquity, a fact which explains its long gestation. Over the years, I have also had the opportunity to lecture in various institutions. To them all, I should like to express my gratitude.

In 1998, I was honored to be invited to give the Boutwood Lectures at Corpus Christi College, Cambridge. I was also invited to give a series of seminars at the Ecole Pratique des Hautes Etudes (Section des Sciences Religieuses; in 1997), at the Ecole des Hautes Etudes en Sciences Sociales (in 2008), at the Istituto San Carlo in Modena (in 2001), at the Istituto di Studi Avanzati of Bologna University, at the Getty Center in Los Angeles (in 2007), and at the Princeton Institute for Advanced Study (in 2008).

Among the libraries I used (many years before I was offered a Professorship at Oxford), I should mention the Cambridge University Library, the Archiginnasio and the Istituto di Scienze Religiose in Bologna, the Bibliothèque Mazarine in Paris, the Biblioteca Nacional and that of the Consejo Superior de Investigaciones Cientificas in Madrid, Houghton Library at Harvard, Van Pelt Library and that of the Center for Advanced Judaic Studies at the University of Pennsylvania, Firestone Library at Princeton, the Research Library of the Getty Center, and the Library of the Ecole Biblique et Archéologique Française and the Jewish National and University Library (now the National Library of Israel), both in Jerusalem. Editing the third issue of the *Archiv für Religionsgeschichte* (2001), together with Jan

Assmann, on the study of religion in the seventeenth century, did much to put me on the track of the complex problem at hand.

Insitutions are nothing without those who animate them. Many colleagues, students, and friends invited me to lecture, hosted me, or gave their time to conversations that have helped me a great deal in formulating, reformulating, correcting, erasing, and fashioning anew many of the ideas in this book. Among them, I should like to mention, with particular thanks, Jan Assmann, Aziz Al-Azmeh, Silvia Berti, Corinne Bonnet, Philippe Borgeaud, Hubert Cancik, Hildegard Cancik-Lindemaier, Patricia Crone, Yacov Deutsch, Giovanni Filoramo, Carlo Ginzburg, Anthony Grafton, Alastair Hamilton, Michael Heyd, William Horbury, Jonathan Israel, Maurice Kriegel, François Laplanche, Jacques Le Brun, Sabine MacCormack, Joseph Mali, Winhand Mijnhard, Jack Miles, Peter Miller, Martin Mulsow, John Scheid, Zur Shalev, Mark Silk, Jan Szemiski, and Zwi Werblowsky.

I owe a special debt of gratitude to Sharmila Sen at Harvard University Press, for her swiftness and kindness in accepting the proposal for this book and in dealing with its production at various stages, as well as to the judicious and detailed remarks of the two anonymous readers.

I wish to thank James A. T. Lancaster for having agreed to prepare the index, and having accomplished this task with celerity and intelligence. Doron B. Cohen has kindly picked up many typos in the proofs. Last but not least, Maayan Liebrecht invested considerable effort in editing the manuscript, with great intelligence and *doigté*, to avoid various repetitions, infelicities, and mistakes. She put me very much in her debt, and I hope that she will in the future put her gifts to better use, by publishing her own research.

To all of them, I am deeply grateful. They have shown me what scholarly friendship and generosity can be.

It is no mere formula to state that this book would not have been written without my wife Sarah's persisting requests through many years that I neither give up nor satisfy myself with a dispersed series of focused studies. The least I can do is to dedicate this book to her, as a token of gratitude and love, as well as to our grandchildren, Yotam and Yaïr, with the wish that they may grow in a world less divided and scorched by conflicting religious identities than today.

A New Science

Introduction:

The Study of Religion as Cultural Criticism

Jean Bodin, a bold thinker and harbinger of modernity who died in 1596, could still retain the medieval taxonomy of religions and speak (under the name of Fridericus, one of the characters of his *Heptaplomeres*) "of the four kinds of religions, namely, those of the Jews, Christians, Ismaelites, and pagans."[1] At the time, Spanish missionaries as well as various travelers had started to circulate reports on the religious customs of the peoples they met, from the Indians of New Spain and Peru to those of India, as well as the Chinese, Turks, and Persians. Such works, however, had yet to have their full impact on the transformation of categories through which European intellectuals, both Catholic and Protestant, perceived the religions of humankind. While the multiplicity of mores throughout the world had already begun to register—a case in point is Montaigne's famous essay "On Cannibals"—new categories that could deal effectively with this recently discovered complexity were still to be formulated.

To be sure, the late sixteenth century had seen a series of daring publications, which opened new vistas on the religions of humankind, past and present. Already in 1571, Vincenzo Cartari had published in Venice, one of the *plaques tournantes* of Europe, his iconogaphic study of Greek and Roman deities, *Le imagini dei dei de gli antichi, nelle quali si contengono gl'idoli, riti, ceremonie, e altre cose appartenenti alla religione de gli antichi*. Cartari also published a work called, in the Renaissance fashion, *Theatrum*, a synoptic presentation, as it were, of all "idolatrous cults" of antiquity, including a description of their temples, sacrifices, idols, rituals, and "ceremonies."[2]

Another milestone in the early days of the modern study of religion, Johannes Boemus's *Mores, leges, et ritus omnium gentium,* was first published in Augsburg in 1520. This book, which would go through forty-seven editions in a century and would soon be translated to Italian, French,

English, Spanish, and German, dealt with the cultures of various parts of the Old World, from Ethiopia and Egypt to Persia and India, tackling also northern countries such as Poland, Russia, Lithuania, Bohemia, and Germany.[3] It showed no arrogance vis-à-vis exotic cultures, but rather approached them with sheer intellectual curiosity. Such works, however, were still rare.

Attempts to legitimize the newly discovered cults had already started with the works of some of the Catholic missionaries to the American Indians, such as the Dominican Bartolomé de Las Casas (1474–1566), and somewhat later, the Jesuit José de Acosta (1540–1600).[4] To better understand odd practices and beliefs, they often compared these rituals and myths with those they knew, in particular from ancient Israel and the religions of Greece and Rome.[5] One should stress that in the works of the Spanish *frailes,* comparisons of Greek and Roman paganism with that of America usually turned to the disadvantage of ancient paganism. It should be obvious that such rather primitive comparative approaches can in no way be considered religiously neutral.[6] The missionaries never forgot the ultimate goal of their endeavors. But the practice of comparison, by its very nature, brings at least some fresh open-mindedness and induces a modicum of distance vis-à-vis one's own religious tradition, which starts being perceived from outside and is now judged to be, to some extent, a matter of custom, ruled by historical contingencies. Moreover, I do not wish to argue that the discovery of New World religions was the central factor in the establishment of the new "scholarly" interest in religious phenomena. Rather, my claim here is that the intellectual and religious shock caused by the observation of formerly all-but-unknown religious rituals and beliefs in the Americas and Asia provided the trigger without which the new discipline could not have been born.

A century later, things would have changed radically in some ways. Starting in the 1820s, the first modern multivolume encyclopedia of the world's religions, *The Ceremonies and Religious Customs of the Various Nations of the Known World,* with the famous engravings of Bernard Picart, was published in French and in English.[7] This remarkable achievement was only made possible thanks to a full library of monographs and synthetic studies. These studies, which started to appear in the sixteenth century, were published in more significant numbers throughout the seventeenth century. A genuine revolution in knowledge and attitudes had taken place, which in turn allowed a radical transformation in the perception of religious phenomena. The dramatic events of the sixteenth century were only now having their full impact. The newly discovered continents and cultures were slowly becoming part of the "cultural landscape," or what the French call the *imaginaire,* of European intellectuals. Books were now printed in classical or "exotic" languages, such as Hebrew or Arabic, and the world of European Christendom had been torn asunder. This new knowledge of the diverse religions practiced around the world entailed the urgent need to redefine religion as a universal phenomenon, with a strong emphasis on ritual, rather than on beliefs. It is this paradigmatic change that we will seek to better understand in the following pages.

The "Age of Reason," as in the title of this book, can refer to the seventeenth century, which saw the development of the great philosophical systems of those we call "the rationalist philosophers," such as Descartes, Malebranche, Spinoza, and Leibniz. It can equally refer to the eighteenth century and the application of reason to social structures by the intellectual leaders of the Enlightenment, those thinkers traditionally referred to as the "philosophes," from Bayle to Diderot, Rousseau and Voltaire. Pierre Chaunu has argued that while the seventeenth and nineteenth centuries saw bursts of creativity, the eighteenth century mainly witnessed the assimilation of earlier discoveries and the preparation for coming ones.[8] In this sense, the works and trends analyzed here deal with both the era of invention and that of synthesis.

"A New Science" quite obviously echoes the title of Giambattista Vico's magnum opus. This similarity is meant to signal that *La scienza nuova,* first published in 1724, is itself a central witness to the birth of comparative religion, a science of which Vico thought he had discovered the essential principles. *La scienza nuova* is not usually seen in direct relationship to the comparative study of religion. The failure to connect the two reflects, to my mind, a category mistake. When Vico, like others during the Enlightenment, speaks of *mitologia,* he does not refer to what we call today mythology, but rather, more broadly, to the comparative study of religion. That he oddly excludes from his worldwide inquiry the tradition of Israel, together with Christianity, should not mislead us. Whatever his reasons for limiting so seriously the scope, and hence the value, of his work might have been (and one should not underestimate the differences in intellectual climate and freedom between Naples and Europe north of the Alps in the first half of the eighteenth century), he was searching for fundamental principles to explain the history of religions in ancient societies. In this sense, Vico was a man of his time. The publication year of *La scienza nuova* was an *annus mirabilis* of sorts, as it also saw the publication of the Jesuit Joseph-François Lafitau's *Customs of the American Indians Compared with the Customs of Primitive Times,* a book which has been acclaimed (at least in the French-speaking world) as the founding study of modern social anthropology, and Bernard Fontenelle's seminal *De l'origine des fables.*[9] Despite the highlighted curtsey to Vico (1668–1744), I have no intention of adding yet another book to the continually potent stream of Vicoan studies. Rather, I intend to deal with the views developed in some of the books in Vico's library. Indeed, many of the authors discussed in the following pages are among those whom Paolo Rossi has called "Vico's great interlocutors."[10] They played an essential role in the formation of his ideas and are mentioned at the start of *La scienza nuova.* Vico himself did not work directly as a scholar of religious phenomena, either as a philologist or as an anthropologist, but rather as a philosopher of religious history and myth, making great use of the newly accumulating knowledge. Moreover, Vico's attitude in refraining from dealing with the biblical tradition and his insistence that both ancient Israelite religion and Christianity remained untouched by *mythopoiesis* make him almost irrelevant to many of the topics dealt with below, as it is one of the main arguments of this book that the study of the Bible was central to the birth of comparative religion in early modernity.

If 1724 stands more or less at the center of our investigation, we must start much earlier, with the seventeenth century, and should end with the eighteenth century. In 1614, the year of his death, the great philologist Isaac Casaubon published, in London, where he was living at the time, *De rebus sacris et ecclesiasticis exercitationes XVI.* Using rigorous philological arguments, Casaubon demonstrated in this work the late date and pseudepigraphical nature of the *Corpus Hermeticum.* Dame Frances Yates has called the publication of *De rebus sacris et ecclesiasticis* a watershed, separating the modern age from the Renaissance.[11] According to Yates, Casaubon's work definitively tore down the Renaissance holistic conception of religious history, to make room for the historical and critical approach to ancient texts and hence the early history of religious and philosophical ideas. Thus, as we shall see, the new paradigm for studying religious phenomena, past and present, was born from the scholarly endeavors of the early seventeenth century. To be sure, great minds produced valuable work on religious traditions before and after our period. But a new science is constituted by a series of individuals, acting in a particular context. And this context must be overdetermined and offer a set of reasons that, combined, transform individual oddities into a collective activity.

At the end of the eighteenth century, in the aftermath of the French Revolution and the short-lived *culte de l'Être suprême,* Charles Dupuis' multivolume *L'origine de tous les cultes,* which sought to interpret all religious traditions as so many transformations of an original cult of the sun, marks the end of our inquiry.[12] Soon afterward, Friedrich Schlegel's 1807 *Über die Sprache und Weisheit der Indier* would usher in a strikingly different era for the study of religions, one well anchored in a new philological *rigueur.*

This book explores the epistemological foundations of the new cognitive structures invented for understanding religious phenomena, at the dawn of the modern age.[13] In his magisterial recent book on the conditions and nature of religion in the modern world, *A Secular Age,* Charles Taylor insists that the very idea of religion in 1500 (in Western Europe) was strikingly different from what it is in 2000.[14] Through a series of case studies, I shall try to show here that the birth of the modern study of religion reflects nothing less than an intellectual revolution. This revolution offered a new understanding of religion that had no real precedent in the Middle Ages or during the Renaissance. In this sense, the birth of the modern comparative history of religions can be called the *discovery* of religion.

Intellectual revolutions, however, are not born from a big bang. At least three major historical events were necessary for the emergence of the modern approach to religious phenomena. The first was the Great Discoveries, initially of the Americas and then South and East Asia, which provided the laboratories where new categories were invented by Spanish and Italian missionaries to describe and analyze hitherto unknown phenomena. Without the discoveries, the peoples and religions of the New and Old worlds would have remained unknown and hence a new approach to religion, unnecessary. The second major event was the Renaissance itself, or rather some of its direct consequences, such as the new interest in antiquity and the growth of modern philology. The latter two permitted the study of classical and oriental languages and brought the publication of major texts from different cultures. The wars of religion that devastated significant parts of Western Europe in the wake of the Reformation provided the third impetus for the new science. For many scholars, Catholic and Protestant, the claim of their own faith to express divine truth had lost much of its persuasive force. The violent and painful divisions of Christendom had cast doubt on the validity of Christianity itself. As anyone could see, the Turks, those followers of the "false prophet" Muhammad, showed a much more tolerant attitude toward Christian, Jewish, and sectarian "outsiders" than did Christian authorities toward "outsiders" throughout Europe. This questioning of one's own Christian faith, with its universal pretensions, was a major incentive toward the new understanding of religions as reflecting, rather than perennial truth, the values of the specific society in which they blossomed.

The first to correctly identify a crisis was the French intellectual historian Paul Hazard, who in 1935 published his decisive *La crise de la conscience européenne, 1680–1715*—a complex title overly simplified in its English rendering, *The European Mind*.[15] In this work, Hazard identified the last two decades of the seventeenth century and the first of the eighteenth as a period of "crisis," of the breakdown of old conceptions and emergence of new ones that produced the Enlightenment. Jonathan Israel has recently argued that one should date the start of the "crisis" earlier, around the mid-seventeenth century.[16] The difference between the views of Hazard and Israel need not concern us here, as it may be largely a matter of definition, rooted in how broadly one characterizes the crisis in question. Let us note only that Hazard's identification of a major crisis in European culture was published at a time when various radical movements were sweeping European countries, paving the way to the Second World War. Indeed, that very year, Edmund Husserl delivered in Vienna the lectures that formed the basis of his *Krisis in den europäischen Wissenschaften und die transcendentale phänomenologische Philosophie*.[17] A crisis in culture reflects the collapse of old paradigms and permits the establishment of new ones. The comparative approach to religious phenomena, born of the crisis in European consciousness, created the first modern phenomenological approach to religious phenomena—an approach that would become best known in the 1930s through the work of Dutch scholar Gerardus van der Leeuw.

Hazard provided a magisterial analysis of the intellectual changes that shaped the "Republic of Letters" at the passage from the classical age to the Enlightenment. Just as religious ideas were undergoing deep transformations when modern science was born, so, in a different register, was the intellectual approach to religious questions. This was the case among Catholics and Protestants across most of Europe, but particularly in the

Netherlands, Switzerland, France, and England. The blurb on the back of the 1964 Penguin edition of *The European Mind* reads,

> Paul Hazard conveyed all the excitement—and much of the detail—of what he saw as the most significant single revolution in human thought: the birth of Newtonian science and of comparative religion: the impact of Descartes and Bayle, Newton and Locke, Spinoza and Leibniz; the creation of *our* world.[18]

A generation before Michel Foucault's *Les mots et les choses: Une archéologie des sciences humaines* (*Words and Things: An Archeology of Human Sciences*) was published in 1966, Hazard was able to identify in that period the birth of the human sciences.[19] He also recognized that among the new sciences and disciplines emerging from the crisis of European consciousness, one should include a new approach to religion. Together with the discovery of the New World, the discovery of chronology, of the parallel histories of ancient civilizations, permitted a hitherto unknown conception of the unity of humankind. Beyond the multiple forms of religion, including the most barbarian forms of idolatry, such as the human sacrifices practiced by some American peoples, all religions reflected the unity of humankind. As the Dominican friar Bartolomé de las Casas—a man whose encyclopedic vision of the world's religions remains stunning—would say, "Idolas colere humanum est" (idol worship is human).[20] In this sense too, one can legitimately speak of "the discovery of religion," as it was beyond the multiplicity of religion's historical and cultural forms, and into the essence of religion, that scholars would now start to inquire. In earlier times, religion had remained a binary concept, centered on the Augustinian opposition between *vera* and *falsa religio*. Together with the devaluation of Christianity, both implicit and explicit, the discovery of so many and so different forms of religion permitted, paradoxically, the development of a single concept of religion. Henceforth, religion would be perceived, primarily, as a central aspect of any society, endowed with a different function in each. Religion had become part of humankind's collective identity, and the study of religions would see, gradually, intellectual curiosity overtake polemical animus—although this remains, alas, a never-ending process.

Wilfred Cantwell Smith noted in *The Meaning and End of Religion*, more than a generation ago, the major changes that the concept of religion underwent in the aftermath of the Reformation, as religion became increasingly identified with a system of beliefs and practices.[21] It is a pity that Smith's insights were not fully carried through and seem to have had little impact on scholarship. *Vera religio,* since Augustine's day, was indeed represented through a series of correct actions, both personal and public. It was, however, essentially a personal attitude, the right belief, the correct understanding of the Christian *mysterium.* Whereas heresies were perceived as a multiplicity of ugly movements, or medusa heads, to use Irenaeus's metaphor, orthodoxy was characterized not only by unity but also by interiority. The Reformation was to break this deeply ingrained perception. Polemics between Protestants and Catholics raged more over rituals and outward forms of piety than over belief itself. The polemics on Christian rituals must be seen in the context of the uncertainty created by the discovery of so many odd forms of ritual, observed throughout the world, before one could read the texts and understand the etiological myths that permitted the contextualization of these rituals, or "cults." In the constant pendulum between what one says and what one does in religion, the seventeenth century gave preference to acts, *dromena,* while the following century would witness the turn to the underlying words, *legomena.*

In a recent book, I argued that a series of major transformations in the very concept of religion can be discerned in late antiquity: from the suppression of blood sacrifices to the new central role of books in religious identity and ritual. The victory of Christianity entailed not only the passage from polytheism to monotheism but also the radical transformation of the very concept of religion, which included its internalization.[22] In modern times, the medieval concept of religion, with its late antique roots, would be ushered out. This book investigates the implications of this transformation for the modern comparative study of religions.

Although secularization is a striking and obvious characteristic of modernity, its implications for the study of religion are not commonly understood. We readily acknowledge the role played by biblical criticism, as first undertaken by Richard Simon and Spinoza, in the fast erosion of revealed religion in Western European countries. Much less well known, however, are the contemporary efforts by a long list of scholars, both Protestant and Catholic, to describe and analyze religious phenomena across the world and throughout history, as adequately as possible. The secularization of modern times is usually seen as having permitted, or imposed, a privatization of religion, together with religion's progressive disappearance from the public space. Religion now became more and more the affair of the individual, whose choices need no longer be shared by the whole community. This is certainly true. But it is as true, although less commonly recognized, that secularization also transformed religion into a major facet of any society. In that sense, ethnology would now replace theology on the front stage of the study of religion. From the individual's point of view, religion was now privatized, meaning that one was free to choose among different possibilities of religious—or, for that matter, nonreligious—behavior. The development of religious toleration, thanks to its great advocates from Locke to Lessing, would become one of the main benefits of this privatization. From the point of view of religious scholarship, however, the progressive weakening of Christian revelation as the only form of truth meant the opposite: in all cases religion should be studied, rather, as an individual endeavor, but within its social context.

Throughout history, since the great figures of Karl Jaspers's "axial age,"—Zarathustra, the prophets of Israel, the Buddha, and the Greek philosophers—any reflection on religion has also been a *Kulturkritik*.[23] Reflecting on religion entails a certain distancing from current religious beliefs and religious practice, even on the part of theologians, who in principle write on their tradition as insiders. The early modern study of religion is no exception to this rule. Its close connection to the critique of Christianity, by both Catholic and Protestant practitioners, is too obvious to need elaboration. What is less obvious, however, is that this new science was born from the relationship between Catholic and Protestant intellectuals. Neither the Catholic missionaries playing ethnologists nor the Protestant theologians turned philologists would have been able, by themselves, to assert the premises upon which the modern comparative study of religion is established. This book will hopefully shed some light on the dialectical process between them.

Indeed, this dialectical process took place between not only Catholic and Protestant intellectuals but also two kinds of scholarship. On the one hand, were missionaries groping to understand the language and mores of those they were seeking to convert, who discovered, almost unwillingly, the principles of ethnology. On the other hand, were philologists studying various oriental languages and learning to appreciate, sometimes despite themselves, the content of the texts they were trying to edit and translate. From Las Casas to Lafitau, the Catholic missionaries to the New World were establishing, at least implicitly, some of the principles of social anthropology. One can also say, moreover, that the modern study of religion, comparative by nature, involves by necessity a complex

9

mixture of philology and ethnology, in the analysis of both sacred acts and sacred words. If the religious world of contemporary savages is similar to that of ancient pagans, then comparison is not only possible, legitimate, and necessary between similar or comparable texts, such as the Bible and the Koran, but also between what ancient texts and contemporary mores teach us, when studied together.

I have referred above to a new paradigm of religion and to cultural criticism. While freethinkers, such as François de la Mothe le Vayer (1588–1672), showed a great interest in the comparison of pagan and Christian myths and rituals, with the aim of demoting the latter, early modern scholarship on religion remained, by and large, an enterprise of Christian believers.[24] The intellectuals and scholars with whom we will deal here were no freethinkers, but rather "enlightened" Christians. Intellectual curiosity about religious traditions different from their own (including Christian heresies) permitted them to overcome, to some extent, religious and theological prejudice, and to quiet polemical instincts. As enlightened Christians, they were all critical of various forms of religion, past and present, and able to recognize similarities, both in structure and content, between rituals and beliefs from different religious traditions, including their own. In that sense, Vico, who draws a hermetically sealed border between the tradition of Israel and its Christian sequel on the one hand, and all other traditions on the other, is strikingly out of tune with the attitude of most contemporary intellectuals and scholars.

That the modern comparative study of religion was born in Christian milieus is not only due to the fact that the dawn of modernity occurred in Western Europe. As Max Müller saw so well, Christianity itself was particularly fit to become the humus of such a development:

> In no religion was there a soil so well prepared for the cultivation of Comparative Theology as our own. The position which Christianity from the very beginning took up with regard to Judaism, served as the first lesson in comparative theology, and directed the attention even of the unlearned to a comparison of two religions . . . [25]

Comparative religion is still too often perceived as having been born, like other comparative sciences, in the second half of the nineteenth century, under the influence of biology, in particular of Cuvier's comparative anatomy and Darwin's evolutionary theory.[26] Such a perception must be strongly qualified. The real breakthrough in comparing cultures and religions and the most significant passage from the medieval worldview, still represented by Bodin, to modern approaches, stems from the seventeenth-century transformation of discourse on religion.[27] A few scholars, both Catholic and Protestant, then learned to recognize, although in different ways and from different perspectives, the multiplicity of observable religions, past and present. Eventually, comparison, no longer mainly perceived as a polemical tool, would rather be used to recognize the irreducibility of differences, as well as the similarities between cults and beliefs, ancient and modern, from near and afar.

Meanwhile, some form of unity was provided through all this diversity, mainly thanks to the traditional concept of natural religion—a concept inherited from medieval and ultimately from ancient philosophy. It was natural religion, permeating the multiplicity of rituals and beliefs, which retained the unity of humankind. As we shall see, however, the appeal to natural religion would eventually become a powerful instrument in the hands of those who sought to undermine adherence to Christian supremacy, as it presupposed an identical approach to all observed religious rituals, irrespective of their beliefs. Even in its strangest or most objectionable forms, such as human sacrifices, religion could now be perceived as reflecting natural religion and even a powerful religious faith. That clearly dealt a serious blow to the idea of revelation.

One should seek, then, to understand more precisely the conditions under which the modern study of religion first appeared and grew. The main question lies in identifying the kind of discourse that made its birth possible.[28] As we have seen, the profound transformation of scholarly *western* approaches to the religions of humankind and to the phenomenon of religion itself that occurred between the Renaissance and the Enlightenment must be seen in the context of the three major phenomena referred to above. The great discoveries, the birth of modern philology, and the wars of religion deeply transformed intellectual and religious attitudes. It is only the joint effects of these three distinct phenomena that would permit the formation of a new kind of intellectual *curiositas* and the birth of comparative religion. This last point is essential. As Edward Said has shown in his book *Orientalism*, the birth of orientalism in France and England, for instance, is certainly related to imperialist designs and attitudes.[29] But this is true only to a certain extent. What Said did not see, and what too many forget or fail to remark, is that for scholars to invest so much energy throughout their lives in the study of difficult languages, abstruse mythologies, and odd literatures, they must be inspired by intense intellectual curiosity. Such intellectual curiosity goes a long way toward

11

transforming traditional perceptions and patterns of thought. Crossing all traditional boundaries—ethnic, cultural, religious, or ideological—intellectual curiosity provides a necessary condition for the blooming of "la science pour la science."

The heroes of our story all had personal stakes in their research. And yet, it would be misleading to think that their lack of disengaged objectivity entailed a deeply flawed method and to deny that their work has real scientific value. One of the claims of this book is that thanks to their deep personal involvement with the subject of their inquiry, they developed some sympathy for those whose beliefs they were studying. Their intellectual curiosity, therefore, permitted them to overcome, at least to some extent, their personal attitudes and prejudices. To be sure, the idea of scientific objectivity, which is always problematic in the humanities, is all the more so in a field as complex, as fraught with deeply engrained personal attitudes and beliefs, as the study of religion. Whether scholars of religion are ever able to develop a completely *wertfrei* (value-free) approach to the phenomena they study, either within or without their own tradition, remains a moot point. But we deal here with the inception of the secularization process, at the time of the discovery of American and Asian civilizations. In the study of all cultures and religions involved—from those of the native Americans to those of the Jews, from those of the Muslim world, of India, China, and Japan—European Christians could not be devoid of old and engrained prejudices and were often moved by the temptations of imperialism. The snares of colonialism would only come later.

It is not only due to a greater cultural and linguistic familiarity on my part that the following chapters devote much space to the early study of ancient Israelite religion and of Judaism, as well as to that of biblical mythology and of the other "Abrahamic religions." As we shall see, reflection on and around the Bible, and the religious phenomena this reflection represents, embodies a capital moment in the birth of the modern study of religion. This introduction seeks to present the early modern study of religion as cultural criticism and to provide some *points de repère,* rather than a full-fledged overview of the intellectual scene. Chapter I deals with the discovery of the world's religions together with that of the New World; it also introduces some of the "heroes" of our story. Chapter II, on ancient Israelite religion, highlights the fact that, for modern minds, the roots of religious history were grounded in biblical soil. Chapter III focuses on the deep interest shown by Richard Simon, one of the fathers of biblical criticism, in postbiblical Judaism, and on his structural and genetic comparison

Western

12

between Judaism and Christianity. How biblical mythology offered the most obvious starting point for reflecting on the religious traditions of the whole earth is examined in chapter IV. From there, we move to orientalism with the early study of Zoroastrian and Manichaean dualisms in chapter V, while chapter VI is devoted to the changing perceptions of Islam among early modern Arabic scholars. Finally, chapter VII, dealing with Roman paganism and Chinese "atheism," probes the idea of civil religion, showing how the discourse on religion was inscribed, for eighteenth-century European intellectuals, in their reflection on society. The epilogue investigates the new turn that the study of religion would take in the early nineteenth century, with Romanticism and the clear separation of fields. In various ways, these chapters echo one another, explicitly and implicitly. I have sought to call attention to such echoes, in what might at times sound like repetitions. The course I have followed here is by no means the only one possible, but I hope that its meanders will reflect for the reader the fascination that the story of the discoverers of religions as continents of the mind has exerted on me for many years.

I

Paradigm Shift:

Exploring the World's Religions

1. A New World: Religions Unthinkable

On October 12, 1492, Christopher Columbus steered the *Santa Maria* to an island of the West Indies called Guanahani by its inhabitants, and which he baptized San Salvador. In his diary that day, he wrote that the peaceful population walked naked, without any shame, "as if they stood out of the original sin." Columbus added that it would be easy to convert them to Christianity, as they appeared to be without any religion and were not even idolaters.[1] That the "Indians" lacked a recognized religious identity, as they did not belong to any of the traditional "sects," probably stemmed in his view from their practice of natural religion, which had been implanted in men since the beginnings of humankind. The natives of the New World did not belong to the sect of idolaters. They were pagans without a "law" of their own, hence living under natural law. As they did not have a precise conception of the divinity, they were more open to the idea of conversion to Christianity than either Muslims or Jews, who belonged to *"sectas de perdición."* As noted by Alain Milhou, Columbus's remark reflects the medieval taxonomy of religions, according to which, side by side with Christians, Muslims, and Jews, the fourth "sect" includes all idolaters. For Columbus, the inhabitants of the New World represent a hitherto unknown category of religious identity.[2]

Is the existence of humans remaining unstained by original sin at all conceivable? If so, how should one think about them? Do they possess a soul? Are they destined, by nature, to become slaves, as postulated in Aristotle's theory? The urgency of such questions would soon preoccupy Spanish theologians throughout the sixteenth century, a fact reflected, for instance, in the famous debates at the University of Salamanca.[3]

It was, then, in religious terms that European intellectuals first learned to reflect on the nature of New World inhabitants in the time of "the first globalization."[4] This reflection would soon transform anthropological conceptions, eventually launching the modern human sciences in the seventeenth century.[5] In contemplating the various religious systems of the Amerindians, which should at least be understood, if not respected, one learned then to think the unthinkable. Indeed, some at least among the missionaries in New Spain and Peru soon recognized that doing so was a necessary condition for the conversion of the Indians. These missionaries made a remarkable effort to describe, analyze, and understand these strange religions, with their sometimes violent and repugnant practices. Human sacrifices, in particular (especially among the Aztecs), remained for the Spaniards major stumbling blocks preventing the toleration of Amerindian religions.

From the beginning of the Spanish conquest, the religious identity of New World peoples presented a capital problem. When referring to the practices and beliefs of the conquered empires, those established by the Aztecs in Mexico or by the Incas in Peru, the Spaniards remained unable to speak of natural religion. The only available way to understand these practices and beliefs was therefore to compare them with already-known practices and beliefs, in an effort to think about the new religions with the help of existing concepts meant to describe the religious multiplicity of the world. In some of their rituals, American religions were reminiscent of various aspects of Old World religions. For a long time, the missionaries' knowledge of American myths and beliefs remained quite vague and was mostly limited to rituals that they could observe and describe. They compared these rituals with those of idolatrous religions, of course, such as those of the Greeks, Romans, or Carthaginians. But these rituals also reminded them of Islam (they often called temples in the New World *mesquitas,* mosques), and even of the religion of Biblical Israel (for instance, when dealing with sacrifices). Sometimes even similarities with various Christian rituals were noted: the missionaries called some Indian purifying rituals with water "baptisms." In other words, those monks, who have often been called the first ethnologists (but whom we should rather describe as "ethnologizing," as both their approach and their instruments were directly linked to their missionary role), succeeded in describing and understanding the curious phenomena that they could observe.

In an important study of religion in early colonial Peru, Sabine Mac-Cormack notes that the Roman Catholic Church was able to accept the comparative and historical study of religions, provided this study did not deal with Christian doctrine.[6] Descriptions of Inca practices and beliefs redacted by *fráiles* in the sixteenth and seventeenth centuries do not usually refer to Christianity. And yet, ecclesiastical authors could not always avoid comparing American religions to Christianity. Similarities were usually interpreted as manipulations of Satan, who ever likes to appear under the form of our Lord. Eventually, some but by no means all Roman Catholic intellectuals became instrumental in the emerging new approach to religion. In this context, various works authored by the Spanish missionaries document the birth of the comparative history of religions.

The discovery of the New World opened the door to knowledge of previously unknown societies that did not fit in the traditional categories for analyzing religious phenomena: revealed religion, heresy, idolatry, and natural religion. To what extent were these categories transformed by this new knowledge? On the other hand, did the creation of new categories for thinking about religion permit a new curiosity to express itself? It is on these corollary questions that I want to reflect here. In doing so, I wish to weigh both the stakes involved in these questions and the consequences of the meeting between European scholars and American religions for the idea of religion. I propose to begin this reflection with examples taken from works written by missionaries to Peru.

Confronted with the religious practices of the Incas, our authors asked themselves two sorts of questions: how can one explain the existence of these religions, and how can one understand them in depth. The first systematic study to be written on the Incas, Piedro de Cieza de León's *Crónica del Perú,* was published in Seville in 1554. Cieza de León insists on the relationship between the Indians and the demon (whom they call Xixarama). Yet, he notes, the Indians could not be real idolaters, as they possessed neither idols nor temples.[7]

The most important work, in both ambition and impact, written by a missionary on Amerindian religions is certainly José de Acosta's *Natural and Moral History of the Indies.* Acosta, a Jesuit qualified by Marcel Bataillon as one of the most intelligent men of his times, learned the Quechua language and visited various towns in Peru, where he had requested to be sent.[8] On returning to Spain in 1587, he held a series of lengthy meetings with King Philip II and was then appointed rector of the University of Salamanca.

Historia naturál, published in Seville in 1590, was the first book written by a Jesuit in the New World.[9] A huge success, it was translated to
French in 1600 and to English in 1604. As underlined by MacCormack,
its publication permitted the radical transformation of European discourse
on Amerindian religions.[10] Book 5 is dedicated "to religion, or superstition, to rites, idolatries and sacrifices of the Peruvians." For Acosta, the
very existence of idolatry proved the Indians' deep religiosity, even if this
religiosity was hijacked by demons *(huacas)* and deprived of its rightful
identity. Paradoxically, reasoned Acosta, only God-fearers could become
involved in such odious practices. Acosta revealed his intention: although
some of the Indians' rites and customs may appear barbarous, this was
not reason enough to consider them inhuman and diabolical, as the rites
of the Greeks, Romans, and other ancient peoples were basically similar
to those of the Indians. Referring to the Old World divinities,[11] Acosta
mentions Osiris, Isis, Amon, Athena, and so on. If the Indians were idolaters, he reasoned, this stemmed from the malicious manipulations of the
devil. Their error was essentially that of the ancient Greeks and Romans.[12]
Different forms of idolatry were to be distinguished; some, like that of
the Mexicans, were clearly more pernicious than others, like that of the
Incas. The latter accept rather easily the idea of a supreme God, even if it
was harder for them to recognize the idea of a *single* God. Regarding their
priests, Acosta noted that "among all the nations of the world," some men
devoted themselves exclusively to divine worship, be it true or false.
These men were in charge of offering sacrifices and of the interpretation
of divine messages to the people.[13] He also noted the existence of monas-
teries, for both virgins and men, "invented by the devil for his service and
for superstition" and refers to the Buddhist bonzes in China and Japan,
according to the reports of Jesuits in East Asia.[14] Elsewhere, Acosta
speaks of the circumcision practiced on the sons of kings and nobles, as
well as of "baptisms" among the Indians.[15] Some of the Indian festivals,
according to him, appeared to imitate the mysteries of the Holy Trinity.
At one such festival, the Indians seemed to celebrate the feast of Corpus
Christi.[16] These were, no doubt, the devil's effort to imitate true religion.
Acosta compared some of the Incan rituals with those of the Church,
others with those of the Hebrews, Muslims, or ancient polytheist religions.
Altogether, the comparative method was obviously of great importance
for Acosta.[17]

Having described religious practices in detail, Acosta then inquires
about their origin. He had questioned the Incas, but was not convinced

by their myths. He also rejected the two most common theories about the Incas' provenance. According to him, they could not be the offspring of either Plato's Atlantis or the ten tribes of Israel.[18] All in all, Indian idolatry, which appeared to be novel, revealed the universality of religious phenomena.[19]

Acosta was a Jesuit, and his efforts reflected those of the Jesuit fathers in Asia and America to understand in their own terms the cultures of the peoples they sought to convert. Accommodation entailed a systematic comparison between cultures. Such a comparison underlined the similarities between different expressions of religious feeling, a feeling found in all religions, even those that seemed to have been deeply perverted by Satan's efforts.

Acosta devotes book 6 of his *History* to Indian customs and political organization. His explicit goal in this book is to show that they are not savages lacking any understanding and that one should strive to govern them according to their own rules when these do not contradict Church law. In the introduction to his *De procurando Indorum salute,* published in 1576, Acosta classifies the peoples of the New World in three categories. Side by side with "republics" of peoples of "high culture," such as the Chinese or Japanese, one finds those of peoples without scriptures, from Mexico or Peru, and finally, the "savages" devoid of writing, who remained more or less in the state of nature.[20] Such a taxonomy, which delineates the limits between cultures and periods, highlights the distance from the Aristotelian tradition. The systematic comparison between cultures announces the spirit of modern anthropology.

The Jesuit Acosta echoes the approach of the Dominican Bartolomé de las Casas, whose work Acosta had read. True to his Thomist education, Las Casas recognized in the Incas the voice of natural law, dictated by reason, beyond and despite the devil's stratagems. In his *Apologética Historia,* Las Casas, who knew well the writings of Eusebius of Caesarea, defends the idea that Amerindian civilizations could be compared with those of the ancient Mediterranean, representing, like them, a *praeparatio evangelica.*[21] For Las Casas, the Incas, whose main ritual was that of the *huacas,* or idols, were not endowed with a concept of God similar to that of Christianity. And yet, Las Casas presents himself as a fighter for Indian rights; in his own words, "idolas colere humanum est (offering cult to the idols is human)."[22]

To be sure, not all missionaries shared Acosta's attitude. Bartolomé Alvarez, for instance, was at the antipodes of José de Acosta and objected to Las Casas's views. His represents a militant antinative attitude, and in 1588, he published *De las costumbras y conversion de los Indios del Perú*, a book written as a *Memorial a Felipe II* to convince the king to let the Inquisition fight against non-Christian practices in Peru. This work, incidentally, did not convince the sovereign.[23]

Garcilaso de la Vega, a remarkable figure known as the Inca Garcilaso, was the son of a Spaniard and an Incan princess. In his *Commentarios reales* (1609), he made a further step toward systematic comparison, as he strives to integrate Incan culture with that of Western Christendom. For him, Incan religion prefigured Christianity, as it brought civilization, monotheism, and spiritual cult to barbarian peoples. According to Garcilaso, the Incas followed the divine scheme and prepared the way for the coming of Christianity.[24] For Garcilaso, Incan religion is a form of natural religion, not perverted by the devil and thus preparing for the Gospel. To claim that the Incan religion is not idolatry, Garcilaso explains that it is incorrect to translate *huaca* as "idol." Andean religious terms, he contends, do not have true equivalents in European languages. We find here an intuition that will be of capital importance for the comparative study of religions: religious systems have each their own structures and cannot be compared on all points.[25]

Throughout history, it is only by the brutal confrontation with radically new facts that categories open up and new cognitive structures eventually appear. As has often been noted, modern ethnology is rooted in the observation of the mores of newly discovered peoples. It is not only ethnology but also the modern study of religion, in its essence and forms, that is rooted in the violent, unexpected meeting with the religious practices of the Amerindians, a fact that has not received the attention it deserves. The Christian missionaries, Dominican and Jesuit, did not hide their repulsion for some of the religious practices of the peoples they met, whether they called them forms of idolatry, Satanic religions, or natural religion corrupted by Satan or his demons. Sometimes they even learned to love these peoples, even while "extirpating" their native religious practices so as to anchor the Indians' conversion in daily life. In the sixteenth and seventeenth centuries, indeed, many manuals for missionaries on the "extirpation of idolatry" were published in Peru and New Spain.[26]

John Elliott, the eminent historian of the Spanish in early modern times, has argued that the confrontation between Europe and America followed patterns developed during the long conflict with Islam, and that the European inability to assimilate American cultures and religions reflects European attitudes toward Islam.[27] For centuries, there had been a confrontation, at times acute and at times dormant, between Islam and European societies; the Iberian Peninsula, in particular, stood at the forefront of the conflict. The parallel suggested by Elliott is striking. Indeed, to understand the rituals of indigenous peoples of the New World, the missionaries could only compare them with ones they knew: in some cases to Christian sacraments, but usually to the rituals of the Hebrews, Romans, or Muslims. In contradistinction with the Hebrews and Romans, with whom Christians considered themselves in some way related, Muslims represented the radical enemy in Iberian consciousness, both before and after the final Christian victory in 1492 over the last Muslim kingdom of Granada. For Christians, the religious practices of this enemy were at the antipodes of their own. Since the first half of the eighth century when John of Damascus called Islam the last and worst of all Christian heresies, Islam was usually conceived as a heresy in Christian consciousness.[28] In contradistinction with Islam, Amerindian religions represented multiple versions of idolatry, a religious perversion of which the rigorous monotheism of Islam could hardly be accused. It was thus as new and radical forms of idolatry that Christian theologians perceived Amerindian religions.[29] In particular, the only way for the missionaries to explain human sacrifice and cannibalism was as the direct result of the devil's activity and his perverse distortion of the natural religion of primitive humankind. The monks, who sought to justify the natives as much as possible and protect them against the most brutal exactions of the conquistadores, were also able to express their admiration for the strength of religious feeling that brought people to offer human sacrifices.[30]

The Catholic missionaries' analysis of idolatrous rituals appears to parallel that of the Protestant theologians to Catholic rituals, which Protestants tended to define as "magic," and thus as essentially outside the pale of religious legitimacy.[31] Only later, in the seventeenth century, would English and Dutch Protestants be confronted with the religions of Asia and America. The broadening of the concept of religion by Catholic missionaries played a significant role in the polemics between Catholics and Protestants. Hence, when the Jesuit Joseph-François Lafitau analyzed the religious system of the Iroquois in New France, he pointed out that acknowledging the religious nature of their mores and customs offered him a weapon for the fight against Pierre Bayle's "atheism," which saw only human culture where Lafitau identified divine providence.[32] Indeed, Catholic thinkers succeeded in acknowledging the diversity of religious phenomena much more than did Protestant theologians.

As we have seen, under certain conditions the Catholic Church was able to accept the comparative history of religions.[33] Beside missionaries turned ethnologists, such an attitude is also found in Vico's *Scienza nuova*. The essential contribution of Catholic intellectuals to the birth of the comparative history of religions must be spelled out here. It was thanks to their own heritage, that of the Church Fathers, that they were able to recognize as religions the belief systems of the newly discovered peoples. Indeed, because of their education, the best minds among the missionaries were able to return to the late antique theologians and polemicists against Judaism and paganism and use their works in discussing the religions of the newly discovered peoples. Rather than continuity, underlined by the Catholics, it was mainly rupture that Protestants insisted upon: rupture in faith as well as Scripture. The Protestant intuitive vision of the world was dualist, whereas that of the Catholics was unitarian. The Jesuits soon understood they must accommodate the mores of peoples they hoped to convert. To justify this accommodation, they needed to discover equivalences between religions and cultures. A series of similarities permitted them to overcome the radical otherness of the newly discovered religions and to understand them within the intellectual framework of their own culture.[34]

The early encounter between Christianity and New World religious phenomena, for which traditional categories stemming from medieval theology offered no adequate concepts, entailed a broadened idea of religion.[35] As Lafitau noted, the New World savages were quite similar to the men of the earliest times. This collision between the contemporary world and the *Urzeit* enhanced the comparative reflex for analyzing new phenomena. In particular, the simplest way to answer the question of the Indians' origin was to invoke biblical mythology, more precisely the dispersion of Noah's sons throughout the earth or the lost ten tribes of Israel.[36] The effort to internalize the deep nature of the Amerindians' religious feelings recalls what Wilhelm Dilthey called *Verstehen*. As idolatry was the main religious category through which new religions could be understood, a series of parallels allowed Catholic thinkers to better grasp the unknown by comparing it to the known.

As pointed out by Max Müller, the great herald of comparative religion in the late nineteenth century, it was not by chance that the comparative study of religions was born in a Christian cultural milieu. According to Müller, Christianity is by its very nature engaged in a constant comparison with Judaism.[37] But this is only partly true. First, because it was the Roman Catholics, rather than the Protestants, that first encountered the religions of Asia and America. And second, because if it was true that ancient Christianity had prepared its adherents to compare religions, this was due not only to the basic polemic with Judaism but also to the polemics with Greco-Roman "idolatry." The "divine scheme" *(esquema divino)* referred to by Garcilaso echoes Justin Martyr's *logos spermatikos*.[38] In the first half of the second century, Justin Martyr's conception of the *logos spermatikos* sown by God among all peoples, pagans as well as Jews, and barbarians as well as Greeks, had established the basis for the reasoning of Las Casas and Acosta. Throughout the Middle Ages, the Jews were the only religious outsiders to be (relatively) tolerated in Christian society. Their disturbing presence had been too familiar to generate a real ethnological curiosity about them. Only with the great discoveries of early modern times would such a curiosity arise.

Conceiving themselves the intellectual heirs of the Church Fathers, the Catholic missionaries were as prepared to confront paganism in its various garbs as they were to meet Muslims and heretics. The creation of the *Sacra Congregatio de Propaganda Fide* by Gregory XV in 1622 would only confirm the recognition by the Roman Catholic Church of the complex cultural contexts of the missions.

With the goal of accommodation, the Jesuits would offer a justification for various rituals that they considered to belong to "civil religion."[39] As the goal of civil religion is to maintain social identity, the Jesuits did not consider such rituals to be "religious practices" in the traditional sense; since these practices did not represent a cult of the divinity, they should not be condemned as idolatrous. A broad spectrum of religious practice was thus legitimized and religious phenomena were no longer conceived through the traditional binary approach that recognized only true or false religion. This broadened concept of religion thus permitted the contemplation of even the strangest and newest of the world's religions.[40] As we have seen, the earliest comparisons were made essentially between contemporary phenomena and ancient traditions. After Acosta, for instance, Garcilaso did not express any curiosity toward Islam and Arabic culture and referred mostly to Roman history to understand Incan religion. The comparative reflex to explain religious change thus became anchored in diachronic thought.

Claude Lévi-Strauss referred to three successive types of humanism in the modern age. The first appeared in the Renaissance, with the rediscovery of the cultures of the ancient world. The second, dating from the nineteenth century, arose with the discovery of oriental cultures. The third, implicit in twentieth-century social anthropology, addresses for the first time peoples with neither Scriptures nor script.[41] Lévi-Strauss was correct to perceive different forms of humanism. However, the idea itself is more convincing than its proposed chronological frame. In fact, the three forms of humanism described by Lévi-Strauss seem to be corollary and to have appeared simultaneously, at the start of the modern age. Classical philology, the study of oriental languages and cultures, and the observation of the American "savages" date from the same time: the sixteenth and seventeenth centuries.[42] Thanks to their *bricolage* with the instruments of their cultural baggage, the missionaries had succeeded in understanding, sometimes with sympathy, the religions of the Amerindians. To be sure, they remained theologians at heart, and their ethnological approach remains vastly different from contemporary social anthropology in its sources, methods, and goals. But through their faith and culture, the missionaries were able to transform their inherited cognitive categories.[43]

As Sabine MacCormack notes, contemporary Europe, at last liberated from its own demons, seems now to have lost a capacity to engage other religions and cultures with passion.[44] For a long time, Christian Europe did not know how to reflect on foreign religions. Has the secularized West now lost its interest in them? Is it true that serious, sustained thinking about religion demands some equilibrium between religion and reason or some ambivalence toward religious traditions? The consequence of too great an intellectual detachment would be the loss of the comparative perspective.[45]

Let us summarize. The encounter with Amerindian religions engendered a series of conditions necessary for the modern study of religious phenomena. The concept of natural religion came to Hobbes and Locke from Acosta, whom they read. The insertion of Christianity within the comparative history of religions, the loss of its absolute character, as was the case, already, with Montaigne, stemmed from the missionaries' reflection on Amerindian religions.[46] The notion of religious change was explicit in the writings of Las Casas and Garcilaso. The concept of "world

23

religions" would later reflect the need to insert the religions of the New World into the general framework of the study of religious phenomena. Similarly, the interest in the sociological dimension of these phenomena (which can be understood only within the societies in which they appear) comes directly from the writings of the Spanish *frailes*. The transformation of the concept of religion permitted, in dialectical fashion, a more precise and better comprehension of religious facts. Last but not least, it is in great measure thanks to American "idolatry" that modern students of religion learned to free themselves of theological blinkers and, in the practice of scholarship, put the idea of truth inside brackets.[47]

2. A New Science: Explorers of Religions

The emergence of a new science requires the discovery of new facts and the crafting of new methods, but more importantly it requires the arising of a new sensitivity. The great discoveries aroused intellectual curiosity about cultures previously unheard of, from Central and South America to South and East Asia—although, as John Elliott argued, there was a certain "slowness to respond" to these discoveries.[48] The new interest in ancient and oriental languages permitted the introduction of serious philological approaches to sacred and classical religious and cultural texts, a fact that suddenly and dramatically broadened intellectual horizons. The Reformation encouraged new approaches to biblical text and to ecclesiastical history, while its violent aftermath forced on scholars of all sides a subtle but deep-reaching distance from, or even questioning of, their own religious attitudes, implicit as well as explicit.

It would be a mistake, however, to perceive the new religious attitudes as dependent solely on the Reformation and the intellectual storm it generated. Religious attitudes were eventually transformed just as much, if less directly, by the two other phenomena mentioned above, the great discoveries and the new philology brought by the Renaissance. The discovery of new worlds and with them of religions and cultures previously unheard of, entailed the invention of new categories through which they could be studied. It was no longer possible simply to refer, as Bodin still did, to "paganism."

To sum up the key characteristic of the transformation of the concept of religion in the early modern age, one could perhaps speak of its *externalization*. As a concept, religion always had a double edge, referring both

24

inward, as a set of beliefs, and outward, as a pattern of behavior. In antiquity, however, religion had primarily been perceived as collective or public behavior within the city. Among both Jews and pagans, religion was essentially a pattern of behavior, most clearly exemplified by public animal sacrifices. In this respect, late antiquity had shown a deep transformation of the very idea of religion, which now became interiorized, as it were, reflecting essentially a set of beliefs. True religion (*vera religio,* in Augustine's terms) was now orthodox Christianity, while all other forms of religion were identified as heresies or forms of idolatry and hence false. In many ways, this internalized conception of religion would remain prevalent throughout the Middle Ages.

The externalization of the concept of religion in the early modern age is best expressed, perhaps, in the new interest in the political aspects of religion. More precisely, to salvage exotic religious systems from being categorized as "idolatrous," several scholars claimed that they were actually "civil religions" and hence that the category of idolatry was irrelevant to their analysis. The most famous such case is that of Confucianism, which was often compared, in its status within the state and its role in supporting the state, with Roman religion, as well as with the religion of Israel. The Jesuit missionaries, who sought to "immerse" themselves in Chinese customs and culture, were accused by their enemies, in particular the Dominicans, of adopting idolatrous rituals and practices. To defend themselves, Matteo Ricci and his friends argued that these rituals were meant to help the good functioning of society and could not therefore be understood as "religious" in the traditional, Christian meaning of the term. Accepting elements of Chinese culture, then, could in no way be understood as violating Christian beliefs. The polemics between Jesuits and Dominicans on this issue, famously known as the *Querelle des Rites,* was a major affair in the Catholic world of the early eighteenth century, with its acme at the 1700 condemnation of the Jesuits by the Sorbonne.[49] That same year, as we shall see in chapter V, a similar claim was made by Thomas Hyde, the first orientalist to offer a scholarly study of Zoroastrianism. The fire cult, according to Hyde, was endowed with a clear civic quality and thus could not be identified as a pagan ritual, nor condemned as such.

Side by side with the study of the Greek and Latin pagan literatures of antiquity, the Hebrew Bible and postbiblical Jewish literature had been studied since the Renaissance with a new energy. This energy is already reflected in Guillaume Postel, the first incumbent of the chair of Hebrew and Arabic at the *Collège des trois langues* (soon to become the *Collège de France*). The college was established by François I. Postel, an early member of the newly founded Company of Jesus and a visionary who could dream of a council in Jerusalem, in which wise Jews, Christians, and Muslims would hold religious peace-talks and eventually establish universal peace. Guillaume Postel's name is enough to refute the mistaken but widespread notion that the Reformation alone encouraged the study of Hebrew letters. The seduction of Hebrew studies and the occasional infatuation with Jewish texts had begun with Christian kabbala in late-fifteenth-century Italy, in the circles of Marsilio Ficino and Pico della Mirandola, who were also pivotal in the transmission of Greek classical literature from Byzantine to Western intellectuals. Johann Reuchlin, who was profoundly drawn to kabbalah, launched modern Jewish studies through his studies of Hebrew grammar.[50]

By the early seventeenth century, the intellectual climate had undergone drastic change. After the religious wars, the search for a utopian unity in the intellectual and religious heritage of humankind could no longer attract the best minds. An epistemology of discontinuity, insistent on a specificity of fields of inquiry, was the order of the day in the humanities as well as the sciences. Scientific curiosity was also applied to the irreducible differences among the world's languages, cultures, and religions.

In this changing climate, the seventeenth century witnessed a new intellectual interest in Hebrew language and literature and Jewish tradition. The best-known example of this new attitude is that of Johannes Buxtorf the Elder, the great Hebraist from Basel, who published in 1603 his *Judenschul,* a detailed compendium of Jewish practices, which soon appeared in Latin as *Synagoga Judaica.*[51] Just as people had learned to observe and describe, sometimes even with a modicum of sympathy, the religious behavior of the most foreign peoples, they also learned to observe the religious practices of contemporary Jews. Only in the context of the new ethnological curiosity can one understand the importance of the work of early modern Hebraists.

Scholars learned to observe Jewish customs, in a way, just as they had those of the American Indians, the Turks, or even, already, the Persians and Chinese. The Renaissance's "romantic" discovery of the wonders of the world had made room for not only philological scholarship but also ethnological curiosity. What is most remarkable, however, was the fluid boundaries of these young disciplines and the willingness of their early practitioners to cross them: ethnology came to the help of philology and vice versa. Canonical texts were thought to be best understood in their original tongue, but anthropological observation also contributed to the meaning of ancient texts. There was a clear realization that one was dealing with foreign civilizations, distant either in space or in time and that the religious behavior of contemporary Turks, for instance, could shed light on various biblical practices, such as circumcision—or even on mores in the days of Homer.

Gifted, original, and isolated as they may have been, scholars remained very much the product of their times. In the seventeenth century, for example, the deep abhorrence of free spirits from religious warfare constituted the immediate context of all intellectual activity in the field of religion. Intellectuals often perceived religious traditions as idolatrous or superstitious. After the Council of Trent, Catholic as well as Protestant intellectuals stressed the need for "cleansing" both beliefs and practices.

At the same time, a fast-growing literature of travelogues was revealing the existence of foreign religions. Written in Spanish, French, Italian, English, German, or Dutch, these works were soon translated and thus circulated in many languages. One should insist on the international and interreligious character of the *République des Lettres*. Ideas traveled fast and often crossed the Channel back and forth. Intellectual communication between the Netherlands, England, and France functioned remarkably well. For a variety of reasons, however, Germany, Spain, and Italy remained rather different cases.[52]

In various countries, stories about the Indians of America challenged the traditional definitions of the human inherited from medieval scholasticism. Moreover, the ethnological reports on the Indians' mores gradually forced the Europeans to acknowledge their religious (though idolatrous) dimensions.[53] It should not come as a surprise, then, that the first to speak of the *religions* of the world, in the plural, were the Catholics (as early as 1508). Through their missionaries in China, Central and South America, and elsewhere, they had been confronted, earlier and more concretely than Protestants, with the variety of faiths and practices around the world. Henceforth, religion would no longer refer to personal vision but to systems of beliefs and behavior. This radical semantic externalization of "religion" and its transformation from inner piety to social patterns of behavior occurred in the seventeenth and early eighteenth centuries—a fact recognized by Wilfred Cantwell Smith more than forty years ago. This transformation both reflected and served the clash of conflicting religious parties, the emergence of triumphant intellectualism, and the new information coming from overseas about patterns of religion in newly discovered societies.[54]

Besides the Amerindians, the other powerful presence of a foreign religion in European consciousness was that of Islam. In 1685, the Turks stood at the gates of Vienna. They were a traditional enemy, identified in popular and intellectual consciousness with Islam, and as such despised and feared at the same time. Yet, since the Renaissance, a new sensitivity, developed mainly by travelers and diplomats, was finding an exotic charm in Islam, which began to exert a certain attraction on some of the more curious minds. The traditional anti-Islamic polemics, which was as old as Islam, had by no means disappeared. But since the sixteenth century, a curiosity about Muslim mores and customs was added to the traditional polemics. More and more, diplomatic contacts with the Sultan's Seraglio added intellectual and ethnological curiosity to the traditional themes. To be sure, one cannot speak of a completely "intellectual" curiosity, devoid of any interest or calculation, be they military, political, or economic. Such calculation could even be of a religious nature, since through the Turks, Christian Europe discovered the Eastern Christians, whom both Catholics and Protestants sought to draw to their side. To better understand both the Muslims and the Eastern Christians, who were then subjects of the Ottoman Sultan, and to publish and translate their writings, some scholars began to learn oriental languages: Arabic, Turkish, Persian, and also Syriac and Armenian. As to Coptic, despite the wild theories of Athanasius Kircher, it would remain, basically, terra incognita until Champollion succeeded in deciphering the Egyptian hieroglyphs.[55]

The second half of the seventeenth century thus saw the birth of orientalism. The term itself, however, would not appear until a century later. The "East" meant, then, first and foremost Muslim lands, from Istanbul to Mongolia, as discovered by intrepid travelers (most often merchants), such as Jean-Baptiste Tavernier and Jean Chardin. To be sure, there was also an awareness of other Asian civilizations, those of India, China, and Japan, due to the reports of the Jesuit missionaries, such as Matteo Ricci or Saint Francis Xavier, and travelers such as Pietro della Valle.[56] In contemporaneous taxonomies, however, East Asian religions remained classified as belonging to the "fourth form" of religion, the other three being Judaism, Christianity, and Islam. Here too, travelers' reports were soon translated, but the full implications of the opening to Asia would only be recognized later.

Hence, much of what one knew of the different religions around the globe was what the few European witnesses, mainly travelers and missionaries, had described. This meant that it was largely the rituals of the "new" religions that were first described, while their theologies, or sets of beliefs, would long remain much less clearly perceived. Ritual also formed the main bone of contention between Protestants and Catholics. Thus, in the age of the great discoveries and the Reformation, religion came to refer mainly to a system of ritual practices. A turn can be detected to a new perception of religion as a public activity—a return, as it were, to the primary sense of the word in the ancient world. Ritual would thus become the defining component of religion, and the plurality of religions on earth reflected the multiplicity of ritual practices. Under these conditions, it was the idea of natural religion that provided humankind with an awareness of the unity of its essential religiosity.

The paradigm of religion emerging in the seventeenth century thus privileged ritual over belief, and abandoned value-judgment for observation, as a chief classifier of religious attitudes; more than anything else, this fact highlights the major transformation in intellectual attitudes toward religion. Rituals were observed, they were not judged as right or wrong (except in marginal cases such as human sacrifices), as were beliefs, such as idolatry, false prophecy, or heresy. The great divide between old and new, ancient and modern, had now been passed. When studying the religions of humankind, one sought to understand their origin and history. Let us note here a similar polarization of ancient and modern within literary circles at the turn of the eighteenth century, with the famous *Querelle des Anciens et des Modernes,* about the esthetic value of Homer.[57] All seemed to agree on the original unity of humankind and, consequently, of religion. Diversification, radical as it may have become, was a product of history and geography. That the two *Querelles,* that of ancients and moderns and that of rituals, blew up more or less at the same time, does not seem to have been fortuitous. In both cases, the polemic was between those identifying with the values of their own society and those searching for alternative traditions in foreign societies, past or present.

The dimension of time gained new importance in the seventeenth century—a development the significance of which cannot be overemphasized. Following Joseph Scaliger, John Marsham established the basis for historical, that is, first of all, chronological comparisons between religious ideas and cults. As a science, chronology did not last long.[58] Its impact, however, would be crucial and its effects long-standing. Understanding a phenomenon now meant grasping its origins, and even the Scriptures had to be understood as documents of past civilizations. Chronological awareness, combined with ethnological observation and a new philological approach to the biblical texts, led to a major breakthrough. Symbolic thought, which had remained so much in fashion throughout the sixteenth century, now lost much of its power. Instead of a single *prisca theologia,* or *philosophia perennis,* expressing itself in different garbs in various religions and philosophies, the plurality of ancient cultures was now recognized. It was the differences rather than similarities among religions that one underlined. And these differences were to be found in their ritual systems, rather than their mythologies.

Comparison was now complementing the chronological study of religious ideas and customs, and during our period different models of comparison were used. The new could be explained by the old: for instance, the Indians of India or America, or even the Chinese, could be compared with the Jews, or Phoenicians, or Iranians. Conversely, the old could be explained by the new: thus biblical idolatry was better understood when compared with idolatrous practices observed among the Indians, and Indian mores, for instance, could shed light on Egyptian idolatry. Following the same method, one could also compare two ancient religions, such as those of Phoenicia and Greece (the former being the source of the latter), or two religions of the present (those of the Indians and the Chinese, for instance).

One of the earliest and most influential comparative studies of religion in the seventeenth century was perhaps the voluminous work of the English clergyman and polymath Samuel Purchas, oddly entitled *Purchas His Pilgrimage.*[59] The first part of the book offers a "theological and geographical" study ("historie") of Asia, Africa, and America and propounds a chronological study of the traditional taxonomy of non-Christian religions: "Heathenish, Jewish and Saracenicall." In each category, Purchas offers to analyze the various

> opinions, idols, oracles, temples, priests, fasts, feasts, sacrifices, and rites religious; their beginnings, proceedings, alterations, sects, orders and successions.

30

From this ambitious, all-encompassing list emerges Purchas's intention to study all aspects of the religious phenomena of humankind through the ages, but mainly the cultic. *Purchas His Pilgrimage* also underlines the obvious links between the origins of comparative religion and travel literature. Purchas offers to intersperse his book

> with brief descriptions of the countries, nations, states, discoveries, private and publicke customes, and the most remarkable rarities of nature, of humane industrie . . .
> He is obviously quite conscious of the novelty of his enterprise, when he writes that the newnesse also makes it more difficult, being an enterprise never yet (to my knowledge) by any, in any language, attempted.

Let us not imagine, however, that such an open mind would be completely free of prejudice or of any vested interest beyond scientific curiosity. One of the avowed goals of the book, indeed, was to demonstrate the pagan origins of "Popish rites." Like other humanistic disciplines, comparative religion remained a product of its age.

In 1614, a year after the publication of Purchas's *Pilgrimage,* Edward Brerewood published his *Enquiries Touching the Diversity of Languages and Religions through the Chief Parts of the World.*[60] Here too, we can see the deep influence of travel reports, to which Brerewood often refers. One of the most remarkable characteristics of *Diversity* is its insistence on the close link between language and religion, and the importance of oriental languages and philology for the study of religions. Like Purchas, Brerewood still used the old taxonomy and divided the religions of the world into four categories: "idolatrie, Mahumetanisme, Judaisme and Christianity."

Both Purchas and Brerewood were perfectly aware of the dispersion, lowly status, and social insignificance of the Jews in the seventeenth century. Their taxonomy reflected, however, the traditional place of Judaism in Christian consciousness. The religion of Israel was granted a special place, side by side with its daughter, the religion of Christ, and in clear contradistinction to other religions, Islam included. Israelite religion, however, was now transformed into Judaism, which included also the religious practices of contemporaneous Jews (it must be remembered that before Cromwell allowed the Jews to return to England, they remained a rather mysterious and abstract group for English intellectuals). Another phenomenon Brerewood noticed was the existence of diverse

31

forms of Christianity—what he called its different sects. Greeks, first of all, but also Syrians, Melkites, Georgians, Moscovites and Russians, Nestorians, Indians, Copts, Maronites, and so on. Oriental Christians appeared in their diversity as so many cults, which should first be described as truthfully as possible. Brerewood also called these various "sects", "religions." The interest that Eastern Christians presented is obvious: both Catholics and Protestants sought to draw them in to their camp. Hence, their liturgies were analyzed, and similarities to synagogue cult were noted. Ethnological curiosity, mission, ecumenism, and philology: all of these elements would play a role in the new organization of knowledge.

Another landmark in the discovery of the plurality of religious traditions is *Pansebeia; or, A View of All Religions in the World,* by the English polymath Alexander Ross.[61] *Pansebeia* uses questions and answers to propose that religion, or rituals and collective actions, is the cement of any society. Establishing himself mainly on biblical religious history, Ross thus sought to identify what one may call, in Durkheimian fashion, "the elementary forms of religious life." In particular, he was fascinated by antediluvian history: the sacrifices of Cain and Abel, the Tower of Babel, and so on. Using the various testimonies at his disposal, Ross analyzed the religions of different continents. He discussed the religions of Guinea, Virginia, Florida, New Spain, Mexico, Yucatan, Brazil, Peru, and Hispagnola. He also analyzed the ancient religions of Europe, those of the Greeks and Romans, and those of the early Germans, Gauls, Brittons, Saxons, Danes, Swedes, Moscovites, and Lithuanians. He described their pantheons, priests, sacrifices, matrimonial and funerary ceremonies. As to contemporaneous religions in Europe, Ross considered them to be Christianity and Islam. To be sure, the confrontation between Christianity and Islam did not take place only in Europe: the decline of Christianity in the Levant was due to the victory of "Mohametanism." From a sociological point of view, Islam was in Ross's day, as it is again in our own, a European religion. It is worth noting that a few years before Cromwell granted the Jews permission to return to England, Ross raised the question of religious freedom for them, and supported it, adding that a tolerant attitude was more likely to encourage them to convert than persecution.

Ex oriente religio and *ex oriente idololatria* were major methodological presuppositions of the times. Thanks to the development of a comparative chronology of ancient nations, the Orient was now recognized as much older than Greek antiquity. Of the peoples and religions of the ancient Near East, one referred in particular to those of Syria and of Egypt, while Babylonia remained terra incognita: the tension between *"Babel und Bibel"* would become a major polemical theme of orientalist scholarship only in the late nineteenth century.[62]

In a series of brilliant though diffuse and often far-fetched comparisons and parallels, the Jesuit Athanasius Kircher presented in the first half of the seventeenth century a series of hypotheses and suggestions on the possible contact among early languages, civilizations, and religions.[63] Few of his intuitions, however, would survive: he had little method, and his universal ambitions remind one more of the Renaissance than the seventeenth century. But this should not diminish our appreciation for his most important intuition: that the various cultures of the ancient world must be studied together.

Gerard Vossius's *De Theologia Gentili* is probably the most important work of comparative mythology in the seventeenth century, at least as approached from the classical perspective.[64] Vossius, or De Vos (1577–1649), was a Dutch scholar and canon of Canterbury, whose loyalist sympathies are apparent from the dedication of the first edition of his work to King Charles I. John Selden's influence on Vossius's book is evident and even reflected in its full title: *De Theologia Gentili et physiologia christiana, sive de origine ac progressu idololatriae,* which picks up the main theme of Selden's *De Diis Syris.*[65] Although much read and cited, Vossius's book was not rigorously constructed. It did not deal solely with the ancient Near East but employed all the available pieces of information on polytheistic cults around the world, from the Brahmins of Calcutta and the Chinese to the native inhabitants of Peru and Mexico (as described by José de Acosta) and those of Virginia (as described by the English traveler Thomas Avioth).

Such works as Vossius's *De Theologia Gentili* were officially intended to expose idolatry wherever it hid by searching for its roots. Yet, it is hard to avoid the impression that these works also reflect a hidden attraction to the richness of polytheistic mythologies and cults. Moreover, they certainly encouraged an avowed sympathy for such ancient beliefs in the gods. Edward Herbert, Lord of Cherbury (1583–1648) and the father of English deism, is an excellent case in point.[66] Herbert had read Vossius, whom he quotes concerning heathen practices such as star worship. Here too, evidence from ancient and contemporary idolatry is used simultaneously, to search for what Herbert considered the five innate ideas, or axioms, of natural religion, which could be found everywhere under different garbs. Hence, according to Herbert, the various rituals of all religions were devised by priests, impostors seeking to hide the truth from simple people, who disseminated superstition and idolatry. In this way, idolatry, which had originally derived from the Egyptians, came thence to the Syrians and neighboring nations and later to the Greeks and Romans—"for almost all Religion and Superstition came from the East," adds Herbert. Beyond the obvious influence of contemporary literature on idolatry, such as the work of Selden and Vossius, one detects here a new meaning of religious imposture, a concept that previously had been applied mainly to Muhammad, considered by most Christian scholars as the false prophet par excellence.[67] As is well-known, the radical deists would later suggest the imposture of religious leaders throughout history, with the help of the anonymous tract *De tribus impostoribus* that circulated throughout Europe in the eighteenth century, and according to which Moses, Jesus, and Muhammad had each in turn succeeded in lying to their naïve believers.[68] Already for Herbert, imposture was a universal feature of priestly religion, not a feature of Islam.

Herbert's views provoked a nearly universal hostility. It was clearly felt that a generalized attack on priesthood throughout the religions of humankind could not stop at the doorstep of reformed Christianity. And indeed, Herbert's ideas soon became the backbone of deism. In his *Diana of the Ephesians* (1680),[69] Cherbury's professed disciple Charles Blount plagiarized *De Religione Gentilium,* and in *The Origins of Idolatry* (1695), he developed the thesis that

> Before Religion, that is to say, Sacrifices, Rites, Ceremonies, pretended Revelations, and the like, were invented among the Heathen, there was no worship of God but in a rational way.

Similar ideas were to be repeated and developed in the following decades, in particular by John Toland (1670–1722).

The search for the origins of religion, however, was not limited to Protestant intellectuals. Catholics, too, learned to ask similar questions, although they usually started doing so a little later. Hence, Bernard de Montfaucon's monumental *Antiquitates Graecae et Romanae* (the French edition was published in 1719) starts with a short introduction *de Origine idololatriae,* where he refers to Varro's work as summarized in Augustine's *De Civitate Dei.* In the early eighteenth century, the Benedictine scholar Dom Augustin Calmet would feel the need to write a *Disssertation sur l'origine de l'idolâtrie,* where he argued that the idols worshipped by the Israelites in the desert must have been Egyptian deities.[70]

Bernard Picart, whose name is associated with the *Ceremonies and Customes of the Several Nations of the Known World* thanks to his magnificent engravings, was born in France as a Catholic and emigrated to The Hague in 1710, after his conversion to Protestantism. Like many other Huguenots in the *Refuge,* he underwent a series of religious transformations, and eventually became, in London, one of the founders of the pre- Masonic order of the Knights of Jubilation. Picart, whose religious affiliation and sympathies remained ambiguous, argued for the rejection of old religious customs. At the same time, he produced his multivolume encyclopedia of religion, which did much to present accurate ethnological knowledge of various religions to a large public audience. The work appeared, simultaneously, in Amsterdam and London (in French and English, respectively) in 1723. The French original was republished at least eleven times in the eighteenth and nineteenth centuries.

The preface of *Cérémonies et coutumes religieuses,* entitled *Dissertation sur le culte religieux,* speaks (already) of the *Être Suprême* in whom all peoples, including the most savage, believed, although usually under different names (Dieux, Démons, Génies, etc.). This similarity among religions was often hidden by the great cultic differences—hence the need for a preliminary dissertation on religious cult, comparative and phenomenological in essence. The study of the "étrange bizarrerie" found in cultic practices was meant to underline the common theism of humankind, which crossed religious boundaries, and to insist on the relativity of religions. In the eighteenth century, indeed, the religious unity of humankind was used by the deists as an argument against the established churches. The introduction of a later edition of the work, published in 1783, refers explicitly to natural religion as the original and purest religion of humankind, of which all the various observable rituals are only later derivations. The conclusion of *Dissertation sur le culte religieux* concurs with this view and adds that the oddities of the various rituals hide the essence of religion itself, the simple cult of *l'Être Suprême.*

As is made abundantly clear from the numerous references in the text of the *Scienza nuova,* Vico was able to offer his new approach to the study of myth and society only thanks to the major progress made in the seventeenth century in understanding religious phenomena. To a great extent, this progress had already been registered by Pierre Bayle, in his *Dictionnaire historique et critique,* first published in Rotterdam in 1697 (the publication year of Barthélemy d'Herbelot's *Bibliothèque Orientale*). If religion, in all its manifestations, could now be studied as one phenomenon, this was because the new scholars had learned to recognize the plurality of religions and retain a certain distance between them and their own religious culture.

The Enlightenment is usually associated with the idea of progress. In early scholarship on religion, however, the main paradigm was that of a constant deterioration from the pristine status of religion's origin. It was in the most ancient societies that religion in its purest form could best be observed. In contradistinction with knowledge, religion did not progress but degenerated with time. Primitive religion was, then, religion at its best, the religion of the *bons sauvages,* of the Sabians and of the Indians.[71] The older a religion was, the closer it was to natural religion, and the less it had been perverted by historical and cultural evolution. Such statements are found in the introductory prospectus to the new, revised edition of *Cérémonies et coutumes religieuses,* published in 1783. Religion as it was observed at the time, in particular contemporary Christianity, was indeed perceived as a late, bastardized form of religion. The path to the *Culte de l'Être Suprême,* which one could call "the cult to end all cults," was not only that of anticlericalism but also that of the modern study of religion. Comparing religions, rather than encouraging tolerance, seems to have fostered a will to eradicate contemporary forms of Christianity.

The Christian context of the early modern study of religious phenomena points to a fact of major importance: it was not only other religions of the world that were being discovered and studied critically but also Christianity itself. Our topic is by no means "the West versus the Rest." The attempt to understand, critically and with sympathy, the various religious traditions was ipso facto a quest for self-understanding. Indeed, the birth of biblical criticism and the *Auseinandersetzung* between Protestant and Catholic scholars about the nature and history of Christianity (in particular its origins and heresies), as well as biblical hermeneutics, is too often studied in isolation from the discovery of "other" religious traditions.[72] Such compartmentalization is bound to misrepresent the intellectual parameters of the new discipline. One should remember, furthermore, that early modern scholars never forgot that the religious identity of Europe was manifold and always pointed eastward: the Muslim Turks were at the gates of Vienna, and the roots of Christianity were known to lie in Palestinian Judaism. In other words, it was only later that the "Christian identity" of Europe would become a source of narcissistic self-satisfaction—a self-satisfaction now sometimes broadened to include its "Judeo-Christian" or even "Abrahamic" roots.

This paradigm shift at once permitted and demanded that all religious traditions be studied according to the same method. The discovery of the unity of humankind was also that of the plurality of cultural and religious forms. To be sure, the idea of religion could not but retain its essentially Christian parameters. Nonetheless, one can speak of an intellectual revolution, as the idea of divine revelation was emptied of its theological potency. The plurality of religions (and that of cultures) did not entail, however, a complete disparity between them. All, including Christianity, were now perceived as so many variations on the single theme of natural religion. Natural religion, with its implicit and powerful rejection of any claim of religious superiority for Christianity—because revelation had been dealt a powerful blow—was the obvious solution to the quest for a common substratum beneath the multiple aspects of religion. On the other hand, the plurality of religious forms could also be explained through the idea of civil religion. As a social phenomenon, religion was perceived by our scholars as the expression through specific cultural forms of a universal and natural need. Any religion, in that sense, was more than a set of beliefs, as it represented the public form of a universal drive, different for each people and in each culture. In that sense, any given religion was an eminently social phenomenon, and one of its major expressions would be civil religion, the public expression of social interaction with the sacred.

The discovery of the New World, then, meant the concurrent recognition of the unity of humankind and the multiplicity of cultures. From those intellectuals and scholars who were particularly interested in the essence as well as the multiplicity of religion, a twofold effort was demanded: to understand both religion's single nature and multiple forms. Armed with the notions of natural religion and civil religion, they groped with this complex task. These scholars, mostly forgotten today, were certainly not all equally brilliant minds. But the reading of their often-demanding texts, with their oddities and at times wild interpretations and extrapolations, leaves one with a sense of great respect for their effort and achievements, as well as a sense of humility at the revelation of

37

our own inadequacies and ignorance. These intellectuals and scholars forged many of the concepts that later generations, from the nineteenth century onwards, have used to study religious phenomena.

As enlightened Christians, these scholars, even those who were no "public intellectuals," were what the French call *intellectuels engagés,* and their conception of religion as a universal phenomenon could not but reflect their own understanding of Christianity. It was there, as I hope will become clear in some of the following chapters, that the concept of civil religion permitted these scholars to overcome the limits of Christianity. With the notion of civil religion, they could conceive forms of religion that with a purely Christian vocabulary could only have been understood as idolatry. It was the combination of these two concepts, natural religion and civil religion, that enabled their *Kulturkritik* to bear fruit by setting the foundations for the science of religion—a science left aside, or forgotten, by Michel Foucault's "archaeology of knowledge in the age of reason."

Intellectuals and scholars, missionaries and theologians, ethnologists and philologists: the characters in our story represent many different types of mind. Those most remembered today, thinkers such as Spinoza, Leibniz, or Voltaire, surely had valuable things to say in the story that concerns us, but they are not its main characters. Other intellectuals, Fontenelle, Bayle, and their like, played a more direct role in the process of the *haute vulgarisation* of knowledge on religious phenomena. The real heroes, however, are those, least remembered today by the public at large, who accomplished the actual work of deciphering. Names such as José de Acosta, Thomas Hyde, Isaac de Beausobre, even Athanasius Kircher or Bernard Picart, do not often evoke much interest today, and yet, they and their like were the real explorers of the world's religious traditions, as we shall see in more detail in the following chapters. The paradigm shift they achieved reflects the dialectics of the Enlightenment. It could not have happened without a modicum of critical attitude toward religion on the part of enlightened Christians. And it would eventually lead to the radical undermining of biblical revelation.

II

Respublica Hebraeorum:
Biblical Religion and European Culture

1. *Antiquitates Judaicae:* The Early Modern Study of Israelite Religion

For Church Fathers and medieval Christian scholars alike, ancient Judaism was the precursor of their own faith, and a deep interest in the Hebrew Bible (or, more often, in its inspired translations, the Septuagint or the Vulgata) was a matter of course. Occasionally, this interest included a serious involvement with the rabbinic exegetical tradition. Except for a few rare cases, however, Christian Hebraism essentially remains a modern phenomenon, directly linked to the radical change that occurred in the early modern period in the scholarly approach to ancient texts. At first glance, this change seems to have had less to do with understanding Jews and Judaism than with new attitudes about the past, its documents and monuments. A new critical approach to ancient classical texts was emerging toward the end of the sixteenth century in Western Europe, and new rules for understanding the past were being formulated by a small group of dedicated intellectuals—all convinced, enlightened Christians, whom we usually call the antiquarians. One should insist here that ancient Israel was for them a Gordian knot of sorts, whose understanding would solve, at once, the main problems of ancient history, Christian theology, and European politics. And so, many brilliant and well-trained minds set to work, from various viewpoints, beginning with biblical philology.

Joseph Justus Scaliger (1540–1609) is of course the prime example and model of this new kind of scholar.[1] Although he was primarily a classicist, his philological genius new no boundaries and was also applied to things oriental and Jewish. Witness his claim that the *Book of Enoch* was a (late) case of pseudepigraphy, a reasoned claim that jump-started the modern, critical study of ancient Christianity and its heresies as well as that of Judaism and its early postbiblical history. Here, a direct, straight line leads from Scaliger to Pierre Jurieu and Isaac de Beausobre, both early-eighteenth-century Huguenots in the Amsterdam *Refuge* who emphasized the importance of the Enoch traditions for postbiblical Judaism, early Christianity, and Manichaean origins.

Despite the significance of Scaliger's contribution to oriental studies, however, his main focus was on classical Greek and Latin texts. It was left to others, no less critical and diligent, to consider the early history of Israel. One of the first to do so was Benito Arias Montano (1527–1598), the "Jeronimo español," as his fellow students already called him, who had been appointed to head the Antwerp Polyglot. Alongside his textual studies, in order to highlight their historical context, Arias Montano composed a series of preliminary studies, first published in 1572 in volume 8 (*Apparatus*) of the *Biblia Regia,* and later often reprinted under the title *Antiquitates Judaicae.*[2] Most of these studies dealt with the Holy Land, the Temple and its service, prophecy, and chronology. The first study, however, entitled *Phaleg, sive, de gentium sedibus primis, orbisque terrarum situ,* aimed to draw the broadest possible background for the emergence and development of ancient Israel, beginning with the partitioning of the earth and the dispersion of all its peoples. As we shall see, both the title of this volume and its topic would reappear in one of the major works of seventeenth-century biblical scholarship.

As mentioned above, the century following the endeavors of Arias Montano would see the beginnings of the modern study of ancient Judaism.[3] The modern methods and greatest achievements of biblical criticism, as well as the birth of the *Jewish* study of Judaism, the so-called *Wissenschaft des Judentums* (which dealt mainly with postbiblical Judaism), both date from the nineteenth century. This belatedness is (partly) due to a serious case of intellectual myopia, from which we still suffer, that has kept the real intellectual origins of modern Jewish studies hidden from view. To a great extent, it was the now-forgotten intellectual struggle of a few impressive figures in the seventeenth century that established the ground on which these modern achievements rest.

Michel Foucault's *The Order of Things: An Archaeology of the Human Sciences* enabled us, one generation ago, to recognize more clearly the depth and shape of the intellectual shift that transpired in the seventeenth century. From the scrutiny of deep-seated similarities among phenomena, which had governed Renaissance study, the scholar's mind now learned to focus on differences and to build taxonomies. What Foucault was able to diagnose in fields such as linguistics and grammar was also true in the field of religious phenomena. Since the sixteenth century, the discovery of new cultures had also permitted the birth of an ethnological curiosity to an extent previously unknown, at least in Europe—the eleventh-century Persian polymath Al-Bīrūnī is proof that serious ethnology was possible in Medieval Islamic civilization. The missionaries, first and foremost the *frailes* in New Spain and Peru, were writing the first chapter, now too-often occulted, in the history of social anthropology. The Jesuits and other missionaries in the Ottoman, Chinese, and Japanese empires, soon learned to observe and describe the beliefs and practices of these new peoples. Such curiosity was then applied to still other peoples. For Western European Christians, the Jews were the only foreigners, and sometimes the only enemies, within. Although Jewish life had been precarious in all European countries, Jews had remained a noted presence throughout medieval Europe. Now, the medieval tradition of anti-Jewish polemics faced the need to renew itself. Christian polemicists sought to understand Jewish customs and their traditional background, as reflected in Talmudic and rabbinic literature. It may not be mere chance that the first important study of Jewish rites, in this vein, was that of a Protestant scholar, who sought to base polemics on a firmer knowledge of contemporary Judaism. Johannes Buxtorf's *Judenschul,* or *Synagoga judaica,* was published in German in 1603 and in Latin the following year. To be sure, Buxtorf's book can in no way be considered "value-free," but it opened a new era for the study of Judaism. The first modern ethnological presentation of Judaism written by a Jew for a non-Jewish public, Leone Modena's *I riti degli Ebrei* (published in 1637, but written some twenty years earlier), was probably composed as a response to Buxtorf's slanderous insinuations.[4] In 1674, Richard Simon published his translation of Modena's book, to which he later added (in the second edition, published in 1681) an important *Comparaison des Cérémonies des Juifs et des sacrements de l'Eglise.* This publication stands as a major testimony to the breadth of this great biblical scholar's horizons.[5]

To what extent were the contemporary Jews heirs of the ancient Israelites? This question was beginning to be asked in slightly de-theologized terms, but it is from the early modern times that the dichotomy between the study of ancient Israel and that of postbiblical Judaism dates. Few scholars were interested in both past and present Jews, in both philology and ethnology. The forefathers of the diasporic Jews remained by far the preferred topic of investigation. And although biblical scholars had usually received an excellent training that allowed an extensive use of rabbinic exegetical literature to better understand the Old Testament, few expressed a real intellectual curiosity or respect for postbiblical Judaism. In this sense, Richard Simon was the exception rather than the rule, although for him, too, rabbinic Judaism was interesting less for its own sake than because it provided the real, necessary background for a better understanding of Jesus as a historical figure.

Eventually, however, the phenomenon observable in various branches of orientalism and in missionary anthropology arose in the study of Judaism as well. Here, too, one can detect a gradual transition from theological concern to academic research. The sheer power of intellectual curiosity was able to overcome theological preoccupations, and at least some Hebraists learned to observe Judaism, just as missionaries had learned to observe more exotic religions. The long list of books attempting to compare the religion of the Jews with those of the "Turks" (i.e., Muslims), Americans, Indians, or Chinese is a clear indication that these two phenomena should be seen as directly connected.

It is only in the seventeenth century that the chronological element came to play a central role in the evaluation of cultures. Anthony Grafton has shown how the short-lived science of chronology nonetheless had an immeasurable influence on the early modern comparative study of ancient cultures.[6] The chronological tables set by John Marsham (1602–1685) and others made it crystal-clear to all intellects of good will that Greek and Roman antiquity was neither the oldest nor the purest. Still more significant, accumulated evidence suggested the Bible was not the earliest extant text. The Bible had tilted from its traditional pedestal and began to lose the absolute advantage it had long held over other ancient texts. From now on, the Bible, like Homer, would be only a highly respected and respectable text, a document of the past, to be considered critically, using the same standards applied to other texts. With their groundbreaking publications of the 1670s, Baruch Spinoza and Richard Simon are the obvious early heroes of this story, that of the new, oriental philology. As we shall see in the second part of this chapter, the Bible and Homer could now be compared, as they were now, for the first time, placed on the same level; while the Bible had been demoted, as it were, Homer had been upgraded. A new insight into the nature of ancient cultures was gained, offering a picture dramatically richer than anything previously known.[7] What began as the study of the Hebrew text of the Bible went on to include the study of ancient Near East religions as presented in the Bible, and, from there, more generally, to the study of religious language and experience. The Bible (specifically, the Old Testament), however, retained a clear advantage over Homer: it was older, and came from the east, as all religion did: *ex oriente religio,* or, as the Huguenot theologian Pierre Jurieu would say at the turn of the eighteenth century, "Toutes les religions viennent d'Orient."[8] Orientalism and the study of religions, indeed, have the same roots. To seek the origins of religion, one had to go east, hence to read the Bible in a new way, as one of the oldest documents of the past. Read in this manner, this single document was found to retain not only God's revelation to Israel but also, through the early history of that people, the description of ancient polytheistic religions, subsumed under the generic term of idolatry. The Bible was now read by philologists, using methods first developed for the study of Greek and Latin texts. But the Bible, in its turn, permitted to extend the limits of philology (from Latin and Greek to Hebrew and Aramaic), promoting the flourishing of orientalism in the *République des Lettres.* Throughout the seventeenth century, a series of intellectuals offered major contributions to the study of ancient Israelite religion. The most consistent theme in these contributions remained the comparative study of the polytheistic *Umwelt* of ancient Israel, the "idolatrous" religions of the ancient Near East, mainly those of Phoenicia and Egypt.

As a direct consequence of these studies, the great dichotomy shifted. There was no longer the divide between the great chain of Divine Revelation, first to Israel and then through Jesus Christ, on the one hand, and idolatries of all kinds, times, and figures, on the other. Rather, the unbridgeable gap would from now on be that between religions and cultures of the past and those of the present. There was no essential difference between ancient Israel and other peoples of antiquity, and ancient religions were to be studied together. Israel, just like the Greeks, was now known not to have been the most ancient people. It was commonly agreed that idolatry came first, then monotheism. It was also agreed that ancient Israel could not have escaped the influence of ancient Near Eastern religions; the only question was which ones. Scholars were now divided between supporters of the Phoenician and of the Egyptian cause, as it were. Religious history, *Heilsgeschichte* itself, came to be seen as inseparable from the history of religions, which was by definition universal. There was no such thing as a history of Israel (or of any other people, for that matter) that would not be ipso facto a chapter in universal history. No people could draw impermeable borders around itself and its beliefs. Indeed, the Bible reveals much about the extent to which the history of Israel is fraught with idolatry. As the introduction to *Moeurs et coutumes* strikingly states: "Un peuple est sur cet article le singe d'un autre"; on that topic, peoples ape one another.

The interest in ancient Israel also reflected the imperative need to offer a new model for the integration of politics in society. In the wake of the wars of religion, the traditional relationship between religion and society had been eroded or questioned in various countries. A new understanding of the concept of religion was emerging in the seventeenth century. According to this understanding, religion had a place in every society, and by providing a system of beliefs and practices, religion structured societies' identity and daily functioning. As we have seen, to justify their accommodation of foreign, oriental societies, such as the Chinese, and their acceptance of practices easily dubbed as "idolatrous," the Jesuits learned to counter that such practices were not of a religious nature. Rather, they should be considered reflections of "civil religion," rituals needed for the preservation and well-being of society. This line of argument reflected a long tradition that had its roots in antiquity.

The modern discourse on civil religion is usually considered to start with Rousseau's brief but capital discussion of this concept at the end of his *Contrat Social*. Indeed, the long history of the concept before the Enlightenment is too-often forgotten. Starting with the Stoic Chrysippus, it found its most famous surviving testimony in the writings of the first-century B.C.E. Roman polyhistor Marcus Terentius Varro, whose *Antiquities* have been partly preserved in Augustine's *City of God*. Varro divided theology into mythic, natural, and civil. According to him, the first king of Rome, Numa Pompilius, had also been its legislator, or *nomothetès,* and had given Rome its religion, which was meant to offer a rule to the city. The figure of Numa was thus of major importance in Latin and in later Greek literature, an importance that was amply echoed by patristic authors.[9] The idea of civil religion, which largely remained dormant in the Middle Ages, suddenly came to the fore of intellectual discourse and debate: was it possible, and if so, under what conditions, to discover the principles at the root of any civil religion? Just as Christian medieval theology and philosophy had not been able to develop a conceptual reflection of idolatry, the European tradition had no ready-made tool to define and analyze the elements of civil religion. In such a situation, trial and error was the only available method of investigation.

From Bodin to Rousseau, through Hobbes, Locke, and Montesquieu, the history of political thought until the Enlightenment is a series of such attempts. Of course, concepts of natural law, and to some extent natural religion (as any religion was, mainly, the law of a nation), already had a long history. But in their search for the elementary forms of religion in all societies, these thinkers received unexpected help from a medieval Jewish precursor. The influence of Maimonides on seventeenth-century European intellectuals has indeed been recognized, but it seems to me that his impact on the development of a new discourse on religion has not yet received the attention it deserves.[10] In his *Mishneh Torah,* the philosopher Moses Maimonides (1136–1204) discusses at length the seven Noahide Laws, which according to rabbinic tradition were the clear criteria differentiating civilized societies from barbarous ones. Maimonides' discussion, in this as in other matters, seems to have had a powerful effect. All of a sudden, and for a century, the Noahide Laws became a central concept in the history of religions. They offered a thread of Ariadne, as it were, through which one could retrace the early religious history of humankind and the place of religion in ancient polytheistic societies, as reflected in the Hebrew Bible.

From our current perspective, one of the most influential books throughout the seventeenth century and beyond was John Selden's *De Diis Syris Syntagmata.* Selden sought to collect all extant information (from the Bible and classical and patristic literature) on ancient Near Eastern religions. This book, which students of Selden too-often ignore as an early, immature work, has been largely overlooked. The great jurist John Selden (1584–1654), whom John Marsham called "Seldenus noster," was one of the most learned and best minds of his generation. He published in 1617 his *De Diis Syris Syntagmata,* which was written as early as 1605. This book represents the first serious effort to deal with ancient polytheism from a nonclassical perspective.[11] Its dramatic influence on all subsequent studies of ancient Near Eastern religion cannot be overemphasized.

The single most important topic Selden discussed in the *De Diis Syris* is the description of ancient Phoenician mythology, more precisely the creation myth, as had been registered by the Phoenician writer Sanchuniaton and translated to Greek by Philo of Byblos.[12] Philo's work is lost, but excerpts were preserved by the fourth-century Christian writer Eusebius of Caesarea, in his *Praeparatio Evangelica*. Selden devotes only few pages to this text, but these pages would be echoed in many learned works, at least to the end of the eighteenth century. It is to a great extent thanks to Sanchuniaton, as much as to Greek and Roman myths, that early modern European scholars discovered the study of mythology. Selden's *De Diis Syris* taught his contemporaries how to think about the religious history of the Near East and the pagan background of the Bible.

The third chapter of *De Diis Syris* is entitled: *De tès polutheotès seu Deorum multitudinis origine et processu.*("On polytheism, or on the origin and evolution of the multiplicity of gods"). Rather than looking for the roots of polytheism in Greece and Rome, Selden goes back to the biblical testimony on idolatry, which constitutes the core of his evidence, although by no means all of it. Selden refers not only to Hebrew but also to other Semitic languages. His references, which are derived from epigraphy as well as from classical, patristic, rabbinic—and kabbalistic—as well as Arabic literatures, show an amazingly broad field of research. Selden, however, keeps the reader confused as to his real goal and method. He certainly works as a comparativist (the first chapter, for instance, is entitled: *De Gad, seu Fortuna*), but he is mainly interested in discovering genetic links, not simply parallels. For him, religion stems from the East: *ex oriente numen*. Since the evidence from the ancient Near East (Syria, Egypt, Persia, as well as the Hebrew Bible) antedates preclassical times, it is there that one has to search for the roots of European religion. Comparativism, then, is put here at the service of history, and Selden's method (which he uses in his legal studies as well) can be described as "historico-philological." For him, polytheism is basically the effect of a multiplicity of symbols. With time, distinct images came to be perceived as different gods. This highly original theory about an early misunderstanding of the symbol would soon influence Ralph Cudworth's *True Intellectual System of the Universe* (London, 1678). Through Daniel Heinsius, a prominent Dutch humanist who had become closely associated with Selden when living in England, *De Diis Syris* was reprinted in Leiden in 1627. Thence, it had a direct influence on later studies of ancient polytheist cults, on the continent as well as in England.

The mature Selden's more famous work, *De jure naturali et gentium* (London, 1640), had a remarkable influence on the transformation of natural law theory and its abandonment of scholastic conceptions of natural law, which had been confined to the strictly Aristotelian tradition. In this work, Selden discovers and highlights the rabbinic conception of the seven Noahide commandments, of which he had learned in Maimonides' *Mishneh Torah* (*Hilkhot melakhim* 8.10).[13]

Maimonides discusses there the rabbinic teaching about the seven commandments given by God to Noah's sons after the Flood. These commandments, the seven Noahide Laws, are both religious and civil in nature, and according to the rabbis, these laws were a necessary and sufficient condition for "pagan" societies to be considered decent (and hence for those who observe them to be saved). These seven commandments, in short, represent God's expectations from all peoples, while the Decalogue was revealed only to the Hebrews. For Selden, natural law reflects the dealings of God with men immediately after the Flood. In fact, he conceives the Noahide Laws to be quite equivalent to natural law: indeed, the full title of his work reflects this perception: *De jure naturali et gentium iuxta disciplinam Ebraeorum, libri septem.*[14]

From Selden's discussion, it is clear that he discovers in the Noahide commandments a new way of reflecting on natural law and natural religion, one more congenial to him than that offered by the scholastic tradition. The seven Noahide Laws represent a mixture of personal ethics (the prohibition of bloodshed), rules for the proper functioning of a decent society (tribunals), and directives for religious behavior, properly so-called (divine cult).

For Selden, the ancient Near East meant mainly Syria: Mesopotamia was still largely unknown, and the "Bibel und Babel" controversy does not antedate the nineteenth century and the decipherment of cuneiform writing. The other obvious direction in the search for the origins of Israelite religion was, obviously, Egypt, a path that would be followed by other scholars. In this case too, research remained highly speculative, as no Egyptian text could yet be deciphered. But the image of a culture has little connection with real, solid knowledge about it, and Egypt, known at least since the Renaissance to have been the oldest civilization, had appealed to the European imagination. Athanasius Kircher (1601/2–1680) among others had written some daring comparative analyses of foreign cultures and religions, in which Egypt played a central role, such as his *Oedipus Aegyptiacus.* But Kircher, a German Jesuit living in Rome, still belonged in a sense to the Renaissance world, and his hermetist mind was interested in analogies more than in careful distinctions.

The major work to discuss directly and in a sustained fashion the political dimensions of ancient Israelite religion was *De republica Hebraeorum* by

Petrus Cunaeus, a law professor at Leiden.[15] Others, such as Cunaeus's friend Hugo Grotius, were devoting efforts to the topic, but the work of Cunaeus soon became the standard reference, a fact reflected by the book's many reprints. For Peter Miller, if this text "marks an epoch in this genre," it is "because of its reliance on post-biblical sources."[16] Such reliance, however, can also be found in other contemporaneous works. It seems, therefore, that the success of Cunaeus's book is due, rather, to the conceptual framework in which he places his discussion and, more precisely, to his Maimonidean approach to political realities, which was unknown in Christian Europe. Cunaeus, in a sense, was offering a study of theocracy, as he was trying to search in ancient Israel for a convincing model of the place of religion in the state.[17]

Moses was the Lawgiver, as were, later, Lycurgus and Numa Pompilius. His Law and rule had established, at once, both society and religion. Moses' Law was perfect, and, if observed, it permitted the blooming of a perfect society, the *Republica Hebraeorum*. Here again, it stands to reason that we have a significant (though, it seems, unrecognized) Maimonidean influence. Maimonides had read al-Farabi carefully and was strongly influenced by al-Farabi's views on Plato's political philosophy as developed in the *Republic*. For Maimonides, the philosopher king was the prophet, and the best prophet of all was Moses, the Lawgiver. In *Guide of the Perplexed*, Maimonides had thus applied to ancient Israel the description of an ideal society as discussed by al-Farabi.[18] In its turn, Maimonides' argument now formed the backbone of Cunaeus's work. Cunaeus refers to Maimonides on various occasions in his book, in particular to Moses as the Lawgiver, as developed in Maimonides's legal code, the *Mishneh Torah*.[19]

Spinoza, too, was a reader of Maimonides. More than any of his contemporaries, however, Spinoza is highly critical of him, while accepting in part (but only in part) Maimonides's understanding of the political dimension of religion. In his *Tractatus Theologico-Politicus* (ch. 14.10), Spinoza rejects Maimonides view on the Noahide Laws, but offers seven principles that seem to be fashioned on the seven Noahide commandments as a blueprint for a civil religion that will bring peace to the state.[20] Although Spinoza's *Tractatus Theologico-Politicus* falls beyond the scope of our concern, its central role in the birth of biblical criticism cannot be ignored.

What is clear from the two pivotal cases of Selden and Cunaeus is the extent to which ethnological observation and the comparative study of religious systems coincided: Judaism observed was also Judaism compared. Indeed, the study of ancient Israel lies largely at the root of the orientalist quest. The recognition of Israel's oriental background as the natural framework for its serious study broadened the scope of both biblical and oriental studies. Early biblical scholars, moreover, were well-read Hebraists, who often possessed a strong knowledge of rabbinic literature, and made good use of it. A better understanding of ancient Israel helped explain other religious systems, including polytheistic ones, while other religions shed new light on that of Israel. At the time, the religion of biblical Israel still held a place of honor in intellectual reflection, which it would gradually lose throughout the eighteenth and nineteenth centuries.

2. *Homeros Hebraios*: Homer and the Bible at the Origins of European Culture

Ex oriente lux! This formula—whose origin remains unknown—reflects the attraction of the East throughout the cultural history of Europe, from antiquity to modern times. The "East" serves as a generic term through which one refers to exogenous or exotic civilizations, heirs to a perennial wisdom whose key has been lost. Western Europe has always known that its cultural and religious roots were elsewhere, in Athens or in Jerusalem.[21] From biblical Palestine, one moves to Egypt, or even to Babel, and to the world of Islam—as in Goethe's *West-östliche Diwan*. One of the oldest major theses of the Eastern roots of European culture is found in the relationship between the two canonical texts which stand at its roots, the Homeric epics and the Bible.

Around the mid-seventeenth century, European intellectuals began exploring the relationship between Homer and the Hebrew Bible. This was actually more of a new question than a renewed interest, as the Church Fathers of late antiquity dealt with the relationship between Plato and Moses, rather than with that between the Bible and the pagan Homer. For centuries, actually, Homer's texts remained terra incognita for Christians, and Homer himself was a dubious character in patristic literature.[22] According to Justin Martyr, and to many subsequent theologians, it is in Plato, not Homer, that one finds the "spiritual seed" planted by God in peoples other than the chosen people. Such an attitude toward Plato was not limited to Christian authors, and Plato is presented, for instance, as an "Atticizing Moses" by Numenius of Apamea, a neo-Pythagorean philosopher of the second century.[23]

The context, causes, and significance of the new perception of links between Homer and the Bible in the early modern age need to be carefully examined. We shall follow here the origin and the main trends of this perception. To a great extent, indeed, the comparison between Homer and the Bible stands at the root of the historical interpretation of the Homeric epics and biblical criticism. In the eighteenth century, the center of these studies moved from France to England, and only later to Germany. In the nineteenth century, the very success of modern classical philology and the study of the ancient Near East encouraged the fast dissociation between the two fields. The mutual ignorance between disciplines was emphasized by the location of biblical studies in theological faculties and by the development of anti-Semitism in academic circles, particularly in Germany.[24] Happily, we can witness today, among classical philologists, a new acknowledgment of the importance of the cultural and religious contact between Greece and other civilizations of the Near East throughout antiquity. In this context, the name of Walter Burkert comes first to mind, although he is by no means the only one to recognize what Greek mythology owed to oriental mythologies.[25]

We must beware of anachronisms. What appears today to stand as common sense was not necessarily obvious three centuries ago. Various conditions were necessary for the comparison between Homer and the Bible to take effect. The first of these was clearly modern philology, both classical and Semitic, the study of Greek and Hebrew, and the publication of biblical or parabiblical texts in critical editions. The greatest pioneer here, Joseph Justus Scaliger (1540–1609), does not erase the enormous philological achievements of numerous classicists throughout Western Europe.

The second condition, closely tied to the first, is the new perception of both the Bible and Homer that permits their comparison. The birth of biblical criticism in the second half of the seventeenth century led to a devaluation of the Bible's text. From a religious canon, a revealed and unchangeable text, it became a venerable text from antiquity, like others, to which textual and historical criticism could be applied. In a sense, one can say that the Bible was transformed from a religious canon into a cultural one.[26] Like Homer, the Bible was now perceived, for the first time, as a historical document. This historicizing of the Bible entailed a certain distantiation: it was now seen as arising from a society quite distant from modernity, even if the latter's religious identity was rooted in that ancient society.

While the Bible was, in this sense, "devalued," the inverse phenomenon occurred with Homer. The *Iliad* and the *Odyssey* were edited and translated and became the object of a series of polemics. The most famous of these, the "Quarrel of the Ancients and the Moderns," raged in late-seventeenth-century France and in the first two decades of the eighteenth century. The Jesuits, who had at first strongly objected to teaching Homer (whom they considered dangerous for young minds) in their schools, eventually authorized it. Homer achieved then the status of cultural canon. To be sure, from late antiquity up to the modern age, European cultural identity was always built as bi-cephalous. Despite Tertullian's literary phase, Athens and Jerusalem were perceived throughout European cultural history as its two complementary poles—what I have called, using a metaphor borrowed from the field of biology, a "double helix."[27] Now, for the first time in history, the Bible and Homer could be read by the same persons, with more or less the same hermeneutical rules.[28]

Let us note that these two antiquities, that of Israel and that of Greece, were not the only ones to compete in the early modern age. There was also Rome *bifrons,* or two-faced, pagan, then Christian.[29] But the first is linked to Greece through the notion of the classical world, while the other is perceived, in a sense, as the *continuatio christiana* of the sacred history of Israel. As to the ancient Near East, while it seems close to Israel from a cultural point of view, it resembles Greece and Rome in its polymorphous idolatry.

Once the principle of comparison between these two textual bodies was established, various theories could explain the similarities and differences between them, which are sometimes perceived as striking. The starting point for any comparative reflection was biblical monotheism versus Homeric polytheism. Both were (and are) often conceived as only superficial and hiding a more fundamental unity of the various religious traditions. In patristic literature as well as in medieval thought, two leading models were proposed to explain the historical relationship between polytheism and monotheism in the ancient Near East. The first model proposed the degeneration of an original monotheism into polytheism; the second, the accommodation of Israelite monotheism to preexistent cultures imbibed with polytheistic ideas. The first model explained and justified the existence of various pagan cults; the other explained the persistence of "pagan" beliefs and practices (in particular, sacrifices) in

Israelite religion. Oddly enough, these two options would reappear in later approaches. The second is obviously more "modern," as it is more in line with contemporary scholarship that assumes the preexistence of paganism to monotheism; John Spencer, in *De legibus hebraeorum ritualibus* (Cambridge, 1685), is the great advocate of this approach.[30]

Textual criticism reflects the new scholarly attitude: to restore texts stemming from the oldest past and to consider them in their original historical and cultural context (what will be called later *"Sitz im Leben"*). How should the similarities between the Greek and Hebrew texts be explained? Once again, one should insist here on the importance of compared chronology. John Marsham, perhaps the best-known representative of this discipline, discovered that both classical Greece and biblical Israel were younger than other civilizations of the Ancient Mediterranean and Near East, in particular Egypt.[31] The Greeks appeared rather late on the scene of world history. Similarities between Homer and the Bible, then, must reflect influences from the ancient Near East, biblical or not.

In the comparison between Homer and the Bible, then, one finds *in nuce* the fundamental principles of the new comparative study of religions. This study deals with both structures and chronology. Beginning in the seventeenth century, a series of serious works offered a historical and comparative study of ancient Near Eastern religions. We discussed above one brilliant example of this genre, the pioneering *De Diis Syris,* written by the young John Selden (London, 1617), which draws an impressive panorama of the milieu in which the Bible was born. This milieu, of course, was that of idolatry, and thus similar to that of Greek fables, or myths. These fables, be they Greek, Roman, or oriental, were posited in contradistinction to biblical history. But scholars also start to speak in the plural of stories transcribed in the Bible, moving from there to speak about fables, first in the Jewish postbiblical traditions (Richard Simon, for instance), then within the Bible itself.[32] By "fables" one means what will later be called myths.[33] In the eighteenth century, the new term "mythology" referred to what is today called the comparative history of religions. Such use of the term is recorded, for instance, in the entry "Mythologie," in Diderot's *Encyclopédie.*[34]

The comparison between Homer and the Bible represents a chapter in the birth of the history of religions. As we have seen in chapter I, the publication and diffusion of ethnological reports coming from Catholic missionaries to exotic cultures, both in Asia and the Americas, did much to permit this birth. Did contemporary nonmonotheistic religions reflect idolatry, like the religions of the ancient world? What seemed evident when dealing with Amerindian religions became much more problematic when applied to the Chinese, for instance. One has here the nucleus of the other famous polemic of the times. Like the *Querelle des Anciens et des Modernes,* the *Querelle des Rites* focused on the problem of cultural relativity and would divide the Catholic Church for a good part of the eighteenth century. Ethnological curiosity played a role in this problem. In the eighteenth century, the study of the relationship between the Bible and Homer would use, well before William Robertson Smith, albeit in a rather simplistic way, ethnographic material coming from the observation of Bedouin mores, which were thought to reflect, *mutatis mutandis,* those of ancient societies such as the Hebrews or the Greeks.[35]

The comparison between biblical and Homeric mores, however, represents the last stage of a process. The study usually starts with philological observations. Edmund Dickinson, for instance, published in Oxford in 1655 *Delphi Phoenicizantes.* According to the author's thesis, it is in the story of Joshua in the Scriptures that one must look for the origin of the Delphic oracle. For Dickinson, the pagan gods represent the transformations of the Hebrew heroes, in a sort of transcultural euhemerism. Apollo and the "Egyptian Hercules," in particular, are identical to Joshua, whose father, Nun, became Jupiter. In an appendix, Dickinson shows that Noah, who reached Italy in his ark, is inter alia at the origin of the druids.[36]

Dickinson dedicates his book to his friend Zachary Bogan, the author of *Homerus Hebraizon* (Oxford, 1658), the first work, it seems, to deal specifically with our theme. As its subtitle clearly indicates, it is meant to compare the wording of Homer to that of the Bible ("comparatio Homeri cum Scriptoribus Sacris quoad normam loquendi.") Bogan, who refers to the works of Meric Casaubon and Vossius, lists expressions found in both Homer and the Bible (in particular the Old Testament). The analysis of such isomorphisms does not go far, and the implications of such linguistic parallels are not fully pursued. Bogan deals mainly with expressions, for instance, anthropomorphic expressions, and grammatical and syntactic resemblances between the two ancient languages.

Another book, similar in its approach, is *Homeri Gnomologia,* published in 1660 in Cambridge, where its author, James Duport, was the Regius Professor of Greek. The main idea of this work is that the parallels one can observe between Homer, the oldest of the pagan authors, and the Holy Scriptures, in particular the Pentateuch and Job, can be explained by the chronological precedence of Moses to Homer. These parallels are thus often interpreted as allusions, quotations, or else parodies of the biblical texts. Regarding the Homeric text, Duport is critical: the division of the *Iliad*, for instance, is late and is ascribed to Aristarchos. His orthodox attitude toward Moses, the author of the Pentateuch, should not however mislead us. From the moment one accepts that the argument must be philological and historical, new data permits another vision of the relationship between the two texts. The main fact is that they can be compared.

A few decades later, Gerard Croese published a book entitled *Homeros Hebraios*.[37] Croese attributed the similarities between Homer and the Bible to the fact that the authors of the Homeric books were refugees from Palestine who concealed their original traditions within the Greek text. Thus, for instance, the story of the fall of Troy would hide that of Jericho's conquest, while Ithaca, Ulysses' fatherland, would stand for Mesopotamia, Abraham's fatherland. Croese also claimed to identify various allusions to Isaac in the Homeric text.[38] These works often make for tough reading and are quite simplistic in their argumentation. Their importance lies in that they announce more serious philological studies.

A series of articles in the *Histoire Critique de la République des Lettres*, perhaps the first important scholarly journal, reflect the start of such studies. In the issues from 1713 to 1716, for instance, one finds various discussions (often signed by Jacques Masson) on some difficult passages in both Homer and the Bible. The solutions proposed usually rest on comparisons with other writings of antiquity. The thunder in *Odyssey* (V, 113–114), for instance, is directly linked to the various theophorous mentions of thunder in the Bible and elsewhere. The thunder is "a sign of Divinity among the Orientals, the Greeks and the Romans."[39] The author of the same article notes that "without a significant knowledge of Antiquity, it is not possible to understand correctly various passages of the Holy Writ." Elsewhere, one reads: "This is how Profane and Sacred Letters help one another." Here, the cloud taking Jesus Christ is clarified in the *Iliad* (XVII, 551).[40]

The idea that the Scriptures were anterior to all other ancient literatures was a theological conception that sought to explain parallels or similarities between the Bible and Homer (or other ancient texts) as reflecting the imitation of the former by the latter. This idea, undergoing a transformation, would become the basis of modern comparative philology. The Bible and Homer would now put on the same level: both are ancient literatures, reflecting the *realia,* the psychology and the religious conceptions of civilizations quite foreign to our own, but rather close to one another. As representatives of similar cultures, they could indeed be better understood each in the light of the other.

Thus Richard Bentley, Regius Professor of Divinity in Cambridge in the late seventeenth and early eighteenth centuries, who discovered the digamma, considered the description of Homer and Moses as authors of collections of ancient writings to be pious fictions. One detects here, essentially, the approach that would permit the intuitions of Heyne and Wolf toward the end of the eighteenth century. That this approach has been called "Homeric atheism" should come as no surprise.[41]

The remarkable objectivity of the *Histoire Critique de la République des Lettres* did not conquer all minds. Apologetic undertones would remain for a long time. To give only a single example, Guérin du Rocher postulates in his *Hérodote historien du peuple hébreu sans le savoir,* the anteriority of the Bible to all other literatures, pointing out the many parallel features in the histories of Egypt and Israel.[42] What the various mythologies of the ancient world share with Hebrew religion stems from the latter, and reflects pagan alterations. Du Rocher, a Roman Catholic priest, speaks of "antiquités fabuleuses" (i.e., mythical histories).

Even a short review of seventeenth-century authors cannot avoid mentioning three great French names, the Protestant Samuel Bochart, the Bishop of Avranches Pierre-Daniel Huet, and Claude Fleury, also a Catholic priest. François Laplanche has called Bochart's oeuvre "une montagne d'érudition,"[43] while Ernest Renan had already noted that "Bochart established around 1650 the basis of the comparative science of Semitic antiquities."[44] As Bochart will be discussed in chapter IV, I shall only mention here his opus magnum, *Geographia Sacra,* including *Phaleg,* a monograph on the dispersion of peoples on earth after the destruction of the Tower of Babel.[45] *Phaleg* starts as a commentary on Genesis 10, on the origins of all nations. In this work Bochart explains the plurality of ancient civilizations through their propagation from Palestine and the biblical Near East. Relevant here is Bochart's polemic with the Catholics about Phoenician navigation and colonies in the Mediterranean. According to Bochart, it is the Phoenicians who gave shelter to shipwrecked

Ulysses and brought him to Crete. On this topic, the Homeric scholar
Victor Bérard observed that it is high time we return to some of Bochart's
conceptions.[46]

Bochart's ideas thus represent the link between acknowledging the
cultural and religious pluralism of the ancient world (in Selden, for instance) and borrowings from the Semitic world on the part of Homer.
Bochart was, first of all, a philologist, and it is as such that he reveals
both his strength and his weakness, as comparative Semitic philology
was then only budding. For him, for instance, the name of Aeolus stems
from Hebrew *aol,* "gust of wind" (*sic!*). About Charybdis and Scylla, he
refers to Hebrew *scol* (=*she'ol*), "pit of perdition." Similarly, Siren comes
from Hebrew *shir,* song. Bochart kept constant contacts with contemporary scholars. One can find him in Oxford (where he converses in Latin);
he studies Arabic with Erpenius in Leiden, and also meets Vossius in the
Netherlands. It is with his young pupil Huet that he went to Stockholm,
upon the invitation of Queen Christina.

Huet's *Demonstratio Evangelica,* first published in 1679, with Bossuet's
blessing, immediately became a great success and was reprinted four times
within five years. Huet, an excellent Hebraist, read Hebrew texts for a few
hours every day, according to his own testimony: the Bible, but also the
rabbis.[47] For him, the various mythologies in the world represented so
many disguised versions of the story of Moses. The Egyptian Thoth, the
Greek Hermes, the Roman Mercury, the German Wotan, the Gaul Tautates, Osiris, Bacchus, Adonis in Arabia where Moses sojourned, and many
other gods, were all masquerades of Moses. Huet states explicitly that he
establishes his argument on the works of Scaliger, Vossius, and Bochart.

As noted by Alphonse Dupront, Huet's epistemological principle is
that "truth comes first . . . Truth must exist before lie."[48] It is not only in
ancient civilizations that Huet finds the biblical truths. He also discovers
their traces among exotic peoples of the present, such as Peruvians or
Indians.[49] In his remarkable *Essai sur les origines du Roman,* published
in 1669, Huet had already speculated that Homer had visited oriental
lands and had met Egyptians, Arabs, Persians, and Syrians. From all
these peoples, Homer could have received Hebrew traditions, at least indirectly, side by side with the teachings on poetry that he received from
oriental peoples.[50]

Claude Fleury published in 1681 *Les moeurs des Israélites*—like
Huet, with the approbation of the powerful Bossuet. He starts by ac-

knowledging the distance, geographical and chronological, between contemporary society and those of the ancient world, such as Greece or Israel. This distance, however, did not exist between the ancient societies
themselves.

> One must be totally unaware of history in order not to see the
> great change brought to mores by time and space. How far are we
> from the life style [of Gauls and Romans] . . . And in our own cen-
> tury, what is the relation between our mores and those of Turks,
> Indians or Chinese? Then, if we add the two sorts of distance, we
> will not be surprised by the fact that the mores of men living in
> Palestine three thousand years ago were different from our own.[51]

This sensitivity to everything that separates us from the ancients should
certainly not prevent our sympathy for them. The ancient Hebrews represent "an excellent model of human life, the most conform to nature."[52]

Fleury did not keep his sympathy only for the Hebrews. He was also
a friend of Homer. In 1665, at the age of twenty-five, he published his
Remarques sur Homère. In this work, Fleury submitted the idea of a link
between Homer and the Bible, which he later further developed in his
Moeurs des Israélites.[53] One finds in Homer, he wrote, "an infinity of
peculiarities of the lifestyle of his time which are very helpful for the understanding of the Bible." Like Huet, Fleury spoke of biblical anteriority
("the world was quite old in Homer's times, and the East quite cultured"), but the various speculations on possible channels of influence
between ancient societies did not seem to interest him, even though he
followed Huet in things oriental. This was due to the fact that Fleury's
sensitivity was more that of an ethnologist than a philologist.[54] When he
compared Homer with Job, noting in both a mixture of dialects, he did
not linger to draw consequences from this fact. He simply noted the existence, in Homer as well as the Bible, of various "extraordinary" words,
that one must often explain as coming from Arabic, Aramaic, or Syriac.
For him, indeed, Homer

> lived in the time of Solomon, and one agrees that he was born in
> Asia, although one does not agree on the place. Thus Greeks and
> Trojans follow in Homer the same lifestyle as that of the Hebrews
> in the Bible. That is, pastoral and agricultural kings, except for the
> fact that the Greeks are even less cultured. We can detect, more-
> over, very similar patterns of speech.

Fleury concluded his work by noting that Homer "is one of the best interpreters of Scripture for those who only look for the literal sense."[55]

It is not only for the freshness of his approach, so much more modern than that of Huet and even Bochart, that Fleury is remarkable. It is also because his work had a deep and lasting influence. Until the nineteenth century, *Les moeurs des Israélites* and *Les moeurs des Chrétiens* were constantly reprinted. The young François Fénelon, who had met Fleury, was deeply influenced by him, as can be seen in his *Télémaque*.[56] Fleury's influence can also be detected in other seminal works such as La Bruyère's *Caractères,* Montesquieu's *Esprit des lois,* and even, perhaps, Rousseau's *Contrat social.*[57]

Fleury's essay appeared together with the translation of the Homeric epics by Anne Dacier, the famous protagonist of the "Querelle des Anciens et des Modernes" (1687–1717). Madame Dacier sought to defend Homer and the archaic quality of his poetry against the moderns, for whom Homer belonged to a rough age with which the "politeness" of modern taste had nothing in common. To do so, Dacier called attention to the fact that Homeric mores were rather similar to those of the biblical patriarchs. "These are the same mores that one sees in the Sacred Scripture," she wrote, adding that Homer's "style is the same as that of the books of the ancient Hebrews."[58] He who decried the one also decried the other—which would entail a rejection of the Scriptures, or at least a total lack of respect toward them. Here too, Fleury's mark is clear. Dacier expresses her views, in particular, in the preface to her translation of the *Iliad*. "I like to see Homer's heroes do what the Patriarchs were doing"[59] (XXV). For her, the Homeric gods were identical to the angels in Scripture (XV). She refers to Grotius, who had compared Homer with Ezekiel. Where do these parallels come from? Dacier was here following Huet, a friend of her father, the Protestant scholar Tanneguy La Fève. She greatly respected the authority of Homer, whom she believed to have travelled across the Mediterranean, and in particular in Egypt. As we know from Herodotus that most of the Greek gods and their cult come from Egypt, Homer was probably "educated in Egypt in many aspects of the doctrine of the Hebrews."[60] Here too, there is a refusal to consider modern civilization as superior to that of these times, rough, indeed, but "happy, when one knew neither luxury nor softness, and when glory consisted only in work and virtue, and shame in sluggishness and vice."[61] Since the moderns rejected Homer for his poor artistic quality, for the suspect ethics that he reflected, and for his paganism, the ancients had to defend him on all three levels.

With Madame Dacier, we are solidly in the eighteenth century. Now, Homer seems to be attractive mainly on the English side of the Channel. The two great names here are Thomas Blackwell (1701–1757) and Robert Wood (1717–1767). With both of them, the comparison between Homer and the Bible has opened the way to a new, comparative approach to the Homeric epics, which is not necessarily limited to Hebrew literature. It is with the various cultures of the ancient Near East that one must now compare Homer. One can detect here a certain secularization of knowledge. The comparison with the Bible has legitimized Homer. He can now abandon, as it were, his "Hebrew crutches."

Thomas Blackwell was in strong disagreement with theories popular in the preceding century. He objected to Vossius, to Bochart, to Huet, and also to his contemporary Étienne Fourmont (1683–1745), who followed the trace of these great philologists and mythologists.[62] Blackwell first expresses his ideas in *An Enquiry into the Life and Writings of Homer* (London, 1735). He proposes to read Homer as literature, rather than as a sacred text: Homer was not inspired by heaven; he was "not a Prophet, nor an Interpreter."[63] For Blackwell, Greek religion came essentially from Egypt, a land visited by Greek sages. It was thus in Egypt, rather than in Israel (via Egypt), that the first wise men picked up their religious ideas. "The first sages among the Greeks drew their Science from these countries, and their Theology in particular from Egypt."[64] Such Ethiopian influences were spread in Crete and in various areas of Greece. The Egyptians were not the only ones to influence the Greeks. Other influences came from Asia Minor (music) and from Phoenicia (the arts). From all peoples of antiquity, only the Jews did not contribute anything to the common good: "The Jews alone of all the rest have contributed nothing for the publick good."[65]

This represented a dramatic break with the various options possible until then. The rejection of Israel did not entail that of the whole East. The contrary was perhaps true. Liberation from the chains of the Bible permitted scholarly imagination to spread its wings. The East was vast, one dreamt of it. It was now multiform, colored, mythical. To be sure, the variety of archaic religions and cultures had already been articulated in the seventeenth century. Through Maimonides, one knew of the existence and importance of the mysterious Sabians and of their books full of an exotic and lost wisdom.[66] Now, one could do better. The great oriental mythology of the eighteenth century was that of Sankhuniaton. Eusebius of Caesarea had revealed for us, with the fragments of his work, the lost mythology of the Phoenicians. Blackwell was far from original when he mentioned Sankhuniaton in his *Letters Concerning Mythology*.[67] During the Enlightenment, many scholars would get involved in similar studies.

If Blackwell reached notoriety, Robert Wood surpassed him. Wood was a traveler, one of the very first in a long list of British scholars who fell in love with the Near East. In 1753, he published *The Ruins of Palmyra (Tedmor)*, and in 1757 *The Ruins of Balbec-Hieropolis*, magnificent folios with a series of drawings and plans from temples and ruins. It is for his *Essay on the Original Genius and Writings of Homer*, published in 1775, that he is best remembered. Although it was criticized by Gibbon, the work soon became a "best seller" in Europe. Soon, it was translated to French, German, Italian, and Spanish, and would eventually captivate Goethe.[68]

Wood's central idea was, again, comparative. He did not cast doubt on Homer's oriental predecessors. Rather than searching for written sources, he argues that the present can offer important insights for understanding the past. The subtitle of his book reads: "with a comparative view of the ancient and the present state of Troad." In his travels in the East, Wood attempted to find whatever could contribute to an explanation of Homer's writing. Wood accepts the idea that Homer was "Asiatic," probably Ionian or Eolian, coming perhaps from Chios or Smyrna. In any case, he was a Greek and could have learned the rules of navigation from Greeks, so that we can dispense with the need to imagine Phoenician teachers. While some of the figures or scenes in his epic might have come from Egypt or from the East, the action and mythology are Greek, more precisely Ionian, Wood contends. To understand Homer, then, there is no need to postulate any Jewish influence through Egyptian priests. Rather than following this traditional theory, which appears to have mislead research, writes Wood, it may be better to compare Homer with contemporary mores. In the East, where mores evolve slowly, contemporary populations still exhibit ancient behavioral patterns, he observes. It is mainly the Arabs that Wood has in mind, in particular the Bedouins he met during his trip. His book, indeed, is rich in ethnological observations.[69]

As for future Homeric studies, it was mainly in Germany that Wood's impact would be felt. In his study on Homer in eighteenth-century England, Donald Foerster points out that Herder may have been the first to draw attention to Wood's *Enquiry*.[70] For Herder, in striking contradistinction to Vico, the same principles ruled the history of all peoples. In 1769, however, six years before its publication, Wood had sent his manuscript to Johann David Michaelis, the great Old Testament scholar from Göttingen. The latter had shown it to his classicist colleague Christian Gottlob Heyne, the teacher of Friedrich August Wolf, the formulator of the "Homeric problem."[71] In his Göttingen publications, Heyne could thus refer to Wood, who represents the link between England and Germany in the parallel study of Homer and the Bible. When Wolf published his *Prolegomena ad Homerum*, in 1795, Heyne protested, claiming that Wolf had stolen some of his main ideas. Wolf answered (in January 1796), that all these ideas actually came from Wood.[72]

The other pole of research was mainly that of Robert Lowth (1717–1788), whose *Lectures on the Sacred Poetry of the Hebrews* (Latin 1753; English 1787) represent the first attempt, in England, to deal with the Bible from a historical and literary point of view. Lowth thus compared the Scriptures with the Homeric epics, arguing for the religious and ritual origins of poetry, and called Homer "divinus ille genius."[73] Here too, the core of future research would now be transferred to Germany.

Through a specific example, the following chapter will show how one could move from the study of biblical religion to that of Judaism.

III

From Biblical Philology to the Study of Judaism

The Oratorian priest Richard Simon (1638–1712) is mainly known for his path-breaking biblical works. Besides his magnum opus, the *Histoire Critique du Vieux Testament,* which was published in its definitive form in 1685, he penned three major works on the New Testament, *Histoires Critiques* of, respectively, its text, its versions, and its commentators. In his preface to the *Histoire Critique du Vieux Testament,* Simon defines "histoire critique" as a *terminus technicus* for an investigation meant to reconstruct, beyond the deformations of time, the original state of a text.[1] Although Simon remains less famous, perhaps, than his precursors, Isaac La Peyrère, Hobbes, and in particular Spinoza (whose *Tractatus Theologico-politicus* was published in 1670), his seminal contribution to the establishment of modern standards of biblical exegesis is well recognized. Ernest Renan, for instance, who called Spinoza "the Bacon of exegesis," referred to Simon as "its Galileo."[2] Despite Simon's revolutionary influence and the constant censorship applied to his works, however, one should note that he never intended to oppose orthodoxy. On the contrary, he always meant to serve it.

In this chapter, I shall mainly refer to Simon's other works, which may perhaps be described as works of *vulgarisation scientifique—haute vulgarisation,* of course. My aim is to shed some light on another side of Simon's work, which reflects, certainly more than his biblical studies, a deep ethnological curiosity and historical sensitivity.[3] Such qualities, which are not always seen as prerequisites for the philologist, are absolutely essential for any work on foreign religions.

As ideas travel, attitudes evolve. Brerewood's *Enquiries Touching the Diversity of Languages and Religions through the Chief Parts of the World,* published in 1614, was translated to French in 1640.[4] An attempt to reprint this translation came from Calvinist Geneva, and it was for this project that Simon prepared, in the 1670s, the eighteen chapters of his *Additions aux Recherches curieuses sur la diversité des langues et religions d'Edward Brerewood.* The first three chapters are devoted to the languages of the Levant: modern Greek, Turkish, Arabic, and rabbinic Hebrew. The fourth chapter offers a schematic presentation of Islam, and the next three treat rabbinic Judaism, the Samaritans (considered by Simon to be a Jewish sect), and the Karaites. The remaining chapters are dedicated to the various Eastern Christian confessions. In his preface, the author states his method clearly: only a historical and comparative study, established on an adequate linguistic basis, will permit the identification of later, secondary additions to the ecclesiastical traditions, so that the original texts may be purged.

For various reasons relating among other things to the vagaries of cooperation between Catholics and Protestants, the project to reprint Brerewood in French did not materialize, and Simon's manuscript remained unpublished until 1983.[5] But Simon managed to incorporate in other works much of what he had written in the *Additions aux Recherches curieuses.* The importance of popularization—and of translations— for not only the transmission of radical theses but also the dissemination of new sensitivities, does not seem to have received the attention it deserves. In a sense, Simon's "nontechnical" works show the new sensitivity for foreign religions at its best, as well as his conviction that the encounters with exotic societies may shed light on our understanding of ancient history, and even on the Holy Scriptures.[6]

Feeling that he was living in ecumenical times, Simon could write that attempts were being made to unite the different "religions."[7] "Religions," in this context, refers of course to the various Christian confessions, in particular the Eastern Churches. Uniate Churches, indeed, had been already established at the time, allowing the faithful from the various Eastern Churches to perform their traditional liturgies and rituals in their own languages, while accepting the primacy of Rome. Hence, Simon's deep interest in the Eastern Churches and his efforts to describe as carefully as possible their theologies and their cult. Simon discussed not only the Greek Orthodox Church but also the Iberians, or Georgians, the Indian Christians of Saint Thomas, the Jacobites, the Abyssinians, the Armenians, and the Maronites.[8] In this context, he appealed to "enlightened Catholics," ["les Catholiques épurés,"] for whom he wrote his *Histoire critique de la créance et des coutûmes des nations du Levant* (Frankfurt,

1684). Those open-minded Catholics were willing, for instance, to accept the fact that the Eastern "so-called" heresies are much more refined than those of Europe, as the Eastern mind is finer *(plus subtil)* than the European mind, which could invent only rather gross and sensual heresies. So much for Luther and Calvin. We should note here how differently the attempts to identify an "Eastern mind" will sound two centuries later, for instance, when Renan speaks of the Semitic simplemindedness, capable only of thinking of a single God, compared with the versatile mythological, intellectual, and esthetical abilities of the "Indo-Europeans."

Girolamo Dandini, a contemporaneous Italian Jesuit, had written a chronicle of his apostolic mission to the Maronites.[9] Like various other missionaries, Dandini showed interest in the beliefs of Muslims and displayed sensibility and understanding regarding their behavior. He knew, for instance, that if the Turks persecuted the Christians, this was not due to religious reasons, but rather to the more universal phenomenon of xenophobia.[10] Simon decided to translate Dandini's book to French.[11] In his introduction, he courageously insisted on the "usefulness of travels for theology" and on the theologians' need to master oriental languages, which alone can safeguard them from the many prejudices they inherited from their scholastic education.

Simon never questioned the Divine Revelation, but he was convinced that biblical criticism could contribute a deeper, more reasoned adhesion to this revelation. Similarly, he thought that the knowledge of various religious beliefs and practices, from religions past and present, permitted a better understanding of Catholic doctrine and ritual and of the conditions in which they were born and developed. By way of an example of the comparative approach and its use in the service of Catholic theology, Simon ends his *De statu mortuorum* with a comparative paragraph on Greek and Roman funeral practices.

Simon, who was no Arabist, knew that the main sources of the theology of Turks and Persians were to be found in Arabic texts. One should not expect to find in Simon any infatuation with Islam. It should nevertheless be emphasized that Simon was not guided by the then-current prejudices against Muhammad "the impostor," and that his tone remained serene, without any noticeable polemical undertones. As he makes clear, his interest in Islam was secondary and stemmed from his will to better understand the Eastern Christians, and also, of course, to win them over to the Catholic side in the competition with the Protestants. He was quite conscious of attempts, such as that of Cyril Lukaris, to establish contacts between Greek Orthodox and Protestants.

Nevertheless, at the end of a series of studies on the various Eastern Churches, Simon dedicated the fifteenth and last chapter of the *Histoire critique de la créance et des coutumes des nations du Levant* to "the faith and customs of the *Mahométans.*" He notes that the majority of the Eastern Christians live under Islam. It is therefore of paramount importance to know what Islam thinks of Christianity in general, and what the Alcoran says about Jesus in particular. Moreover, he writes, "as Islam is a mixture of Judaism and Christianity, one should not be surprised to find among the Turks many things that can also be observed among us. Those who have a perfect knowledge of these two religions can easily show the origin of most Islamic ceremonies."[12] Simon presents here, in a nutshell, what is perhaps the primary intellectual incentive to oriental studies, and the first intuition of nascent orientalism: the structural multifaceted similarity between the monotheistic religions and the genetic interpretation of them. His insistence on the natural complement between textual studies and anthropological observation, between philology and the comparative study of religion, is remarkable indeed; today, such an approach requires collective projects and budgets for interdisciplinary research.

Simon's chapter on Islam in his *Additions aux Recherches curieuses* of Brerewood does not make any claim of originality. It purports to be an extract from a Turkish theological tractate published in 1522 that claimed to offer an "exact summary" of Islam. This extract begins with "the principal article of their belief," namely, God's unity. Then come Muhammad's prophecy, miracles, angelology, paradise, hell, and so on. In passing, Simon points out various parallels; for instance, between the Roman Catholic Mass for the dead and an Islamic prayer. Elsewhere, he writes:

> It would not be too difficult to show that in part, this belief of Muslims in paradise and hell is rather close to that of the Church in the first centuries, and which is still found in the Eastern Church, while it has been altered in various ways in the Latin Church.[13]

After the beliefs, Simon discusses ethics. According to him, "the morals of Muhammadans consists in doing the good and avoiding evil."[14] He says that "They give very beautiful precepts in order to be freed from passions and to avoid vices."[15] Simon then discusses Islamic religious practices, insisting especially on devotional prayers, and comparing them favorably with the often loose mores among contemporary Catholics.[16] Incidentally, this comparison is already present in Protestant polemics. Simon ends the chapter with a brief mention of the different Muslim "sects." In conclusion, he notes that he did not intend the chapter to be exhaustive, but rather to point out what had been ignored by his predecessors. In other words, even when writing for the public at large, Simon sought to call attention to points hitherto unnoticed by scholars. His original contribution consists in the realization that there is no good theology without honest history, and no deep understanding of Christianity without the study of other religions, using both philological and ethnological methods. Simon's novel comparative approach to religious phenomena made enemies for him beyond those in the Catholic Church. His lack of polemical tone in his treatment of Islam caused strong reactions among some Protestant theologians. In a polemical treatise against the *Histoire critique du Vieux Testament,* the Huguenot Jean Le Clerc, expressed his shock at Simon's "horrible comparison" between the New Testament and the book of "the impostor who has misled, alas, most of the East." In Le Clerc's view, such a comparison reflects too much reading of Islamic theology and too little study of the New Testament.

Protestant polemicists, who criticized Simon's alleged sympathy for Islam, became still more vociferous in regard to his attitude toward Judaism. Simon felt much closer to Judaism than to Islam, and he was versed in Jewish classical sources, which he read in their original languages. What annoyed Protestant scholars most was the seriousness with which Simon took rabbinic literature. Such an intellectual curiosity for Jewish postbiblical traditions ran against the grain of minds formed by argumenting over *sola scriptura.* In a polemical discussion between Simon and the great classical philologist Isaac Vossius, the main argument concerned the importance and the truth-value of rabbinic traditions.[17] Similarly, Jean Le Clerc, who taught Hebrew in the Huguenot *Refuge* in Amsterdam, accused Simon of having too much esteem for the rabbis. Answering such attacks, Simon, after pointing out that Le Clerc's knowledge of Hebrew left much to be desired ("M. Le Clerc ne sait rien en Ebreu de Rabbin"),[18] noted that the first polyglot Bible was not that of Walton but that of Cardinal Ximenez (the Alcala Polyglot dates of 1514–1517), and that altogether, Protestant theologians' knowledge of oriental languages, Hebrew included, remained rather weak. Moreover, Simon added, they have no understanding of Judaism (nor, for that matter, of Saint Augustine).[19] He further argued that it would be hard to convince Jews and Muslims of the truth of Christianity on the basis of Protestant and Socinian theological principles. At least in Switzerland and Geneva, Protestants were opposed to freedom of conscience, and they "reason upon facts as if they were metaphysicians." In his respect for facts, the Catholic Simon shows himself to be a true disciple of Cartesian science. And his insistence on the deep structural similarity between Catholicism and rabbinic Judaism reveals the value he ascribed to the idea of a sacred tradition.

Perhaps Simon's most significant insight concerning Jewish traditions was his insistence on their cardinal importance for the study of Christian origins. For him, the Apostles "conformed completely to "already established customs within Judaism *(dans les synagogues)*." Hence, Simon reasoned, it was not only essential to read rabbinic literature to find clear parallels to the Gospels but also to become acquainted with Jewish contemporary practices, since the Jews, even in their then pitiful state, continued to keep God's Law.[20]

In his *Histoire de l'origine et du progrès des revenus écclésiastiques,* published in 1684, Simon insisted on the "synagogal origin of the Ministers of the Church." If we notice the importance of almsgiving as a religious duty among Jews, we may, said Simon, realize that the Apostles "followed synagogal discipline quite exactly." For him, however, the influence between Judaism and Christianity went both ways. He thus pointed out that Christianity had forced the Jews to become more precise in their references to scriptural text.[21]

Arnold van Gennep, the author of a seminal book on *rites de passage,* could hail Simon as one of the founders of the ethnological method.[22] The truth of van Gennep's remark is most clearly seen in Simon's interest in Jewish ritual. As was the case with Islam, there is no reason to speak here of infatuation with Judaism. Simon retained a strong aversion for various aspects of Jewish life and thought. He was particularly averse to kabbala, in which he saw an intellectual and spiritual perversity, an irrationalism stemming from ill-digested Platonic influences. He also took pains to deny the accusations of various kabbalistic texts that Jesus practiced magic. Simon's rationalism resulted in a strong dislike of popular levels of religious beliefs and practices in Judaism, such as magic, although he would of course have similar reactions to parallel trends in Christianity. Simon's new Hebraism was thus quite different from that of the Christian kabbalists since the days of Pico, Reuchlin, and Postel. The new Hebraism was essentially erudite and rational. But Simon's scholarship did not remain of antiquarian interest only, and it was laced with a good dose of philosemitism, sometimes militant, as Le Clerc's reaction, for instance, shows. Simon personally met with Jews, from whom he sought to learn. He mentions his intellectual and polemical discussions with Jews on the biblical texts, including the New Testament, a text of which his interlocutors showed a sophisticated knowledge.[23] In particular, he maintained ties with Jona Salvador, a Provencal Jew living in Paris, who visited him in the church on a regular basis, reporting to him about various Jewish texts and customs and also about Sabbatai Zevi, the apostate Messiah from Symrna. When his help was needed, Simon endeavored to protect Jews from unjust accusations by the authorities, as, for instance, in the case of the Jews of Metz. Side by side with such marks of sympathy, however, Simon was not free from some of the traditional prejudices against the Jews. This is reflected, for instance, in a letter in which he mentions their inexhaustible thirst for money. Nevertheless, the dominant feature of Simon's attitude is his effort to refute religious prejudice on the nature of Judaism:

> One should not imagine, as many do, that all the sanctity of the Jewish Law consists in vain legal observation, and that they consider, for instance, that bodily washings can in themselves perform the expiation of sins. They are persuaded that all these exterior ceremonies must drive them to interior sanctity.

As we have seen, some sympathy for an alien cult was already present in Simon's treatment of Islam. In regard to Judaism, however, this tendency was much more pronounced.

In this respect, by far the most interesting and important discussion is provided by Simon's *Comparaison des cérémonies des Juifs et de la discipline de l'Eglise*. This text was published in 1681, as an appendix to the second edition of his French translation of Leone Modena's *Historia degli riti hebraici*.[24] Leone Modena (1571–1648), perhaps the most colorful figure of the Italian Jewish community in the *seicento*, has been described as the first modern rabbi. He is, in any case, the first Jew of whom we possess a real portrait. While remaining orthodox in his beliefs, he was, like Simon, motivated by a strong rationalist spirit, which brought him to fiercely oppose kabbala and magic. Throughout his life, he kept close contacts with Christian scholars and figures.

Modena also published, in Hebrew, a highly original autobiography, much studied recently.[25] The *Historia degli riti hebraici,* written perhaps as early as 1613, had been commissioned by the English ambassador to Venice for presentation to King James I.[26] It should be remembered that, as there were virtually no Jews in England at the time, knowledge about their customs was of necessity scarce, a situation that could encourage curiosity. The French orientalist and Christian kabbalist Jacques Gaffarel had received the text from Modena himself, as he was looking in Venice for oriental manuscripts on behalf of his master Richelieu. Gaffarel had published it in Paris in 1637, without seeking the author's final permission. A second edition, purged of various views condemned by the Inquisition's Holy Office in Venice, was published by Modena the following year. The book was then to have a long career of reprints and translations. It was soon recognized for its true value: it represented the first sustained effort made by a Jew to introduce his religion to the non-Jewish public, presenting its practices in as much, or more, detail than its beliefs. The book was a shortened and Italianized version, as it were, of the classic sixteenth-century Jewish legal code, the *Shulhan Arukh,* or "dressed table."

Modena's *Riti* was not, however, the first book in that century devoted to Jewish practice: in 1603, Johannes Buxtorf the Elder, the famous Basel Hebraist, had published his *Judenschul,* the first version (in German) of his *Synagoga Judaica.* This bulky and otherwise impressive compendium of Jewish practices reached immediate fame in Europe. The great Joseph Scaliger had written to its author to congratulate him on his achievement. The book was marred, however, by various derogatory remarks and by a rather hostile tone generally toward the object of its inquiry. Modena testified in a letter that one of his main reasons for deciding to write on the topic was to provide an antidote to Buxtorf's book. He succeeded in this task, and the *Riti* underwent various editions and translations, thus becoming the main source of information on Jewish life and practices in Christian Europe.[27] In what may be called the first modern "Encyclopedia of World Religions," *Cérémonies et coutumes religieuses de tous les peuples du monde,* accompanied by Bernard Picart's famous engravings, Judaism was still represented by Leon Modena's *Riti,* although with some additions.[28] To some extent, Modena's text still represented common knowledge about postbiblical Judaism at the time of the French Revolution.

Simon considered the *Riti* to be interesting enough to deserve translation. He signed his translation as "le sieur de Simonville," one of several pseudonyms that he sometimes used to escape censorship. *Cérémonies et coûtumes qui s'observent aujourd'hui parmy les Juifs* appeared in Paris in 1674. The translation of Modena's text was accompanied by two appendices written by Simon, "touchant les Sectes des Caraïtes & des Samaritains de nôtre Temps." Moreover, Simon appended a monographic essay to the second edition, published in 1681: *Comparaison des Cérémonies des Juifs, & de la discipline de l'Eglise, avec un discours touchant les différentes Messes, ou Liturgies qui sont en usage dans tout le monde.*[29] The tome was dedicated to Simon's *nemesis,* Jacques Bénigne Bossuet, the traditionalist bishop of Condom, and the most powerful prelate in France, probably to placate him.[30]

What makes the *Comparaison des cérémonies des juifs et de la discipline de l'Eglise* so interesting is not only that it reflects the passage from a theological to an anthropological interest in Judaism and the Jews. This work also represents the first scholarly comparison of Judaism and Christianity, insisting on similarities of structure and also on genetic relationships, in particular the Jewish heritage of Jesus, his disciples, and early Christianity generally. Moreover, this text sheds light on the status of Jewish rites and mythology in seventeenth-century scholarship. Simon can be said to have ushered in a new approach to Jewish culture.[31] This new approach left its mark on subsequent understandings of Judaism. Simon's works were known in the Enlightenment: Voltaire possessed all of his voluminous works, and Simon's presence is strongly felt in Diderot's *Encyclopédie.* In Germany, Lessing knew him, while orthodox Lutheran writers associated him with Spinoza.[32] In other words, it is no exaggeration to say that Simon's writings, including his *Comparaison,* had an important posterity. It seems, however, that most of this influence took place outside of France, mainly in England and Germany, in particular on such figures as Michaelis and Herder in Germany, and John Dryden, Richard Bentley, and Bolingbroke in England.[33]

Like his literary activity in general, Simon's discussion of Jewish culture and religion should be seen in its polemical context. On the one hand, Bossuet had succeeded in setting the French Parliament and the royal authorities against him, and Simon was seriously criticized and even ostracized for his audacious ideas about the formation of the biblical text. On the other hand, as a good Catholic priest (and he never ceased to consider himself so, even after his exclusion from the *Oratoire*), he argued against the Protestants.[34] For him, the understanding of the nature of Judaism was directly relevant to this argument. Finally, as a Christian arguing against the Jews, he noted what he believed to be the catastrophic implications of the rejection of Jesus as Messiah for the Jewish nation.

The interest of a seventeenth-century intellectual in rituals should be understood in the context of the contemporary discovery of exotic cultures and civilizations. With the numerous ethnological publications on the Indians in the New World, curiosity for different, strange ways of life, thought, and behavior was growing.[35] Indians were also sometimes compared with Jews.[36] For a Catholic, there was an additional dimension to the question of rites: in the Orient lived Christians, like the Maronites, who did not practice the Catholic rite, although they were not tainted by Protestant perversion. In a sense, argued Catholic thinkers like Simon, a different ritual did not necessarily imply another religion.[37] One detects here the deep ambivalence of the term "religion" in Catholic seventeenth-century parlance. On the one hand, ritual practices, as noted by ethnological observation, define religion. On the other hand, close links between the beliefs of the various communities can be detected despite highly differing rituals, and such links point to the common Noahide ancestry of the different peoples.

This argument was quite different from the accommodation theory developed by the Jesuits in China that would lead to the *Querelle des Rites* within the Catholic Church.[38] Yet, both arguments imply that beyond all the ritual differences, there exists a common, pristine tradition, common to believers of different religious persuasions. This alone, the belief in the power in heaven—common, for instance, to Confucians and Christians—was what constituted the kernel of true religion.

The last two chapters of Simon's book (chapters 18 and 19) form an appendix of sorts that reflects Simon's keen interest in oriental Christian communities. These two chapters deal with Mass according to the various Eastern Christian rituals ("discours touchant les différentes Messes,") and with the differences between Eastern and Western cults. Christian ritual originates in Synagogal cult. The problem of the different Christian cults and the interest in oriental Christian rites brought Sixtus V to establish in Rome a new congregation, *de' riti*. Except for this appendix, Simon's essay consists of seventeen chapters, the last of which presents a short, remarkable method for learning Hebrew: "Usus multus, praeceptiones paucae" ("don't bother with grammar, but read as much as you can") is Simon's rule of thumb for rapid progress.

Simon begins his essay with an analysis of the religious foundations of Judaism (chapter 1) and of the principles of Jewish theology (chapter 2). He then moves to Jewish ethics (chapter 3), which he compares, as he had done for theological principles, with Christian ethics. He further describes the organization of the synagogue and the Sanhedrin, comparing it to the organization of the early Church (chapters 5 to 7). Chapters 8 and 9 deal with Jewish prayers, while chapter 10 is devoted to Jewish festivals. The next two chapters deal mainly with Talmudic texts, while chapters 13 and 14 introduce Jewish literature and its possible interest for Christians. Chapter 15 offers a perusal of Jewish interest in the various sciences. Chapter 16, finally, argues for the necessity for Christian theologians to know Hebrew.

In a sense, the whole essay is dedicated to Jewish myths and rituals, to the relationships between them, and to the links between Jewish and Christian belief and ritual. To be sure, Simon did not use the term *mythe,* which seems to appear only in the eighteenth century.[39] But on various occasions, he speaks about *allégories, fables (fabula* is the usual Latin translation of *muthos), contes faits à plaisir, rèveries,* which he identifies as "a mythology of sorts, like among the pagans."[40] This is said, of course, in derogatory fashion, since a myth, or a fable, is essentially a false story.[41] Instead of facilitating access to divine truth, as they were supposed to do, myths become an impediment to knowing the truth.[42] Angels, for instance, are allegories invented to mislead the people.[43]

But what are these Jewish myths? They are not, to be sure, the stories told in the Bible, since these represent the *historia sacra,* the revelation of God. As mentioned above, Simon never rejected the idea of revelation, contrary to the allegations of the fundamentalists of his time. He only argued that the inspiration by the Holy Spirit is in the text as a whole and not necessarily in each of its sentences.[44] He regarded the traditions of the rabbis as Jewish myths that are best expressed in the Talmud and in rabbinic literature, in particular in the Midrashim. The rabbinic traditions have falsified the revealed truth contained in the Bible, Simon purported; they are additions, transformations of historical truth into a corrupt religion. Nevertheless, he conceded, there is a kernel of truth in the idea of traditions completing the written text of the Bible, which can be either exegetical or ritual in nature. Jesus, indeed, had to fight on two fronts: On the one hand, he fought the Sadducees, who rejected the very idea of an oral tradition. On the other hand, he argued against the Pharisees, who had produced, through over-interpretation, a caricature of the religion of their fathers.[45]

Jesus, Simon reasoned, accepted from the rabbis what fitted the true spirit of the Torah and rejected the additions that changed its meaning. This applies not only to beliefs but also to ritual. In a fundamental sense, therefore, he argued, we must recognize that Jesus followed Jewish ritual,[46] while taking exception to the illegitimate additions of the rabbis, such as their prayers, which He condemned.[47]

The Talmud and the Midrashim tell the myths, or false stories, but these myths are not simple idle fantasizing, according to Simon.[48] They are also reflected in Jewish ritual, a direct manifestation of Jewish myth.[49] The claim of the rabbis that their traditions come directly from the Torah is the essential reason for the falsification of historical truth; "*halakha le-Moshe mi-Sinai*" (rabbinic law has the same authority as the Torah revealed to Moses on Mount Sinai); the "great axiom of the Jews," said Simon, is patently false from a historical point of view. It is absurd to claim that people believe and practice exactly the same things as in Moses' day. It is simply impossible to believe that the tradition originating in Sinai is immune to change. But Jews are not permitted to express doubt about the axiom of *halakha le-Moshe mi-Sinai* without falling into the heresy of the Karaites.[50]

The Karaites did not accept the authority of rabbinic law ("Oral Torah"), and Simon's intellectual and human curiosity led him to attach a great importance to them. The Karaites had attracted much scholarly interest in the seventeenth century.[51] Representing another kind of Judaism, strongly scripturalist and highly critical of rabbinic tradition, the Karaites aroused the curiosity of both Catholics and Protestants. According to Simon, Karaite traditions are important, first of all, for a better understanding of the "true" text of the Hebrew Bible. Simon's attitude toward the Karaites was ambivalent, as it was toward the Jews in general. On the one hand, he regarded their rejection of the Talmud as similar to Jesus' rejection of most rabbinical traditions, which were, for Jesus, additions to, or perversions of, the revealed text. In that sense, Simon felt closer to the Karaites than to the rabbanites. On the other hand, Catholics and rabbanites have in common the respect for tradition (of the rabbis or of the Church Fathers). For both, the text of the Bible is not self-explanatory and can be properly understood only with the help of tradition.[52] The Karaites' rejection of this tradition, and their presumption to read the text directly, without any intermediary, struck him as similar to Protestant attitudes. He could thus address letters to a Protestant friend, Frémond d'Ablancourt: "Mon cher Caraïte," and sign them "Le Rabbaniste."[53]

Altogether, in Simon's view, Christianity and Judaism are essentially the same religion, since the essence of a religion lies in its beliefs, not its practices.[54] Yet, there is a great difference between Jewish and Christian ritual: Christians do not observe the purely ceremonial laws.[55] For him, then, Jewish and Christian festivals are similar, but the latter are the spiritualized version of the former.

Simon spoke harshly of kabbala. Whereas the Talmud includes many Jewish traditions, Simon argued, the locus par excellence reflecting the mythical nature of these traditions is *the* Tradition, that is, kabbala. Kabbala represents a chimerical and baseless discipline.[56] Simon also thought that the mythology of the early Christian Gnostics and heretics such as Basilides ("les rèveries des anciens hérétiques") offered a striking parallel to that of kabbala, although he did not want to dwell on this point, which would carry him too far.[57] Simon saw the origin of kabbala in a baroque misunderstanding of Platonic (and Pythagorean) philosophy, on the part of people who were not used to reading philosophical texts because these were forbidden by the rabbis, like all other profane books. In short, both ignorance and the refusal to encourage rational and critical thought are the main reasons for the development of mythical ways of thought among the Jews.[58] The worst kind of kabbala, of course, is practical kabbala: Simon spoke of the fantasies of practical kabbala, which were nothing but lies and magic.[59] Referring to Pico della Mirandola and Agrippa, he lamented that both had an influence on Christian phenomena such as Christian kabbala and magic.[60]

The intellectual catastrophe that befell the Jews was due to the rabbinic prohibition on reading books outside the Jewish tradition, Simon believed, in particular those of the Greek philosophers. This interdiction turned the Jewish encounter with Platonic philosophy into an intellectual trauma, which was in its turn responsible for the creation of kabbala. About kabbalistic works Simon wrote dryly that not a single one was sensible.[61] Simon thus offers a synthesis between a traditional Christian critique of Judaism and modern rationalism. The absence of encouragement for the practice of reason was responsible for the overdevelopment of irrational, mythical patterns of thought in Judaism. In Simon's writing, this intellectual criticism becomes also an anthropological analysis of Jewish society.

The foundation of Jewish ethics, he said, is the Decalogue. But too many precepts and external duties entail a certain depreciation of "good deeds." If Jewish ritual suffers from hypertrophy, Simon argued, Jewish ethics suffer from the opposite evil, atrophy. There is therefore an intrinsic reason that partly explains the observable lack of Jewish ethical behavior. One must note, however, that Simon thought that if the Jews were evil *(méchants)*, this was partly due to their pitiful state (29–32). For about their evilness he had no doubt. The Jews were dangerous for Christians, whom they considered to be idolaters. If the Jews ever gained power, they would no doubt rule in an oppressive way, since according to their conception, the Messiah should enslave all other peoples to the Jewish nation (16–18). Their belief in a Messiah who has yet to come instills the Jews with great pride and a terrible, frightening desire of domination.[62] Simon observed that the importance of messianic conceptions in contemporaneous Judaism had to be understood as the background of the Sabbatean movement.

The cultural degeneration of Judaism meant that biblical scholars would not profit from consulting Jewish books, except for those dealing with ritual. All other works were of no use for Christians.[63]

Simon, a Catholic student of Judaism, was raised as a Catholic theologian and having found his way as a Hebraist, sought to find out the connections between belief and practice in Judaism. He also compared, in a subtle way, Judaism and Christianity along the same lines. Simon showed an ability to move out of the traditional theological stance to a new, ethnological approach to Jewish belief and practice. It was his historical sense that permitted him to ask these comparative questions. Jewish myths were, for him, an overgrowth of belief, due to a lack of historical criticism and common sense on the part of the rabbis. These myths, in their turn, generated the expanded Jewish ritual. With time, this overgrowth of ritual caused a shrinking of ethics. According to Simon, Christianity was (in contradistinction to Karaism) a successful reform of rabbinic Judaism. Christianity established a balance between principles of faith, based on the Bible, and their ritual enactment. Christianity has no myths, and a purer and simpler ritual. But apostolic Christianity did not completely abandon Tradition, that is, the rules of biblical hermeneutics. The Christian

Protestant reform that intended to do such a thing was a repetition, within Christianity, of the Karaite error.

Simon's original discourse remains exemplary of fruitful interdisciplinary scholarship: philology, history, anthropological analysis, and comparative study are all called to contribute to the new science. In Jacques Le Brun's words, "Richard Simon deserves all our attention for having been one of the first to understand what would be the situation of revealed religions in the modern world."[64]

Simon was indeed one of the first but of course not the only pioneer. I have not touched here upon the proximate channels through which the various elements of the new knowledge reached Simon and other directions this knowledge took toward the end of the century. Even if we limit our inquiry to France, we can discern a phenomenon of reciprocal intellectual fertilization between Protestants and Catholics. In Georges Gusdorf's words, the Catholics would probably not have been able to shake traditional authority away were it not for the Protestant challenge. Without the Catholics, on the other hand, the Protestants might well have sunk into a superstitious adoration of the letter.[65] Two of Simon's teachers were Protestants. Louis Cappelle (1585–1658), professor of Hebrew and Scriptures at the Protestant Academy in Sedan, published in 1650 his *Critica sacra,* a work which was to have a lasting influence on biblical criticism. In the next chapter, we turn our attention to Samuel Bochart, another Protestant, who also in 1650 was establishing the foundations of the comparative science of Semitic antiquities.

In this chapter we saw how scholars were able to move from the study of the Bible to the study of Judaism. The next chapter will seek to interpret how biblical myths paved the way to reflection on the various nations and their religious traditions.

IV

Biblical Myth, Religious History, and Idolatry

1. Noah's Sons and the Religious Conquest of the Earth

Traditional discourse on the plurality of religions underwent radical change in the seventeenth century, as did the attempt to solve exacerbated religious conflicts. The first change was the urgency with which some European intellectuals perceived, in the wake of the wars of religion, the need to establish civil and religious peace, both within the different states and between them. These intellectuals became aware of the complexity of the links between religious tradition and political order in ways that had eluded previous generations. The second change concerned the still-recent discovery of continents and peoples from the New World to East Asia. Leibniz is a good example of the passion with which some leading European intellectuals reflected on such issues.[1] Their reflection included both historical and geographical aspects: in order to deal seriously with the problems created by the plurality of religions, one had to understand the origin of the striking dispersion of the diverse peoples on the earth. The *locus classicus* for the opening of any discussion, here, was the Book of Genesis, in particular chapter 10:

> These are the descendants of Noah's sons, Shem, Ham, and Japheth: children were born to them after the flood. . . . These are the families of Noah's sons, according to their genealogies, in their nations; and from these the nations spread abroad on the earth after the flood. (Gen 10:1,32)

From its first to its last verse, this chapter offers the list of peoples stemming from the three sons of Noah, together with their respective lands and languages. It has a clearly ethnological tone, in stark contradistinction to the cosmogony and anthropogony of the first chapters of

Genesis. Nevertheless, the biblical text lists the peoples according to the historical and geographical contacts between them, rather than according to their ethnic affinities. The biblical myth of Noah and his sons affirms the unity of humanity, which may be divided but stems from a common root. It reflects the new start of humanity after the Flood.

In the seventeenth century, some intellectuals sought to base the nascent human sciences on what they considered the oldest preserved document of humankind and foundational scripture of Christianity and Western culture. They therefore invested the Genesis story of Noah's sons with a new, capital importance.[2] This story served as the basis for their reflection on the origins of ethnic taxonomies as well as of languages, cultures, and religions throughout the various continents.[3] The biblical story of the postdiluvian dispersal of humankind permitted the notion of the original unity of humankind. What should be underlined from the start, however, and what I hope will become clearer later, is that the approach and use of the biblical myth itself reflects an attempt at de-mythologization. Although both Catholic and Protestant scholars took the biblical text seriously, they certainly did not understand it in a literal fashion. Rather, they perceived the Book of God as equivalent to the "great book of nature," of which the Bible was a replica.[4] Hence, the myths of Genesis were not to be simply believed and accepted at face value but were to be used as cues to the scholarly or scientific study of phenomena. The biblical myth recounting the new beginnings of humankind after the Flood permitted a reflection on the origins of nations and religions and the historical relations between civilizations. For early modern intellectuals, then, the biblical Flood separated world history from cosmogony and anthropogony. The myth of the Flood freed thinkers from the need to return to the biblical myth of Creation and indicated the dispersal of peoples across the earth as the earliest departure point for any historical inquiry.

In the sixteenth century, the biblical myth of the Flood and its consequences had been applied to new realities in a rather literal fashion. One of the major problems which then preoccupied intellectuals was the origin of the American populations. Spanish theologians often perceived the Americans as offspring of the Ten Tribes of Israel. José de Acosta and Antonio de Herrera described the routes by which the Indians had reached America. From Arias Montano to Gregorio Garcia, Spanish thinkers applied Genesis 10 quite directly to the New World and its populations.[5] Peru was thus identified with Ophir, the biblical golden land, and the various cults practiced by the Indians were seen as pale latter-day reflections of ancient Hebrew religion: Temple, sacrifices, prayers, aspersions, and so on.[6] This approach reflected a rather mythical reading of reality and the still-unchallenged status of the Bible.[7]

For these seventeenth-century scholars, traces of the biblical Flood could be detected in the stories of peoples from various corners of the earth. Grotius remarked on the universality of such stories and noted that the legend of a flood at the dawn of history was also found among the natives of Cuba, Mexico, and Nicaragua.[8] Similarly, in his *Discourse on Universal History,* Bossuet noted that "the tradition of the universal flood [was] found throughout the earth" and could refer to "the ark, at all times famous in the East."[9] Edward Stillingfleet was more specific when he claimed that the Chinese, too, knew the story of the Flood. In his *De Theologia Gentilis,* Gerard Vossius argued that this story depicted a historical event of universal dimensions. Isaac de la Peyrère, on the other hand, claimed the flood described in Genesis had been limited to the Holy Land.

From John Selden on, we can observe a return to the ancient Near Eastern background against which the biblical text must be read: that is to say, one can detect a passage from a mythological to a philological and historical reading. The Bible still retains a very high status as the foundational text of Western culture, but it no longer remains unchallenged. Its antiquity is no longer unique, and it can now be compared with other literary monuments from the dawn of humankind.

In the early modern age, the biblical myth of the Flood, and, more precisely, the story of the sons of Noah and their conquest of the earth can be seen as the midway point between an earlier wholesale acceptance of the myth and its later total rejection. The biblical story is conceived, then, as a prelude to world history, which is, also, the history of the religions of humankind. The Bible serves here as a springboard from which one can probe the dispersion of peoples and diffusion of religions from the ancient Near East to the various continents.

The philological and historical reading of the Bible in the seventeenth century reflects a rare moment of equilibrium in the status of the Bible. At this hermeneutical moment of grace, the two "books," that is, the Bible and "the great book of nature," were read in conjunction with one another and interpreted in light of one another. The biblical text could then be used, together with modern methods of inquiry, to probe either history or nature. Moreover, this new, modern inquiry was also, ipso facto, a scholarly study of biblical text and a search for its true, "literal" meaning.

Since the great geographical discoveries and the development of Christian missions throughout the world, the question whether the American Indians could at all be called humans—a question that had once preoccupied theologians from the University of Salamanca—had been replaced by ethnological curiosity and a genuine interest for the mores and beliefs of the various "pagan" peoples, and also by the complex comparison between their religions and those of antiquity.

For Christian humanists, New World geography entailed a fresh interest in different cultures and religions. While these new cultures were profane and their religions pagan, they nonetheless reflected human nature, which, beyond its changing appearances, was known to be universal. The unity of human nature was based on the testimony of the Bible, which offered both a historical and a theological explanation for the passage from the one to the many expressions of humankind. We can detect a sustained attempt on the part of early modern intellectuals, scholars, and theologians to incorporate the newly discovered civilizations into the model of "History of salvation" (*Heilsgeschichte*) proposed by the biblical text. In a sense, the sacralization of profane cultures is similar to the theory developed by Justin Martyr in the second century of the "spiritual seed" (*sperma pneumatikon*) present even among peoples completely unaware of divine revelation. This sacralization proceeds through "sacred geography" (*geographia sacra*), a term usually referring to the scholarly study of the Holy Land but that often entails more than its original meaning. Sacred geography aims at using the Scriptures (and Genesis in particular) to establish the historical and geographical paths of religions since the beginning of humankind. *Geographia sacra* deals with all aspects of world history and geography, from attempts to identify the precise geographical location of paradise to various hypotheses about the origins of the New World populations.

In the sixteenth and seventeenth centuries, a plethora of essays dealt with paradise and its geographical location. These essays, which offered various admixtures of scholarship with myth, belong in a sense to contemporary literature on fantastic voyages and utopian worlds. Jewish, Catholic, and Protestant scholars contributed to this literature. Among them, we meet authors as different in their approach and outlook as Abraham Peritsol, Adriaan Reland, Etienne Morin, Samuel Bochart, and Pierre-Daniel Huet.[10]

Geographia sacra was a natural extension of the earlier development of a comparative chronology of the ancient world, which had revealed and emphasized the primacy of ancient Near Eastern civilizations over those of Greece and Rome—and over that of the Hebrews. Thus Joseph Scaliger, a leading precursor of comparative chronology, recognized the chronological primacy of Egypt over Israel—and, of course, the primacy of Israel over Greece.[11] Comparative chronology enabled, inter alia, the nascent modern history of religions to begin to detect, for instance, Egyptian influences on Israelite religion, which implicitly destroyed the perception of monotheistic revelation as standing outside world history, or at its origin. As we shall see in the second part of this chapter, it is the recognition of the temporal primacy of Egypt that would prompt John Spencer, in the last decades of the seventeenth century, to build on the theories of Maimonides regarding pagan influences on the biblical conception of sacrifice.[12]

The early works on the history of religions emphasized the rule that the gods, like men, had traveled from East to West. "Diffusionism" was the main principle explaining the plurality of religions, and the original kernel was located in the East. It was therefore in the East that one would search for the origin of Greek gods. "East" still referred then almost exclusively to the Near East. By going West, it was the names of the gods that changed, rather than their identities. Yet under their new Greek names, these gods were presented as natives.

Let us examine some examples of this kind of literature. In 1622, the Catholic scholar Jacques Lapeyre d'Auzoles published in Paris *La saincte géographie.*[13] D'Auzoles reflects the general consensus when he describes Europe as the original land of Japhet, Asia as that of Sem, and Africa as that of Ham. Later, however, the sons of Shem settled in America, the sons of Ham in the Austral lands of Magellan, and the sons of Japheth in the Septentrion. For D'Auzoles, the land promised to Abraham is of necessity the best land on earth, and Canaan is identical with the land of Eden. D'Auzoles diverges here from the consensus of his times, according to which the Garden of Eden was located in Mesopotamia.[14] As noted above, the diffusion of religions throughout the continents is inseparable from historical diffusionism, and the comparative approach to religions in the early modern age is tied to comparative chronology. Hence, in 1632, ten years after his *Saincte Géographie,* D'Auzoles published a *Saincte Chronologie.*

In his *Chronicus Canon Aegyptiacus, Ebraicus, Graecus,* (1672) the *locus classicus* of Comparative Chronology, John Marsham has relied on John Selden's *De Diis Syris.*[15] While Selden considered Hebrew to be the most ancient language, he recognized the different polytheisms of the ancient Near East as reflecting the most ancient testimonies of the history of religions. These testimonies must be studied together and compared with those of the Holy Scriptures, if one wants to follow the paths of the gods from East to West. Like Marsham, Selden willingly accepts the intuition of Scaliger, who noted the oriental origins of Cadmus (*kadim* = *oriens*). It is only toward the mid-seventeenth century, with George Hornius's *De originibus Americanis,* that works on America began to follow historical patterns. Until then, even a highly serious study like Gregorio Gracia's *Origen de los Indios de el Nuevo Mundo,* retained mythical patterns of thought, when it argued for the Chinese or Scythian origin of American Indians.[16]

It is within this vibrant but confused intellectual context that we must understand the achievement of the French Protestant scholar and minister from Caen, Samuel Bochart (1599–1667).[17] Bochart was one of the greatest scholars of the time, "the equal of Estienne, Castellion, Scaliger, Saumaise, Casaubon."[18] But Bochart's oeuvre is not only "a mountain of erudition," as François Laplanche put it.[19] In his youth, after completing his studies at the Protestant academy at Saumur, Bochart studied Arabic with Erpenius in Leiden and mainly deepened his knowledge of Hebrew. Bochart was already famous in his own time. In 1652, Queen Christina of Sweden invited him to her Stockholm court. And the great Dutch orientalist Adriaan Reland could say, for instance, "Ea est Bochartini nominis celebritas."

Renan did not consider Bochart, unlike Spinoza and Richard Simon, to have been among the founders of modern biblical criticism, who had established, around the mid-seventeenth century, the basis for the scholarly comparison between Semitic antiquities.[20] Bochart was a remarkable philologist and Semitist, but he often goes astray when offering fanciful etymologies and moving freely from Hebrew to Greek or Latin. Such adventurous scholarship should not mislead us into considering his search for traces of the ancient Semitic world in Europe as naïve; indeed, many of his intuitions still merit our respect.

Bochart's opus maximum is his *Geographia sacra,* of which the first volume, *Phaleg, De dispertione gentium et terrarum divisione facta in aedificatione turris Babel,* was published in 1646. This title refers to the biblical figure of Peleg, "in [whose] days was the earth divided" (Gen 10:25). The second volume, *Chanaan, De coloniis et sermone Phoenicium,* deals with the Phoenician language and with its fate in the ancient world.[21] Incidentally, one may note, with Zur Shalev, that both names, *Phaleg* and *Chanaan* were borrowed by Bochart (without acknowledgement!) from Arias Montano: these were the titles of two of the tractates in the latter's *Antiquitates judaicae.*[22] It is *Phaleg* that interests us here. In this huge tractate, which started as an offshoot from his work on paradise, Bochart offers a highly detailed commentary on Genesis 10 and the origins of all peoples. The book is divided into four parts: the division of the earth between the three sons of Noah, followed by detailed discussions of the sons of Shem, Japheth, and Ham. Bochart's methodological principle was borrowed from Tertullian, according to whom truth always precedes lie: "Id esse verum quodcuncque primum, id esse adulterum quodcunque posterius" (Truth always comes first, and error always comes later). Thus, the gods of pagan antiquity would be understood as secondary, as derivatives that should be explained by the Bible. In the first chapter, Bochart set to show that the Greek myth of Chronos (Saturn) and his sons, Jupiter, Neptune, and Pluto, who divide the world between them, represents a transformation of the story of Noah's sons, Shem, Ham, and Japheth. Neptune (Poseidon), for instance, is identical to Japheth. Referring to Hebrew, but also to Aramaic and Arabic, Bochart claimed to show that the Semitic root for "spread," *p.sh.t.* (hence, Japheth, according to him!) is identical, after the permutation between the letters d and t, to Poseidon: "Itaque Poseidon et Japhet sunt plane synonyma." Similarly, Noah's sons mentioned in Genesis 10 are identical with Greek divinities: Canaan is Mercury, Nimrod is Bacchus, and Magog is Prometheus. Many others do not bear their own names in the biblical text, but rather those of the cities that they had established. Bochart's linguistic prowess is remarkable, even when he remains rather unconvincing, and his astonishing virtuosity leaves the reader impressed. Bochart, a supreme "bricoleur," used every possible text, from the classical authors and Church Fathers to the Talmud, medieval Jewish literature, and the few Arabic texts then known in the West. He thus discussed Near Eastern gods, from the earliest to late antiquity, including those of the Nabateans and the pre-Islamic Arabs.

Throughout the rest of the work, Bochart's method was simple. He dedicated a chapter to each name mentioned in Genesis 10, using his knowledge and his intuition to identify places and cults. His approach thus represented a curious admixture of reasoning and analogy. Despite his obvious interest in the history of religions, Bochart remained true to his goal: to reconstruct the historical geography of the ancient world from the clues offered by biblical philology. One would be grossly mistaken, however, to think that this "literal" approach reflected the naïveté of a literalist or fundamentalist theologian. If Bochart thought that the biblical text contained all the truth to be discovered by scholarship, at least *in ovo,* his approach to the Bible amounts to nothing less than a critical reading: while it is through the Bible that one does scholarship, it is also through critical scholarship that one reads the Bible. Bochart read the Bible as a rare document, the central witness of a distant antiquity of which we know very little, at least before the Greek expansion in the Mediterranean. If the questions he asked were chiefly those of geography and ethnology, these could not be dissociated from key problems in the history of religions—problems his followers would seek to solve in light of Bochart's intuitions. In any case, Bochart's *Geographia sacra* would remain the *locus classicus* for this kind of biblical scholarship, and his seminal analysis would long retain a place of honor in scholarly literature.

The most prominent among Bochart's followers, Pierre-Daniel Huet (1630–1721), a Catholic who would eventually become bishop of Avranches, came from Normandy, like his teacher. He is mainly remembered today for his theory on the oriental origins of the novel, which, he claimed, stemmed from myths. A brilliant Hebraist, the young Huet had accompanied Bochart to Stockholm, where he not only eclipsed his teacher but also discovered a manuscript of Origen. From his autobiography, we know how much Huet admired Bochart's *Geographia sacra.*[23] Like his master, Huet wrote a *Traité de la situation du Paradis Terrestre,* but it was his magnum opus, the *Demonstratio evangelica,* that earned him immediate fame when it was published in 1679. The book went through four editions in ten years. Huet applied Bochart's method to the names of the gods. His goal was to show that ancient and classical paganisms reflect a mistaken understanding of the Bible. More precisely, Huet claimed that the pagan gods were so many Euhemerian imitations, so to speak, of the figure of Moses. In the preface, where Huet acknowledged his direct predecessors, Vossius and Bochart, he identified Moses with the Egyptian Thoth, himself identical to the Gallic Teutates and the ancient German's Wothan, the Danes' Tis, and the Angles' Teves.[24] Like Bochart, Huet stated as an axiom that truth is oldest, while falsehood imitates truth.[25]

Against Marsham and Spencer, Huet claimed that the Hebrews originally came from Chaldea, rather than Egypt. It was Israelite religion that influenced Egyptian religion, rather than vice versa, as the Egyptians considered Moses to be the god Thoth, the equivalent of Mercury. Thus did Hebrew religious ideas pass to other ancient peoples, although transformed and devaluated by their "paganizing": so the Arabic Adonis is his own sister's son, just as Moses had been educated by his own sister. There is nothing surprising here, if one remembers that Moses sojourned in Arabia. Emperor Julian, in his *Hymn to the Sun*, mentioned Monimus and Azizus, who were worshipped in Edessa. Julian himself, quoting Iamblichus, claimed that Monimus is none other than Mercury. Huet noted that Abraham Ibn Ezra, in his commentary on *Exodus,* stated that Moses' Egyptian name was Monios. Zoroaster and Bacchus are two other divinities whose origins reach back to the figure of Moses. Like Bochart, Huet established the connections between Moses and the pagan gods, first of all, on superficial etymological similarities. From there, Huet moved from people to people: from Iran, Mosaic ideas reached India, and some clues suggest relations between the Hebrews and Eastern Asia. Similarly, since Athanasius Kircher, there had been speculation about possible contacts between China and Egypt. To be sure, such farfetched intellectual acrobatics leave one rather sceptical, but we would be wrong to simply dismiss them out of hand. We can detect here, supported by a rather awkward philology, a thought in search of itself, which would eventually be able to clearly formulate its own implications. This new kind of superior Euhemerism had a modern flavor and would soon permit the deconstruction of ancient myths by enlightened scholars and intellectuals. In other words, we find here the kernel of the emerging comparative study of myths.[26] Huet, moreover, did not stop with ancient myths; he applied the comparative method to recently discovered peoples. Hence, following in José de Acosta's footsteps, whose *Natural and Moral History of the Indies* was already a classic translated to many languages, he could unearth some of the great Christian dogmas hidden among Peruvian beliefs.[27]

The puzzling and far-fetched parallels proposed by Huet were not to everyone's taste. The Huguenot theologians Jean Le Clerc and Jacques Basnage, in particular, often remained unconvinced by his arguments.[28]

Pierre Jurieu, a leading theologian of the Huguenot *Refuge* in Holland and a bitter enemy of Pierre Bayle (although they had been close friends in their early days), published in Amsterdam in 1704 his *Histoire critique des cultes, bons et mauvais, qui ont été dans l'Eglise depuis Adam jusqu'à Jésus-Christ, où l'on trouve l'origine de toutes les Idolatries de l'ancien paganisme, expliquées par rapport à celles des Juifs.* In this work, Jurieu offered a comparative study of the religions of the ancient world, in particular, the Near Eastern and Mediterranean polytheist systems. Jurieu began by noting that it is hard to say anything new in a field so well charted. Yet, he appears to have done just that. His reflection on the notion of idolatry (today, one would say: "polytheism") seems more synthetic and historical than what one finds in his predecessors. In his own words: "We are looking for the origin of the Greek, Roman, Syrian and Phoenician gods" (400). It is in the East ("l'Orient"), from which humankind originates, that "one can find the origin of religion, i.e., of divine cult and service" (201).

The Bible, the only text from the ancient Near East then known, functioned for Jurieu as a privileged witness. Thus, it was as a historical document that one must read the Bible in the context of this research. Jurieu conceived of his work as responding to Richard Simon's *Histoire critique du Vieux Testament.* But he intended to go further than the great Catholic scholar and to go beyond the philological level where Simon had stopped. Focusing on the religions of the ancient Near East, Jurieu noted that the radical distinction between polytheism and monotheism is not always heuristic. He wrote: "The Theology of the Ancients contained all that is essential in religion" (17). Doesn't one retrieve the concept of Trinity in Zoroaster's oracles? Actually, he argued, "the Theology of the Patriarchs before Moses was more similar to Christian Religion than that of the Jews" (14). Elsewhere, he considered "the Religion of Noah . . . as offering salvation, and sufficient for salvation" (salutaire et suffisante au salut)" (52). For Jurieu, there were religious systems before the revelation on Mount Sinai that were not idolatrous, that did not propound a wrong idea of the divine. If religion, like humankind, came from the East, and if pristine religion is true, then idolatry is derivative, and hence must have come later. Thus, Abraham's behavior with Sarah in Egypt, where he had her pass for his sister, "apparently stems from the fact that Egypt and its king were deeply immersed in superstition and idolatry, while the Canaanite nation was not yet idolatrous" (64–65). Balaam, similarly, was neither a magician nor a false prophet. It was only after Moses that prophecy became limited to a single people (39). Religion, then, came from the ancient Near East, more precisely from Palestine and Syria. It was only later that idolatry (*les simulacres*; the Latin *simulacrum* translates the Greek *eidôlon*) was propagated throughout the world. The origin of idolatry, too, was to be found in the East, more specifically "in the family of Nimrod and in Chaldaea." For Jurieu, "the Theology of the Egyptians and that of the Phoenicians are undoubtedly the source of the Theology of the Greeks and of the Romans" (410). Thence, idols, crossing the Euphrates, reached Phoenicia, and from Phoenicia passed to Egypt. From Egypt, they came to Greece, and then, eventually, to all parts of the earth. "As men went seeking for a home from place to place in that time; wherever they went, they brought with them the gods of their country" (482). "One must accept as an established principle," he continued, "the fact that religions, like men, have come from the East, and . . . the gods of the Syrians and of the Phoenicians are the same as those of the Greeks and the Romans." Once Jurieu established this principle, he could search for identical deities among those of the Semites, Greeks, and Romans. Python is thus "the Ob of the Orientals," and Moloch (as well as Teutates among the Gauls) is the Greek and Roman Saturn. But Saturn is also equivalent to Noah; and Jupiter, Neptune, and Pluto are avatars of Shem, Ham, and Japhet, because, Jurieu stated, "I affirm something else as certain, that all the idolatries of the Pagans found their root in the East, and that the Orientals transformed into their Gods the Patriarchs and those whom Tradition taught them to have been the source of their race" (554–555). Noah, moreover, also becomes Bel-Phagor among the Moabites, and Priapus in Greece. One clearly hears here the echo of "l'illustre Bochart," as Jurieu called him, and also of Huet. Their philological intuitions have now become part of a comparative historiography of ancient religions.

The first postdiluvian religion of humankind, the universal religion of Noah's sons, was certainly no idolatry. In the seventeenth century, that religion was the historical equivalent of natural law. This recurrent pattern, which was stated with particular clarity in Grotius's *De Iure Belli ac Pacis* (1625) and in John Selden's *De Iure Naturalis* (1640), stems from Maimonides, as we saw in chapter II.1.[29]

While seventeenth-century scholars recognized the plurality of cultures and religions throughout the world, they remained in their analysis prisoners to a certain extent of their "bibliocentrism" and classical culture. Among eighteenth-century intellectuals, on the other hand, one perceives a move from the "genetic" analysis of ancient Near Eastern and Mediterranean religions to a comparative analysis of religions around the world. To a great extent, the genetic model is not the only or the most obvious one. Noël Antoine Pluche provides one example among many of this analytic shift. In his *Histoire du ciel,* published in 1739, Pluche stated that the many similarities between Hebrew and pagan mores did not reflect an influence of one on the other, but pointed, rather, to their common ancestry: Noah's sons.[30] The religious systems of antiquity were now compared with those observed by the early ethnologists, who were more often than not Catholic missionaries. Thus, the Jesuit Joseph-François Lafitau, a great admirer of Bochart, saw in the Indians the off-spring of the ten lost tribes of Israel.

2. Idolatry and Its Roots

The application of philological methods to the biblical texts combined with ethnological observation led to a major breakthrough in the study of ancient religions. It permitted the historicizing of religious truth and a strong rejection of the symbolic thought that had been so much in fashion during the Renaissance. Truth had become univalent. Rather than different levels of truth, one level now identified its multiple origins. As we have seen in the last two chapters, even the Scriptures had to be understood as documents of past civilizations. Comparison, then, was to be added to the chronological study of religious ideas and customs. In this new world of knowledge, where all forms of religious practice came to be recognized and studied, various forms of "paganism," that is, of religious error, were prominent, from Greece to China, and from the American Indians to the ancient Egyptians. If we were to single out one keyword for the period under discussion, it would probably be "idolatry."[31] The recognition of the multifaceted presence of idolatry and the study of its origins was a major concern for all students of religion in early modern Europe.[32] The presence of idolatry in early modern scholarship on ancient religions and cultures seems ubiquitous.[33] A central problem for any new cognitive structure lies in the need to legitimize its epistemological foundation. As I hope to show here, the search for the roots and nature of idolatry seems to have provided this legitimization for the nascent science of religion. To support this claim, I shall focus on the Cambridge scholar John Spencer, whose work William Robertson Smith has said stands at the very origin of the modern comparative study of religion.[34]

"Idolatry" was a heavily loaded term, constantly used in Catholic–Protestant polemics. The slogan "idolatry" had been a rallying cry for the Dutch Calvinists in their war against Spain and the Catholics.[35] The Cambridge Platonist Ralph Cudworth (1617–1688) popularized the term "polytheism" (although he did not invent it).[36] This term was less loaded than "idolatry," and it put the comparison of religious worldviews on a new footing. Throughout the following century, from Bayle through Hume to d'Holbach and Voltaire, the term "polytheism" was preferred to idolatry and was felt to convey a sense of a religious tolerance usually foreign to monotheistic systems.

Throughout the seventeenth century, writers hesitated between two theories of idolatry. One theory saw idolatry as a degeneration of the original monotheism; the other insisted on progress in religious history. These two theories of idolatry were likewise reflected in the two main theories of biblical history, present since the apologetic Christian literature of the first century. These are (1) the so-called theft theory, according to which Satan seeks to imitate God in history and corrupt the original true religion through plagiarism, and (2) the theory of condescendence *(synkatabasis)*, according to which God deigns to sanction pagan practices—such as sacrifices—since this was the only way in which ancient peoples in general, and the Israelites in particular, knew how to respect God.

Furthermore, much of the intellectual production of the seventeenth century reflects a progressive disentanglement from two traditional ideas. The first was the Renaissance *philosophia perennis* approach: a general identification of the various gods of past civilizations with one another. The second was, again, the "theft theory": whatever is interesting or respectable in pagan religion or philosophy reflects a Mosaic origin. In the late second century, Clement of Alexandria, in particular, had developed the latter theory, especially with regard to Platonism. One could tone the argument down, by speaking of borrowing rather than theft, but the genetic idea remained basically the same: structural similarities between the various ancient cultures and cults testify to historical contacts between them, to the influence of one on the other.

A major trend throughout the seventeenth century was a reworking of this last approach. This trend sought to interpret idolatry as a misunderstanding and an alteration of primitive monotheism, as an intellectual error and moral degeneration. For such an approach, the origins of humankind were ideal, paradisiacal times. This perspective also implied

89

a conception of universally valid statements about religion. In a sense, this approach was typical of the deists and of supporters of the idea of natural religion. Written at the end of the century, Antoine Van Dale's *Dissertationes de origine ac progressu idololatriae et supertitionum* (Amsterdam, 1696), was rendered into French by Bernard de Fontenelle in his own *L'origine des fables*. The latter work was published in 1724 (some twenty-five years after its redaction), the same year that saw the publication of Gianbattista Vico's *Scienza nuova* and of François Joseph Lafitau's *Moeurs des sauvages amériquains comparées à celles des premiers temps*. The idea of universally valid statements on religion, which was reflected in Fontenelle's work, would have a deep influence on Hume, Comte, and nineteenth-century anthropologists.[37]

Discourse on idolatry not only reflected the discovery of nonmonotheistic religions, East and West, but was also directly linked to Protestant apologetics against papism. To give only one instance of the anti-Catholic ethos of this discourse, one may refer to the great Cambridge Platonist Henry More (1614–1688). In his *Antidote against Idolatry*, More defined idolatry as the proper fruit of animal life, a pathological immersion in sensuality and materiality, reflected not only in the worship of the sun and moon in the East Indies but also in Catholic cult.[38]

It should be noted, however, that the search for the origins of religion in general, and of idolatry in particular, was not limited to Protestant intellectuals. Catholic scholars also learned to ask similar questions, although they usually began to do so a little later. Hence, Bernard de Montfaucon's monumental *L'antiquité expliquée, et représentée en figures* (Paris, 1719; 5 volumes) started with a brief introduction on the origins of idolatry, in which he referred to Varro's work as summarized in Augustine's *De Civitate Dei*. In the early eighteenth century, the Benedictine scholar Dom Augustin Calmet also felt the need to write a *Disssertation sur l'origine de l'idolâtrie*, in which he argued that the idols worshipped by the Israelites in the desert must have been Egyptian deities.[39]

What clearly emerges from the collection of the evidence is the central role of idolatry, ancient and modern, East and West, in seventeenth-century discourse on religion, its origins and its historical development. Although apologetic considerations of one kind or another are never absent from this discourse, what strikes the reader is the boundless intellectual curiosity that it reflects, a will to search with the light of knowledge rather than of theology for the truth in religious matters and in the history of religion. These scholars believed that such a truth could be found through historical, comparative investigations. A clear example of this approach is reflected in Hugo Grotius's *Annotationes ad Vetus Testamentum,* which includes a section on idolatry.[40] Like other scholars, Grotius (1583–1645), who happened to be Gerard Vossius's best friend, saw also in Israelite idolatry a phenomenon originating in Egyptian paganism—an approach that would later be developed by John Spencer.

The deist Charles Blount (1654–1693), as well as Herbert, Grotius and, later, the Catholic scholar Augustin Calmet (1672–1757), perceived idolatry as expressed in both the cult of the stars and sacrifices. Can we identify the source of this trend of thought on the origins of idolatry? Here again, the great intellectual hero of the seventeenth century is none other than the twelfth-century Jewish thinker Maimonides. Time and again, the various works I mention here, as well as numerous others, refer to the writings of Maimonides, both to his magnum opus, the *Guide of the Perplexed,* and to his *Commentary on Mishnah Avodah Zarah,* that is, on the Mishnaic treatise on idolatry.

In 1630, Dionysius Vossius accompanied his father Gerard to Oxford and Cambridge, where the son became an ardent student of religion. Bishop William Laud, the great orientalist Edward Pococke, first incumbent of the Regius Chair of Hebrew at Oxford, and Meric Casaubon, all had an influence on the young Vossius. In 1650, incidentally, Pococke published in his *Specimen historiae Arabum* an Arabic text of the thirteenth-century Syriac scholar Bar Hebraeus on pre-Islamic Arabian religion. The greatest catalyst on the junior Vossius, however, which prompted him to translate Maimonides' tractate on idolatry into Latin, was probably Selden's *De Diis Syris,* a book which Vossius, we are told, had read three times. Vossius's annotated Latin translation, ready in 1636, was published posthumously in 1641 by Vossius *père,* as *R. Mosis Maimonidae, De Idololatria liber,* together with his own *De Theologia Gentili.*

Dionysius Vossius's work on Maimonides' study of idolatry reveals the major reason for the strong attraction to Maimonides on the part of Christian intellectuals: more than any other ancient or medieval thinker, Greek, Christian, or even Muslim, Maimonides offered a compelling analysis of the phenomenon of idolatry, reaching dramatic conclusions on its origin and nature. Maimonides' most original insights on idolatry were to be found in his theological work, the *Guide of the Perplexed.* This book, written in Arabic, had been translated (from Al-Harizi's medieval

Hebrew version) to Latin in the thirteenth century, and was thus available to Christian theologians already in the time of Thomas Aquinas and Meister Eckhart, both great admirers of Maimonides.[41]

A new translation of *Guide,* prepared once more from a Hebrew medieval version (this time, from Ibn Tibbon's, the Hebrew vulgate) rather than from the Arabic original, appeared in Basel in 1629, under the title *Dux Perplexorum.* Its author was Johann Buxtorf Jr. (1599–1664). Buxtorf's translation was the version in which the *Guide* would be read from now on by people as different as Leibniz, Malebranche, Newton, and Bayle. Both the Hebrew version and the Arabic original were available to orientalists. Joseph Scaliger, for instance, on receiving an Arabic copy of the work (in Hebrew characters, as the original Judeo-Arabic text was written) from Richard Thompson, wrote to his friend Isaac Casaubon that he valued it as gold.[42]

For us, Maimonides (also known under his Hebrew acrostic, Rambam) was a medieval Jewish thinker—by far the greatest among them—who systematized biblical and Jewish laws and reflected on their origins and reasons. As a philosopher, he stands in the great tradition of Aristotelian Arabic philosophy, together with al-Farabi and Averroes. As a Jewish thinker, he represents a major effort to harmonize Jewish religion with philosophy. Since the Middle Ages, however, Rabbi Mosis Aegyptus was considered by the Christians to be a great commentator on the biblical text, offering precious insights on its true or deeper meaning. In the seventeenth century, Maimonides was perceived by scholars investigating the nature and origin of religion as a great predecessor, a philologist of genius. For them, he was not an object of research, but rather a highly gifted earlier colleague, who had worked long ago on the same problems as themselves. Hence, Constantijn L'Empereur (1591–1648), for instance, who taught Hebrew in Leiden as a professor of *Controversarium Judaicarum* and whose work on Jewish law shows striking similarities to that of Selden, did not consider Maimonides' *Mishneh Torah* a legal code, but rather a description of the history and customs of the Jewish people. As Peter T. van Rooden wrote, "He shared this opinion with almost all the Christian Hebraists of the seventeenth century. They all considered rabbinical literature as an exposition of the Old Testament."[43]

In his *Guide,* Maimonides developed his views on the origin of idolatry in the ancient Near East (see especially ch. 3, 29–33). And in this context, he dealt with biblical injunctions and precepts, such as sacrifices, which seem to have no rational explanation. In part, his theory was highly original—and Maimonides was quite conscious of having discovered sociological laws of religious behavior. In part, it was a further development of a well-known concept in patristic literature, usually called the theory of divine condescendence (Greek *synkatabasis;* cf. Arabic *talaṭṭuf,* "gracious ruse" as used by Maimonides), a concept perhaps borrowed from the second-century-c.e. philosopher Alexander of Aphrodisias.[44] As Shlomo Pines has shown, it is likely that Maimonides was influenced by the patristic theory, although the precise channels through which it reached him remain unclear.[45] Maimonides argued in *Guide* that the Israelites had been influenced during their stay in Egypt by its idolatrous rites, and that it was to help them gradually uproot these evil habits that God ordered them to perform sacrifices. To the idea that both Israelite idolatrous practices and biblical sacrifices have an Egyptian origin, Maimonides added his own original, broader conception of idolatry. He stated that he had the opportunity to read, in Arabic translation, various books written by the Sabians. Traditions about the Sabians from ancient Harran had already developed in Maimonides' own day into a highly complex set of stories that hopelessly mixed historical fact with legend and myth.[46] There is no need to enter here into the nebulous traditions on the Sabians. Suffice it to state that for Maimonides, "Sabians" was a generic name referring to all idolaters, ancient and modern alike, rather than the name of a concrete and distinct people. It referred not only to Egyptian religion but also to the Mesopotamian and Canaanite religions. Their religion was based on the cult of the stars. Far from representing "primitive" ideas about idols, idolatry was a highly sophisticated approach to cultic activity. All this Maimonides could derive from what he considered to be Sabian literature, in particular from a book *On Nabatean Agriculture,* by the tenth-century-author Ibn Waḥshiyya.[47] The title of this book, called in Arabic *al-filāḥa al-nabaṭiyya,* had been translated to Hebrew as *ha-ʿavoda ha-nabaṭit,* (ʿavoda meaning both agriculture and cult). The Medieval Latin translation of *Guide,* however, had rendered it as *De agricultura Aegyptiorum* (rather than *Nabathaeorum*), and also *de servitio Aegyptio* (ch. 38),[48] while Buxtorf, guessing the problem, had retained the Hebrew *ha-ʿavoda ha-nabaṭit.* This did not prevent readers of Buxtorf's translation, such as Leibniz, from referring to the supposedly Sabian book *de agricultura Aegyptiorum.* Samuel Purchas, too, referred to the book of the "Sabij" called *de agricultura Aegyptorum,* still extant in the hands of the Muhammadans, and referred to it as the "Aegyptian service." Maintaining the erroneous translation of the book on Nabatean agriculture was not an innocent slip. It permitted the identification of the mythical Sabians with the Egyptians, and of their cult of the stars with Egyptian religion. Such a perception, incidentally, went together with a sublimating view of Egyptian religion—a view which would become much more prevalent with the eighteenth-century Egyptomania.

Maimonides' interpretation of the roots of idolatry became common-place in the seventeenth century, and Stephen Nettles' response to Selden might serve here as one example among many:

> Moses Ben Maimon in More Hanebucim writes, that the end for which sacrifices were commanded, did tend especially to the root-ing out of Idolatry; for whereas the Gentiles worshipped beasts, as the Chaldaeans and Aegyptians bullocks and sheep, with reference to the Celestiall Signes, Aries, and Taurus, etc . . . therefore (saith he) God commanded these to be slaine in sacrifice.[49]

As mentioned above, the influence of Maimonides on European thinkers did not begin in the seventeenth century. From the patristic po-lemics of late antiquity up to the early modern era, however, idolatry did not have the status of a major problem in Western thought. Hence, the Sabians could not have played the central role they were to play in the seventeenth century. This seems to explain the puzzling fact that the sev-enteenth century saw the best days of Maimonides' theory, a fact the significance of which is still underrecognized.[50] As Richard Popkin has noted, "there is as yet no study of the impact of Maimonides on seven-teenth century European thought."[51] Jean Bodin had already referred to the Sabians and to Maimonides' conception of idolatry in his *Heptaplo-meres*, written in 1596.[52] In the second decade of the seventeenth century, Purchas spared no effort in his *Pilgrimage* to define idolatry and identify its historical sources. The essence of paganism, he said, is the cult of the stars, as if they were divine, and this cult originated among the Sabians, the people among whom Abraham had grown up and against whose reli-gious ideas he rebelled. Purchas did not seem to have read Maimonides, but he referred to the correspondence between Scaliger and Casaubon, and it stands to reason that Scaliger was the likely source of later refer-ences to the Maimonidean theory of idolatry. For Purchas, as for Mai-monides, the Sabians were the representatives of the various ancient Near Eastern polytheistic religions. True religion was defined in opposition to paganism, and Israelite religion was born from the revolt against Sabian cult.

This was the way the Sabians (often written *Zabii,* as in the Latin translation of *Guide*) were perceived until John Spencer. This background to what the French call Spencer's *imaginaire* was needed if we are to understand him in historical context. Indeed, Spencer's book appears to have been cited more often than read, and some quite unsatisfactory interpretations of his thought have been made recently. A monographic study of Spencer remains a desideratum.

When John Spencer (1630–1693) first came to Corpus Christi College in 1645, Cambridge had already had a long Hebraist tradition. This tradition dated back to the early sixteenth century, when Robert Wakefield, "the English counterpart to Germany's Reuchlin," was appointed a lecturer in Hebrew at St. John's College.[53] In 1667, Spencer was unanimously elected Master of Corpus Christi, which he governed "with great prudence and reputation" for twenty-six years, after which he became a great benefactor of the college. He also was dean of Ely Cathedral from 1677.[54] In 1669, Spencer published his *Dissertatio de Urim et Thumim,* a prelude to his larger work, the *De legibus hebraeorum ritualibus et earum rationibus libri tres.* This last work was published in Cambridge in 1685, and in Amsterdam the following year.[55] *De legibus hebraeorum ritualibus* includes the various studies penned by Spencer over some twenty years. It represents a radical new departure in scholarship. As Steven Benin pertinently appraised, "Spencer blazed a new trail and deserted the well-worn paths of earlier commentators and scholars. Later scholars merely follow in his wake."[56] Since the nineteenth century, Spencer's book has been recognized as a *chef d'oeuvre,* but the book has not received the careful analysis that such lavish praise would lead one to expect.[57]

At the time of its first publication, *De legibus hebraeorum ritualibus* did not pass unnoticed. It signaled the beginning of a loud international controversy: Marsham, Le Clerc, Jurieu, stood for him, while Witsius, Waechter, and later Calmet, opposed him. While Jacques Basnage, the great Huguenot historian of the Jews, was influenced by Spencer in his perception of Egyptian impact on Israel,[58] J. Edwards, as well as J. Bellman, opposed him, arguing that the ceremonial rites were meant to fight idolatry. Giambattista Vico, too, who refers to Spencer's work at the beginning of his *Scienza nuova,* was certainly influenced by his theory of accommodation.[59]

Some fine studies of Spencer have recently been published, in particular by Francis Schmidt and Jan Assmann.[60] Yet, the literary genre of *De
legibus hebraeorum* has remained unidentified, and this lack of identification hampers a clear understanding of Spencer's goals, methods, and
achievements. Spencer was an excellent Hebraist, whose abilities and
reading were not limited to the Hebrew Bible. Seventeenth-century orientalists in Oxford and Cambridge mastered the various linguistic levels of
Hebrew and were avid readers of Medieval Hebrew literature. They occasionally wrote a poem or letter in Hebrew. The index at the end of
De legibus hebraeorum ritualibus gives an impressive list of Medieval
Hebrew works referred to in the text, and we now know that many rabbinic books of Italian provenance were available in England.[61] Hence,
Spencer was cognizant with the long tradition in medieval Jewish theology, of discussing the reasons of the Divine Commandments *(ta'amei
ha-mizwoth)*. Since Sa'adia Gaon (tenth century), medieval Jewish thinkers had asked whether the commandments in the Torah, in particular the
odder or more problematic ones among them, had any rational significance, other than that they had been ordered by God.[62] Among the Jewish
medieval thinkers, Maimonides found a solution radical in its rationalism: ALL commandments had a reason; all had a "useful purpose." While
in some cases, the reason was obvious, in other cases, it was not, and the
role of the exegete was to reveal it. It was in this context that Maimonides
referred to Ibn Wahshiyya's *The Nabatean Agriculture* and God's "gracious ruse" to help free the Israelites from their idolatrous mental and
religious habits.

We have previously noted that there were two traditional but conflicting theses on the roots of idolatry. That of plagiarism had reached Vossius, Grotius, Bochart, Gale, and Huet. The condescendence thesis argued basically the opposite; rather than degeneration, history reflected a
progressive refinement of religious beliefs: a Divine *Erziehung des Men-
schengeschlechts*, to use Lessing's phrase.[63] It was in this second tradition
that Spencer, quite consciously and forcefully, decided to inscribe himself:
the title to *Prolegomena*, Cap. I, reads: "Ostenditur leges et ritus Judaicos
non sine ratione a Deo institutos." He saw himself as Maimonides' direct
successor, and the differences between them stemmed from the fact that
he was a Christian, that is, a fully accomplished Jew, who understood the
fuller meaning of God's Law. As a Christian, Spencer was not bound to
keep most ritual laws mentioned in the Torah, since he believed that
Christ offered a more spiritual way of being faithful to God's revelation.

Spencer thus believed that he understood, better than Maimonides, that there was an evolution in history and that God revealed Himself and His will gradually: Moses offered a religion truer than that of the Sabians. Jesus permitted a higher, more spiritual way of serving God than the ritual laws of Moses. And finally, the Reformation proposed a better Christianity than Catholicism, a religion with too many rituals, remnants, as it were, of earlier stages of religious life. In a sense, then, Spencer was aware that the *De legibus hebraeorum ritualibus* is an apologetic work, fighting on various fronts: he was arguing against the Jews, who would be more easily converted once they understood the historical reasons for the commandments. At the same time, he not only fought the papists but also the enthusiasts, Protestants who had left the high road of reasonable religion.

Jan Assmann has argued that Spencer carried Maimonides' views on historical evolution to their logical end. According to him, Maimonides' evolutionary perspective on religious history remains locked in his belief that although the laws of the Torah were meant as a concession to earlier religious conceptions, they themselves could not be superseded. Assmann may not have been quite fair to Maimonides here, since the latter, while not rejecting the idea of religious evolution, insisted that it must be perceived within the frame of the laws of divine revelation. Although Maimonides' arguments were presented, first and foremost, as a historical analysis, his theoretical intentions were clearly and expressly those of a phenomenologist rather than of a historian of religion. Perhaps one could argue that Maimonides—before Ibn Khaldun—discovered the laws of the sociology of religion, rather than of the history of religions. One could say that, whereas Spencer saw paganism only as an early stage in the development of religious perceptions, Maimonides insisted that pagan ideas were inherent to humankind and could occur in every generation.[64]

Spencer's views were those of a Christian theologian. But he was also living in the second half of the seventeenth century, in Newton's Cambridge. His times were those of *ratio par excellence*. If his search for the *rationes* of the biblical rituals was so radical, it was also because he looked into the Great Book of God just as others were looking into the Great Book of Nature. The religious background against which one must understand Newton is now well recognized. He, and his colleagues, searched for traces of God's revelation in nature. The opposite, however, was also true: Spencer searched the Bible for traces of natural laws applicable to humans, that is, historical laws.

If Spencer's *ratio* is such a rich term, it is because it reflects the confla-
tion of two meanings of the word. The first meaning is simply the translation of the Hebrew *ta'am*, reason *sive* significance. The second meaning
is a translation of the Arabic *'aql*, reason *sive* intellect. Spencer was indeed a religious intellectual, like Maimonides, but living five centuries
later. Being a man of his century, he did not only read the Bible (in the
original text) and its commentaries. He could not separate his readings
from the broader context of the momentous discoveries of his contemporaries. Spencer's interests were by no means only antiquarian. Present
discoveries and new methods of inquiry bore directly on the study of
ancient history, while a better understanding of the latter also had direct
implications on contemporary issues. Like others, Spencer compared the
Egyptian pyramids with those of the Aztecs and knew from his vast readings that if the contemporary Turks prohibited the consumption of pork,
this had to be understood in the same religious context as the parallel
biblical prohibition. The reader of Spencer's book is left with a profound
impression of awe or even magic. This impression is not only due to its
monumental dimensions or to the versatile and boundless erudition shown
by its author. *De legibus hebraeorum ritualibus* is so impressive because
it reflects a complete mixture of genres, based on the recognition of the
unity of humankind. If rituals everywhere were similar, after all, it was
because of this essential unity of humankind. The language of rites was,
in a sense, an ideal library, with open stacks and no walls, and infinite
cross-references.

William Robertson Smith credited Spencer with a pioneering role in
the comparative study of religion.[65] "Comparative religion" is, however,
a somewhat static term that does not fully carry the impact of Spencer's
stand and contribution. We may perhaps see him as a pioneer *historian*
of religion. It has been claimed that John Spencer was a deist in disguise,
who used the strategy of Herbert, Blount, and Toland to indict contemporary religion by presenting a history of heathenism. According to this
thesis, the *De legibus hebraeorum ritualibus* was intended as a challenge
to the Mosaic dispensation, an intention carefully hidden beneath its erudition and innovative scholarship.[66] To my mind, such an assessment
shows a complete misunderstanding of Spencer. It was as a historian that
he wrote, seeking to relativize and historicize religious phenomena in order
to better understand their origins. Hence, his great intellectual opponents
are the *allegorizantium natio,* those who seek to understand the biblical
text independently of any context. For Spencer, symbolism was a simula-

crum of reason. He could not have had good intellectual relations with the Cambridge Platonists. Spencer could speak of the *rudes Israelitae,* and of the *vestigia* of idolatry in their religious habits, as so many *ineptiae tolerabiles* accepted by God, but only for a while, as a kind of "withdrawal therapy" (the term is Assmann's). The most obvious of these *ineptiae* were, of course, the sacrifices in the Jerusalem Temple. Spencer offered an archaeology of religion, and his view of history was optimistic, since it was that of the progressive education of humankind by divine providence. Where the deists saw a degeneration from the original pure and natural religion of earliest humankind through the devilish imposture of the priests of all nations, Spencer saw a long but constant progress from the early stages of history, thanks to a God who has no objection to aping the devil in order to free men from the latter's clutches.

Spencer was not only a prolific writer. His footnotes also show him to have been a keen reader, in all the fields of knowledge open to him. Walton and Cappel for the biblical text, Kircher and Marsham for Egypt, Pococke and Hottinger for oriental matters, and many others, from Scaliger, Buxtorf and Da Costa to Purchas, L'Empereur, Reland, van Dale, Leone Modena and Richard Simon. But the greatest figures in his pantheon, *ille respublicae literariae triumviri,* as he called them, were Samuel Bochart, John Selden, and Hugo Grotius.

Spencer launched an intellectual revolution of sorts. He discovered, more clearly than others among his contemporaries, the laws of religious evolution. Like other revolutions, his was definitely over determined, in the sense that many of the conditions necessary for such a breakthrough were already fulfilled. Not only was his perfect knowledge of the Jewish intellectual and religious tradition an essential condition but also the various discoveries of his contemporaries, from Marsham, who showed the chronological prominence of Egypt over Israel, to the orientalists who were discovering patterns of Semitic religions. Finally, another dimension of Spencer's discourse on religion should be mentioned. For him, as for Hobbes, Locke, and many other intellectuals, the political dimensions of the *respublica Hebraeorum* were the object of constant discussions, in the relatively free political and intellectual English climate.

Scholars and thinkers writing at the end of the seventeenth century, and in the first decades of the eighteenth, read Spencer seriously: from Bayle and Jurieu to Basnage, Calmet and Vico.[67] It was the combination of philology and orientalism, of anthropological sensitivity and the will to communicate scholarly achievements to broader audiences that would permit some of the most impressive intellectual achievements of the Enlightenment. In the next chapter, we shall see how reflection on the biblical myths could be expanded into a study of Iranian dualist religious systems.

V

Iranian Religions and the Idea of Dualism

1. The Prophet of Iran and Zoroastrianism

From Plutarch's *On Isis and Osiris* to Mozart's *Magic Flute*, Zoroaster and the ancient Iranian beliefs and cults remained a major topic of fascination throughout Western culture. It is however only with the publication of the *Zend Avesta* in 1771 by Abraham Hyacinthe Anquetil-Duperron that the modern study of Zoroastrianism would begin in earnest.[1] Anquetil-Duperron's achievements eclipsed all previous attempts to understand Zoroaster and his religion. Earlier attempts to come to terms with Zoroastrianism were soon relegated to the "prehistory" of Iranian studies, and often forgotten. From then on, Iranian studies would seek, first of all, to develop the philological study of the Avestan and other ancient Iranian texts.

When the young Anquetil-Duperron (who was born in 1731) decided in 1754 to go to India, he intended to search there for authentic books written by Zarathustra, or Zoroaster. He was trying to answer a nagging question that had preoccupied scholars since at least the beginning of the eighteenth century, regarding the *"ipsissima Zoroastris scripta."* This academic discussion became known as the "Querelle de l'Avesta," and raged (mainly in French) about the existence and the nature of Zarathustra and Zoroastrian writings. It had become, in the fashion of the period, a "cause célèbre," described by Raymond Schwab as a curious episode in the ideological battle of the eighteenth century.[2] It had some common elements with the two other famous intellectual polemics of the time discussed in previous chapters: the "Querelle des Anciens et des Modernes," which dealt with the literary qualities of classical literature, and of Homer's writings in particular, and the "Querelle des Rites," which centered on the true nature—religious or civil—of Confucian rituals.[3] In his

Demonstratio Evangelica, Pierre-Daniel Huet argued against the historical existence of Zoroaster, who had been, according to him, only another
reflection of Moses.[4] This theory proved to be hard to extirpate. The *Encyclopédie,* for instance, denied in the entry for "Perses" the existence of
both Zoroaster and authentic Zend writings.

In 1762, after many years of a terribly exhausting odyssey, Anquetil-
Duperron was able to announce his discovery to the scholarly world.[5]
In this article, he referred to the *Historia religionis veterum Persarum
eorumque Magorum* ("History of the religion of the ancient Persians and
of their Magi"), a book published in 1700 by the Oxford orientalist
Thomas Hyde, as a book filled with "immense oriental erudition," and
added that Hyde remained the uncontested master of Iranian studies.[6]
Hyde, however, said Anquetil-Duperron, was unable to use the *Zend
Avesta,* traditionally attributed to Zoroaster, and only mentioned its title.
Hyde was further chided for his lack of critical sense vis-à-vis Zoroastrianism. Real scholarship needed to look for the original texts of the Zoro-
astrian tradition.[7]

The only recent analysis of Hyde's work is found in Michael Stausberg's
Faszination Zarathustra.[8] Stausberg's work is impressive indeed in its
scope: it seems to encompass almost every single meaningful discussion
of Zarathustra in European literature from the Renaissance through the
Enlightenment. Stausberg, however, is more interested in the reflection of
the figure of Zoroaster than in the history of a scholarly discipline, namely,
Zoroastrian studies. To some extent this approach blurs the originality
and importance of Hyde's contribution to the study of Zoroastrianism.
Stausberg does not offer a real analysis of Hyde's intellectual background
and milieu. Nor does he sufficiently highlight the major mechanisms of
Hyde's general hypothesis, in particular the fundamental importance
Hyde attributes to the Sabians. Moreover, Stausberg's claim (in which he
seems to be following Jacques Duchesne-Guillemin) that Hyde developed
his theory on Zoroastrianism and dualism, to some extent, as a response
to Pierre Bayle's study of Manichaean dualism in his *Dictionnaire historique et critique,* is not established on real evidence, and strikes me as
highly improbable.[9] Hyde could actually have known the first edition
of the *Dictionnaire,* which had appeared in 1697, before he published
his own book in 1700. But he had been working on his magnum opus
for many years, and his main thesis could not have been formulated at so
late a stage. I shall argue, rather, that the relationship between the two

scholars was based on Hyde's deep influence on Bayle, who did much to propagate Hyde's ideas throughout the eighteenth century, through the second edition of the *Dictionnaire*.

The following pages will therefore attempt to highlight some aspects of Hyde's work that offer a particular interest for historical epistemology and the birth of the modern study of religion.

Thomas Hyde (1636–1703) was a versatile orientalist and a dynamic librarian.[10] Since 1665, and until the beginning of the eighteenth century, Hyde remained the Keeper of the Bodleian Library, which then "acquired more oriental manuscripts than under any librarian before or since," as noted by George J. Toomer.[11] Although the *Historia religionis veterum Persarum eorumque Magorum* is undoubtedly his masterpiece, Hyde's publications span a very broad array of fields. One can mention his *De ludis orientalibus* (Oxford, 1694), which contains a history of chess among the Arabs, Persians, Indians, and Chinese, edited on the basis, inter alia, of three medieval Hebrew texts. Mention can also be made of his *Itinera mundi* (Oxford, 1691), which focuses on the publication and Latin translation of Abraham Peritsol's *Iggeret orḥot 'olam,* and includes various discussions of Islamic liturgy and Meccan pilgrimage. Hyde also made a formal proposal to the Oxford Press to edit Maimonides' *Guide of the Perplexed* in Arabic characters, together with a Latin translation, submitting to this purpose a "specimen." The Press, unfortunately, was unwilling to pay him the substantial sums required for undertaking this task, and he abandoned the project.[12] He also conferred and corresponded (in Latin) with Shen Fu-tsung, the first-recorded Chinese person to set foot on English soil, and learned some Chinese from him. As the Bodleian librarian, Hyde had paid Shen Fu-tsung to prepare a list of Chinese books in the library.[13] Hyde had become such a star in the firmament of the Republic of Letters that on hearing of his death, a Dutch professor exclaimed: "Decessit Hydius, stupor mundi! (Hyde is dead, the world is numb)"

Perhaps the most interesting feature in Hyde's work, from an epistemological viewpoint, is that it shows in exemplary manner how a scholar with only limited access to the necessary sources can still deal significantly with a historical phenomenon. In such a case, more than ever, intuition and imagination are called to play a major role. After Anquetil-Duperron's publication of the *Zend Avesta,* Hyde would appear to have earlier been deprived of access to the most important primary sources of Zoroastrianism. But for him, the newly available Arabic sources of Muslim heresiologists (Shahrastānī and Abūl-Fidā), which had been edited by Pococke, meant a radical departure from the previously almost complete reliance on the Greek sources (mainly Plutarch's description of Iranian dualism in his *Isis and Osiris*). Moreover, Hyde's perception of Zoroastrianism was enriched by a late Zoroastrian ethical work, *Sad dar*, or "One Hundred Gates" (which he calls *Sad der*).[14] Hyde translated *Sad dar* from the Persian original, and to a great extent based his main argument about the original monotheism of Zoroaster's doctrines on this text, which does not show any sign of dualism.

Hyde's argument on Zoroaster's monotheism was thus based on the new document provided by the *Sad dar*, which he considered, quite legitimately, to be a primary and important source. It was also predicated, however, on his overall conception of the religious history of humankind. As we have seen in the previous chapter, two models were available to Hyde: one supported the idea of original monotheism, only later perverted by idolatry, the other argued for original idolatry, in reaction to which Israelite religion was born. While the latter view found a strong supporter in John Spencer, Hyde opted for the first.

Spencer's work must have been known to Hyde, as he proceeded with his new understanding of ancient Iranian religion. As we saw in the last chapter, Spencer was following in Maimonides' footsteps when he identified the ancient Near Eastern polytheists as "Sabian" (*Zabii*). This identification was rather common in the seventeenth century. To give only one example, one can refer to Thomas Stanley, *The History of Philosophy* (London, 1655–1662). Book 3 in Stanley's work deals explicitly with Sabian philosophy and argues that Zerdosht, who is identical with Zoroaster, and a contemporary of Terah, Abraham's father, was the "Institutor of the Sabian Sect." His whole analysis is then explicitly based on Maimonides' discussion in *Guide*.

Like Spencer, who had produced what was by far the most systematic study of "Sabian" religion, Hyde was strongly influenced by Maimonides. Now, Maimonides had also identified the contemporary Zoroastrians as Sabians: "It is generally known that according to the usages observed up to our times by the Sabians in the lands of the East, I refer to the remnants of the Magians."[15]

Hyde sought to understand Zoroastrianism and its historical development within the general framework of the religious history of humankind. He postulated three stages in the evolution of Iranian (which he referred to as "Persian") religion. In the first stage, the Iranians were monotheists, offering cult to the true and eternal God: "solius Dei veri et aeterni cultores fuerunt." Later, under the influence of Sabeism, they came to add the sun and the planets to divine cult. This is what Hyde called "interpretatio Sabaitica prima." Later, after Abraham, came a relapse, referred to as "interpolatio Sabaitica secunda." Hyde noted, however, that the Iranians remained innocent of Greek idolatry and did not have temples dedicated to the idols (3). The central Zoroastrian cult was that of fire, as reflected in the Muslim reference to the Zoroastrians as "fire worshipers" (*ignicolae*) (13). For Hyde, this cult of fire was meant to be an imitation of the fire on the altar in the Jerusalem Temple (3).

For Maimonides and his readers, the Sabians were not a people, but a religion or rather a type of religion: "Sabii non sunt certa aliqua gens, sed certum Religionis genus" (ch. 5, 122). The origins of Sabeism go very far, as they claim to belong to the "religion of Noah" (Sabaitae reputant se esse de Religione Noachi, 123), while some go even further, claiming Seth as their ancestor.[16] Hyde pointed out that far from being limited to the East, Sabeism was prevalent also in the West. The ancient peoples of Europe, Germans, Goths, Danes, and Swedes, were all behaving as Sabians when worshipping the planets.

According to Hyde, the Sabian cult of the sun is universal and can be observed throughout the world among ancient nations as well as contemporaneous peoples, such as the Peruvians: "*Solis quidem Adoratio plus quam civilis fuit fere universalis.*" Contrary to appearances, however, it is not idolatrous, as respect presented to the sun and planets does not in any way imply their divinity.[17] These early Sabians were the "good" ones (*meliores*, 5), the group to which the Persians belonged. Unfortunately, with time, some degeneration of this pure religion occurred, and some among the Sabians began to neglect the cult of God and worship stars and angels as if they were divine, thus starting the long and ugly history of idolatry. These represent, of course, the "bad" Sabians *(qui pejores)*. Hyde noted that this taxonomy of good versus bad Sabians stemmed from Shahrastani.

In following Maimonides' model, then, Hyde had placed the Zoroastrians squarely within the general biblical framework. To the Sabian identity of the Zoroastrians, he added the direct relationship between Abraham and Zoroaster, or Zardusht: "*Persae suam nominarunt Religionem Abrahami*" (The Persians called their own religion that of Abraham; 83), following here a tradition known from the Islamic sources, which he presented as preserving an ancient Zoroastrian tradition.[18]

Seeking to rehabilitate original Sabeism, Abraham succeeded in weakening the depraved version of the religion in the world. (84). In contemporary discourse, the reference to the "Abrahamic religions" has become fashionable. This very recent concept is rooted in the Qur'anic concept of *millat Ibrāhīm*, Abraham's religion (sing.). Hyde's discussion reflects a remarkable interest in the early avatars of Abraham's religion in early modern scholarship.

Just as Abraham, "the first Zardusht," had offered the original reform of Sabeism, his follower, Zoroaster, reformed Sabeism among the Iranians. He was able to eradicate idolatrous elements in the cult of the fire, which represented the sun. This cult was *pyrodoulia* rather than *pyrolatria* (3). Hyde was able to confirm his analysis with testimonies given by Persian priests in India to Pietro della Valle and other Western travelers: their prostration before the fire, they insist, is no adoration (5). As the Zoroastrian fires are no idolatry, they are by nature intrinsically different from the sacred fires found among idolatrous peoples such as the Greeks and the Romans (19).

Hyde's terms, *pyrolatria* and *pyrodoulia,* are remarkable: *latreia* and *douleia* had been used already by Thomas Hobbes in his *De cive* to describe, quite explicitly, divine *versus* civil worship.[19] A quite similar vocabulary had been developed in the early eighth century by John of Damascus to argue for the legitimacy of the cult of icons. The *iconodoulia,* he argued, does not partake in idolatry, or *iconolatria,* as claimed by the iconoclasts, since reverence does not mean worship. The renewed use of this vocabulary, in eighteenth-century discussions of divine *versus* civil religion is indicative of the centrality of the preoccupation with idolatry discussed in the preceding chapter.

It was pure monotheism, then, that Zoroaster had preached, and the dualism reflected by the Greek sources and the Islamic heresiographers reflected a later stage of the religion, when the original cult was misunderstood. One advantage of presenting Zoroastrianism as an essentially monotheistic tradition was obvious: it permitted its sympathetic treatment, as a religion akin to that of Israel. The original religious teaching of humankind thus remained within the biblical *Heilsgeschichte;* Israel's religion (and, ipso facto, Christianity) retained its chronological as well as its ontological supremacy.

Persian cult, then, was parallel to that offered in the Jerusalem Temple, and through their cultic fires, the Zoroastrians were actually offering a cult to the one God: "in ipsis Ignibus celebrarunt Jehovam" (3). Zoroastrianism provided the only clear parallel from the ancient Near East to the religion of Israel. Both represented a reaction against the idolatry prevalent among the surrounding peoples, a degenerate form of Sabeism.

To understand this point, one must remember that Zoroaster, the teacher *(praeceptor)* or lawgiver *(legislator)* of both Medes and Persians or the reformer *(reformator)* of their religion, was cognizant of the Old Testament and could maintain intellectual contacts with the Israelites.[20] Hyde offered an ingenious solution to the similarities between Zoroastrian and biblical teachings: as a young man, Zoroaster had worked as an apprentice *(servus)* for an Israelite prophet.[21]

As in other religions, during the course of history, various heresies and sects appeared among the Zoroastrians (more than seventy, 25). One group among these heretics, the "Magi Dualistae" as they are called, were responsible for the theological innovation of two eternal principles, an innovation later developed by the Manichaeans (25–26). Those Greek and Muslim writers who attributed to all Zoroastrians the theology of these dualists were acting maliciously. The *Sad dar,* indeed, contained no allusion whatsoever to dualism.

This is not to say, he continued, that there was no mention in Zoroastrianism of two principles, but that these two principles were of an ethical nature and did not contradict the unity of God. The idea of two principles, good and evil, was universal, as shown by its presence among the Peruvians.[22] Contrary to common opinion, Mithra was not in Persian cult the object of a divine adoration.[23] It was only the Greeks and Romans who would transform the original Persian cult of Mithra and remodel it according to their own idolatrous usage. Since Mithra, representing the sun, was not perceived by the Persians to be a god, his cult in Zoroastrianism was not of a religious nature. Rather, it was of a civil or ceremonial nature.[24]

To understand Hyde's use of the concept of *cultus civilis,* one should keep in mind its intellectual context.[25] As we have seen earlier, the reappearance of this notion in modern discourse had much to do with the Jesuits' efforts to justify their accommodation to Chinese culture and customs. It should thus come as no surprise that in the second edition of his *Dictionnaire,*[26] Bayle notes that Hyde's observations on the civil nature of the original Zoroastrian cult offered to the sun could be used by the Jesuits to support their cause in the "Querelle des Rites," as they claimed that the honors offered by the Chinese to Confucius were of a civil rather than of a religious nature.[27]

Hyde had certainly not been the first early modern student or observer of ancient Iranian religion. Throughout the seventeenth century, various works had dealt with Zoroaster and Zoroastrian beliefs and cult, from different viewpoints. Most of these works, however, remained quite far from Hyde's radical attempt at a historical reconstruction of a religion. J. H. Ursini's *De Zoroastre Bactriano, Hermete Trismegisto, Sanchoniatone Phoenicio* (Nuremberg 1661), still reflected, up to its title, the Renaissance concept of *prisca theologia*. Under various garbs, it was one and the same truth, ultimately a divine revelation, which was reflected in the teachings of the great religious teachers of humankind. From this perspective, which freely mixed history and myth, Zoroaster, the Egyptian Hermes Trismegistus, and the Phoenician Sanchuniaton were the cultural heroes of the three great non-biblical cultures of the ancient Near East, and Zoroaster was the author of the *Chaldean Oracles*. It would remain for Hyde to lay to rest the fanciful Zoroastrian origin of these Greek texts of the "Platonic underworld" of late antiquity.

During the seventeenth century, the emphasis moved from the *prisca philosophia* to the synoptic presentation and comparative study of "philosophical systems." From 1655 to 1662, Thomas Stanley published in English his *History of Philosophy,* a work dedicated to his uncle John Marsham. Book 2 of Stanley's work deals with "Persian philosophy," beginning with Zoroaster, the "Institutor of philosophy among the Persians," and treats both doctrine (relying on the testimony of Eusebius and Plutarch, in particular) and ritual (or " Magick"), following Strabo and Herodotus.

The attention given to Zoroastrian practices by various travelers to India and Persia throughout the early modern times provided a major impetus for the new scholarly interest in Zoroastrianism. Henry Lord, for instance, published in 1630 what purported to be an anthropological description of "the religion of the Persees" of India, insisting in particular on their "idolatrous worshippe of Fire," and describing their "baptismes, marriages, and burials."[28]

Hyde's *Historia religionis veterum Persarum* owed its immediate recognition to a series of long review articles published by Jacques Bernard in the *Nouvelles de la République des Lettres,* between December 1699 and March 1701.[29] Upon noticing these articles, Pierre Bayle decided to add a lengthy entry "Zoroastre" in the second edition of his *Dictionnaire historique et critique,* which appeared in Amsterdam in 1702.[30] In the

Dictionnaire's first edition, there was no such entry, and the reference to the two first principles of Zoroastrianism, in the entry "Arimanius," was established on Thomas Burnet's *Telluris Theoria Sacra*,[31] which reviewed the various cosmogonical theories then known, from those of the Indians to those of the Greeks. Burnet himself had used Plutarch's *Isis and Osiris* as his main source on Iranian dualism.

In the second edition of Bayle's *Dictionnaire,* the main source for the entry on "Zoroastre" was Hyde, while Bayle also refers to earlier scholars such as Stanley, Bochart, or Huet, as well as to Barthélemy d'Herbelot's *Bibliothèque Orientale.* It was essentially this entry in Bayle's *Dictionnaire* that would introduce the word "dualisme" to general discourse, although Bayle basically presented Hyde's main idea about Iranian original monotheism.

The great Edward Pococke had been Hyde's predecessor as the Laudian Professor of Arabic and Regius Professor of Hebrew at Oxford. It was he who discovered for European scholarship the importance of the medieval Muslim heresiologists. In particular, Pococke called attention to the discussion of the Iranian tenants of *thanawiya* ("dualism" in Arabic, referring to the Zoroastrian belief in two principles) and to the followers of Zaradusht in the heresiographies of Shahrastānī and Abūl-Fidā, and thus directly opened the way for Hyde's systematic use of these and other sources.[32] It was thus following in Pococke's footsteps that Hyde invented the concept "dualismus" to translate Shahrastānī's *thanawyia.* Through Bayle's *Dictionnaire,* the concept of dualism would then spread in the eighteenth century in the various languages of the Enlightenment.[33] In the midcentury, it was used to refer to Gnostic doctrines, and a full entry dedicated to "Dualisme, ou Dithéisme," where Hyde's opinion on the original Zoroastrian monotheism is dutifully noted, appeared in Diderot and D'Alembert's *Encyclopédie.*[34] Toward the end of the century, "dualism" became commonly used to describe philosophical doctrines. The influence of Hyde's new concept is particularly obvious in Isaac de Beausobre's *Histoire de Manichée et du Manichéisme,* published in Amsterdam in 1734–1739.[35]

The *Sad dar,* which Hyde had translated from Persian to Latin and on which he had based much of his analysis, had actually become the touchstone of a polemic that raged around Hyde and his perception of original Iranian monotheism. This polemic had been launched by the Abbé Foucher, who had rejected Hyde's conclusions in a *Dissertation* submitted in 1761 to the Académie des Inscriptions.[36] Before the end of the century, the *Sad dar* became known in much broader circles. In 1785, Jean Charles Ponce-lin de la Roche-Tilhac offered a French version of this work (from Hyde's Latin), in his *Superstitions orientales, ou tableau des erreurs et des superstitions des principaux peuples de l'orient, de leurs moeurs, de leurs usages et de leur législation.* The author insisted that the *Sad dar*, which had been redacted much later than Zoroaster, was not cognizant of dualism.

Thus, Hyde's book soon achieved fame. It was reprinted in Oxford in 1760, and throughout the eighteenth century it remained the standard work of reference in the *République des Lettres* for any serious mention of Zoroastrian beliefs and practices. As Voltaire noted in the entry "Zoroastre" of his *Dictionnaire philosophique* (published in 1764), referring admiringly to Hyde's magnum opus: "Hyde's scholarly inquiries lit a few years ago in the heart of a young Frenchman the wish to learn for himself about Zoroastrian dogmas."[37] The orientalist Humphrey Prideaux, in his *The Old and New Testament, Connected in the History of the Jews and Neighbouring Nations* (London 1717) had based on Hyde's work most of what he wrote about the prophet of the Magians (who was "the great Impostor, except Mahomet," 300). Andrew Michael Ramsey (1686–1743), better known in France (where he had settled, staying with Fénelon until his death in 1715) as the Chevalier de Ramsey, published in 1727 *Les voyages de Cyrus, avec un discours sur la mythologie des payens.* This work, inspired by his French mentor's *Adventures of Telemachus,* can perhaps be called a historical *Bildungsroman,* in which Cyrus converses with Zoroaster, who lays open before the king all the secrets of nature. Eventually, it is the prophet Daniel who teaches Cyrus the perfect religion, while all other ancient Eastern traditions were oral and uncertain. Ramsay took his knowledge of Zoroastrianism from Abūl-Fidā, as translated by Pococke, and Shahrastānī, as discussed by Hyde. He also referred to Bayle's discussion of the beliefs of ancient Persians, mistakenly claiming that for Bayle, the ancient Persians were all Manichaeans.

Between 1742 and 1757, Jacob Brucker published, in six hefty volumes, his *Historia critica philosophiae,* which soon became an extremely influential work. Under the general heading of *De Philosophia Barbarica,* Brucker devoted more than fifty pages of volume I to the philosophy of the Persians (143–189). He too based his discussion mainly on Hyde. In particular, he mentioned the cult of the sun throughout the ancient Near East, a point upon which Hyde had insisted. Brucker, moreover, referred to the works of the best-known travelers: Thévenot, Sanson, Tavernier, and Lord. These and other travelers reported on actual Zoroastrian beliefs and practices in India and Persia. These reports permitted, side by side with scholarly achievements, the formation of a new image of Zoroaster and his religion.[38] Admiring references to Hyde go as far as the turn of the century, when Thomas Maurice, in his *Indian Antiquities* recalls how he discovered Wilkins's translation of the Baghavad-Gita (published in 1785) as he had just read "the very learned work of Dr. Hyde."[39] One of the most remarkable works to reflect the direct influence of Hyde's book would be Johann Gottfried Herder's *Schriften zum Alten Testament,* which devotes much attention to ancient Persian and Sabian religion.[40]

In conclusion, we may ask to what extent Hyde's work really represents a "quantum leap" from previous European perceptions, a leap which signaled the birth of the modern study of Zoroastrianism? Or does his book, rather, represent the last prescholarly attempt, doomed to failure? Hyde, of course, dramatically improved the picture of Zoroastrianism by interpreting in a systematic way the sources revealed by Pococke, that is, the Islamic heresiographers, and by adding an important new source, the *Sad dar,* translating it, and analyzing it at length. But one of his most important contributions was also the rejection as invalid and irrelevant, of the *Chaldean Oracles,* a source that until then had been considered Zoroastrian. Indeed, as a modern scholar, Hyde knew that he needed to act as a "deconstructionist" before being able to reconstruct a new "model." In rejecting the value of the *Chaldean Oracles,* Hyde was doing, as it were, an act of de-mythologization, or of "disenchantment" (Entzauberung) of the field.

On the question of dualism, one could almost say that the jury is still out. To this day, scholars (as well as the leaders of the Zoroastrian community themselves) disagree on the extent to which Zoroastrianism is really established on two equal divine principles. As Shaul Shaked has noted, even in the seemingly most rigorous dualist systems, there appears to be no total symmetry between the two principles and the balance is heavily tipped in favor of the good principle.[41] Hyde's complex and dialectic attitude permitted the recogntion of the undeniable dualist elements in Zoroastrianism without ignoring those elements that clearly speak for a monotheist perception. More importantly, Hyde's understanding offers a dynamic "model" that enlightens the crossing of boundaries between monotheism and dualism, and the transformation of the former into the latter. It also had the significant advantage of introducing chronological evolution and historical understanding into the research of a religion that until then had been considered as too exotic to become the object of historical and evolutionary inquiry.

For Hyde, a way to affirm his sympathy with Zoroastrianism was to argue for the existence of deep Jewish influences on the religion of Iran. He lived in a blessed period. A century later, the discovery of the linguistic families of Indo-European and Semitic languages would have, in various ways, a disastrous influence on the history of Near Eastern and Mediterranean religions, building walls between scholars, creating a deep divide between fields, and often implying that kindred languages should be reflected in families of religions that had little in common. Now, of course, we know better, and the religious and cultural contacts between Iran and Israel are seen as reflected in the Iranian influences on Israelite beliefs, rather than vice versa. Yet, in a sense, Hyde stands at the origins of research in "Irano-Judaica."[42]

Hyde had called Abraham "Persarum patronus et legislator primus." In extending to pre-Islamic Iran the Abrahamic heritage, Hyde was stretching the concept of "Abrahamic religions." In his insistence on speaking about the Sabians, and in mentioning even Noah and Seth as the forefathers of the religion later preached by Zardusht, Hyde was affirming, like other great scholars of the seventeenth century, the original unity of humankind, behind the polyphony of the ethnic, linguistic, and religious traditions, past and present. His affirmation of the essentially "civic" character of the cult of fire reflects John Selden's perception of the Noahide Laws, in Maimonidean fashion, as identical with natural law. Hyde, an orientalist who devoted his life to the study of ancient and oriental religions was not only an antiquarian; his effort, rather, reflected his strongly humanist concerns.

By insisting on the universal patterns of religious transformation, across time and around the world, the orientalists were effecting a dramatic "de-theologizing" (one could speak, in Bultmanian fashion, of an *Enttheologisierung*) of the study of religious phenomena. It is there, mainly, that one can detect the paradigm shift that permitted the birth of the modern study of religion. To be properly understood, texts should be studied in context. Philology, history, and ethnology—indeed, all relevant fields—should be called on to contribute whatever insights or evidence they could, to attempt the reconstruction of the grand puzzle. With so many pieces still missing, the reconstruction was bound to remain highly hypothetical. But Hyde's impressive work, including what seem to be his wildest ideas, commands respect and reminds us that great philological insights are also acts of daring. Without speculation and theorizing, indeed, there is no possibility of scientific progress.[43]

2. The Birth of Manichaean Studies

The search for the starting point of any discipline may easily become a futile venture. There are no beginnings ex nihilo in science, and it is a truism to note that every breakthrough is itself made possible by previous developments. In the humanities perhaps more than in other branches of knowledge, however, the history of a discipline remains a must for any epistemological reflection. The questions raised, the methods developed, the problems solved, are directly related to broader issues of social, religious, and intellectual history. In an obvious sense, Augustine of Hippo or Alexander of Lycopolis were not only powerful polemicists against Manichaeism but also first-rate analysts of Manichaean doctrines and practices. Indeed, Christian and Muslim heresiologists throughout the centuries have devoted much thought to the critical presentation of Manichaean beliefs. Yet, the real incentive to the modern, historical, and philological study of Manichaeism did not appear before the Reformation. As is well known, Catholic intellectuals accused the Protestants of being the direct spiritual heirs of medieval heresies, in particular of the Valdensians and Cathars.[44] Since the latter were perceived (and to some extent rightly so), as the spiritual heirs of the late antique Manichaeans, the Protestants were often considered to be Manichaeans *redivivi,* and a renewed interest in the religion of the Prophet of Light was soon raised.

It is not pure chance, therefore, that the father of Manichaean studies was a Huguenot intellectual, writing at the time of the Enlightenment, after Bayle had called the attention of the cultured public to Manichaeism through his Dictionary.[45] Isaac de Beausobre was born in 1659 in Niort, Poitou, in a Reformed family originally from Provence.[46] On completing his theological studies at the famous Protestant Academy in Saumur (where Louis Capelle taught him Hebrew), he first became a pastor in Touraine in 1683, but had to flee France in 1685, having been accused of illicit meetings with former parishioners. He considered moving to England, but eventually reached the Netherlands, where Jurieu helped him to settle first in Rotterdam. Thence he moved to the court of Anhalt-Dessau in 1686, where he was the chaplain to the prince, and then to Oranienbaum and Berlin in 1694, where he became chaplain to Princess

Sophie-Charlotte. In Brandenburg, he played a prominent role in the Huguenot *Refuge,* often giving sermons at the French Dom on the Gendarmenmarkt in Berlin, and overseeing the schools and the hospice of the community, until his death at the ripe age of 79 in 1738.[47] A conservative and orthodox personality, yet free from any fanaticism, his fame went far beyond the Huguenot community. King Friedrich the Great called him "la meilleure plume de Berlin." Since 1720, he published the *Bibliothèque germanique,* which provided French summaries and reviews of scientific publications from Northern Europe. A year after his death, the second volume of his monumental *Histoire critique de Manichée et du Manichéisme* (henceforward: *HCMM*) appeared (in Amsterdam).[48]

Like the theme of *"ecclesiae primitivae forma,"* the study of ancient heresies belongs to the oldest trends in Protestant historiography. Christian origins are in a sense a historiographical myth, and to this myth belong also the founders of Christian heresies.[49] To some extent, these represent the ancestors of the modern Reformers, the first to reject the hegemony of the Catholic bishops. Cyriacus Spangenberg is the author of the first monograph on Manichaeism, written from a Lutheran perspective. Published in 1578, it still spoke of Mani in strongly derogative terms: *Historia Manichaeorum, de furiose et pestiferae hujus sectae origine.* Spangenberg established his analysis mainly on Epiphanius, and therefore he remained unable to break the traditional heresiographical frame.[50] At the turn of the seventeenth century, Baronius, a Catholic, discovered the importance of the *Acta Archelai,* another essential source for the study of Manichaeism.

Throughout the seventeenth century and in the early decades of the eighteenth, both Catholic and Protestant scholars were intensively active in publishing patristic texts. With the edition of such important anti-Manichaean polemical treatises as those of Serapion of Thmuis, Titus of Bostra, Didymus of Alexandria, and Zacharias of Mithylene by the Huguenot Jacques Basnage, the textual basis for the study of Manichaeism was considerably enlarged.

This development, however, cannot in itself explain the dramatic progress made by Beausobre in the understanding of Mani's *Ansatz.* Two other phenomena of cardinal importance should be mentioned. The first is the new interest in early Christian apocryphal literature. Gottfried Arnold, for instance, who published his *Unpartheylische Kirchen- und Ketzer-Historie* in 1699, translated the Pseudo-Clementine *Recognitiones.* For him, the early heretics, persecuted by "Babylonia," were witnesses of truth, of pure Christianity fighting the Catholic process of corruption.[51] To refine our understanding of Manichaeism, Arnold insisted, we must take into account the significant divergences between Western and Eastern sources, as well as recognize the cruelty of Christian repression. As Julien Ries has noted, Arnold already drew the scholarly agenda followed by Beausobre.[52] Another example of this new interest is the two great collections of Johann Albert Fabricius that date from the first two decades of the eighteenth century: *The Codex Apocryphus Novi Testamenti* (1703) and the *Codex Pseudepigraphus Veteri Testamenti* (1713). When Fabricius died in 1736, two years before Beausobre, his reputation as a scholar was immense. He ushered in a new era for the study of early Christian heretical literature.

The second development is the birth, again in the second half of the seventeenth century, of orientalism (and in particular, the birth of the modern study of Zoroastrianism) represented by the two masterpieces of Thomas Hyde, *Historia religionis veterum Persarum eorumque Magorum* (Oxford, 1700), and of Bathélemy d'Herbelot's *Bibliotheca Orientalis* (published posthumously in Paris, 1697). Both d'Herbelot's *Bibliotheca Orientalis* and Pierre Bayle's *Dictionnaire historique et critique* (1696) have entries on Mani, which offer a digest of contemporary knowledge.

To be sure, Bayle did not claim to contribute any new piece of information on Mani, but he reflects, and to a great extent enhanced, the passage from polemics to a study of religious history *sine odio et ira*. Bayle opened his entry by speaking of the "infame secte," adding that Manichaean doctrines were so miserable that their presentation was in itself their refutation.[53] In this, he made a clear move of method from slander to accurate, objective description. He further stated that the root of Manichaean doctrine—dualism—was much older than Mani himself and reached back to Pythagoras on the one hand, and Zoroaster on the other. He also insisted that in order to approach historical truth in such matters, one must confront all the different sources in a critical way. Ipso facto, he carried the scholarly discussion of Manichaeism beyond the bounds of Christian heresiography.

In other words, one can say that at the beginning of the eighteenth century, the progress in various fields of knowledge on religious history, together with the intensive philological work on early Christian literature that had been carried out for a century, permitted a new approach to Manichaeism. Furthermore, the polemic between Catholics and Protestants on the interpretation of Christian history brought with it a renewed interest in

Manichaeism. These two conditions, philological knowledge and polemical drive, lie in the background of Beausobre's work, but are insufficient to explain it. It may be called a work of genius, because Beausobre integrated into his research all the various threads and wove them creatively and convincingly into a new approach fit for the study of syncretistic religious phenomena. We should now move to an overview of the *Histoire critique,* of its alleged goal, contents, and methods. Only then shall we be able to assess its achievement and impact on later scholarship.

Although Beausobre's *Histoire de la Réformation* was published posthumously in 1785, it was written before *HCMM.*[54] For its author, indeed, as for other Protestant scholars, Manichaeism as well as medieval heresies were perceived as precursors of the Reformation. It also seems that Beausobre intended his book on Manichaeism, which he saw as a digression from his study on the Reformation, to be followed by a study of the Cathars and Valdensians.[55] But what enabled the author to write a groundbreaking work was the breadth of his intellectual endeavors. He did not study Manichaeism only as an early precursor of the Reformation, but was also deeply interested in other early Christian heresies, as well as in the scholarly study of the New Testament. This interest is reflected in his *Examen de la nouvelle hypothèse de Mosheim touchant les Nazaréens,* as well as his *Remarques historiques, critiques et philologiques sur le Nouveau Testament.*[56] In the *Examen,* Beausobre argued against Mosheim ("le savant Professeur de Kiel"), for whom the sect of the Nazareans emerged in the fourth century. Mosheim intended to refute John Toland, who in his *Nazarenus* proposed to see in the Nazareans the inheritors of the oldest Christian community, retaining the teaching of Jesus in its purest form. For Mosheim, on the contrary, the Nazareans were fourth-century Jews, who, seeing the impressive success of Christianity, started to believe in Jesus as Messiah. Mosheim had mainly based his argument on Epiphanius, the oldest source on the Nazareans. According to Beausobre, this argument, powerful as it might be in refuting Toland, the "enemy of Christian faith,"[57] was founded on illegitimate scholarly assumptions.[58]

This is not the place for a detailed discussion of Beausobre's argument. Let us note only that he did not only refer to patristic heresiologists on early Jewish-Christianity but also to modern and contemporary scholars: the names of Le Nain de Tillemont, Richard Simon, Pierre-Daniel Huet, Denis Petau, Hugo Grotius, Isaac Vossius, John Spencer, Fabricius, and Jean Le Clerc appear, time and again, in his text. All these names, and the various branches of scholarship associated with them, would reappear in *HCMM*.

The preface to *HCMM* reflects, besides Beausobre's ambition to study the Manichaean heresy as a precursor of the Reformation, his critical attitude to modern scholars such as Le Nain de Tillemont. While he readily admitted their intellectual excellence, Beausobre noted that their theological commitment prevented them from reading the sources in a critical way (vi). Beausobre clearly intended to create a work of honest scholarship: he would give precise references to the texts quoted and would seek to translate these texts himself. Otherwise, he would refer to the translator in a footnote. This is what was meant by *Histoire critique* (xxiii).

The second volume broadens the scope. Beausobre intended to deal there with the early dualist and Gnostic theologians, such as Basilides, Marcion, Bardaisan, in whose thought, he claimed, one finds the root of various Christian heresies. In other words, the book was meant to discuss also the main precursors of Mani himself. For various reasons, Beausobre did not include Valentinus in this list.[59] Beausobre started by postulating four basic principles of Manichaeism. These are (1) the idea that the Paraclete is the apostle of Jesus Christ, (2) Mani's rejection of the Old Testament, (3) his acceptance of "oriental prophets" such as Seth and Enoch, and (4) his extensive use of New Testament Apocryphal writings attributed to Docetists and Encratites.

These principles were relevant, however, only to the extent that Manichaeism could be considered a Christian heresy. Beausobre did not go so far as to speak of a "religion," but he knew that Mani's system could not be understood only from a Christian viewpoint. He insisted that the main Manichaean dogmas were directly derived from "the theology and the philosophy of the Orientals." These dogmas were essentially the foundations of dualist beliefs, particularly as represented in Zoroastrianism. Now, a similar dualism was to be found also among Greek philosophers, in particular Pythagoras and Plato. The reason for this apparently double origin lay in the fact that Greek philosophy, too, ultimately stemmed from Eastern wisdom. Altogether, Mani built a "système fabuleux," that is, a mythology.[60] In a sense, therefore, *HCMM* can also be seen as one of the earliest modern studies of mythology.

Following scholarly rules, part 1, which is divided into two books, presents the main sources for the study of Manichaeism, as they were known then: book 1 analyzes the Greek and Latin sources, starting with the *Acta Archelai*, until then the main source for the study of Manichaeism, then moves to the apocryphal writings, which Christian theologians unjustly accused Mani of having forged. Book 2 studies the oriental sources, written in Syriac, Pehlevi, and Arabic. Part 2 deals with Manichaean dogmas, ethics, cult, and church organization. As mentioned above, Beausobre started with a word of caution against modern scholarship, which, he said, was seriously lacking in critical approach. Of all modern scholars, he said, only Gottfried Arnold discussed the early Christian heresies in a critical fashion. Volume 2 includes books 4 through 9, dealing respectively with Basilides and other precursors of Manichaeism, the material principle, the intelligible world, anthropology, Christology, and finally, again, cult, ethics, and Manichaean church discipline. Only here did Beausobre approach Manichaeism as a full-scale religious system. The text contains a large number of remarks, discussions, and digressions, some of great interest, on a variety of topics and not necessarily in a rigorously organized fashion. We shall here call attention to some of these topics.

Beausobre knew that the state of the sources did not permit a clear picture of Manichaean beliefs and practices. The direct sources were few and fragmentary, and one should be deeply suspicious of the heresiological sources. After all, even if Mani's ideas are considered to be perverse, the opponents of his followers were the representatives of that same Catholic Church that, as every Huguenot knew, was prone to vicious slander and cruel persecution. Hence, one must be particularly critical when reading patristic sources. The most complete of these texts was Augustine's magisterial treatise *Against Faustus (Contra Faustum)*. And yet, it would be a mistake to think that Augustine presents a trustworthy picture of Manichaeism (I.231). In the near-complete absence of objective sources, Beausobre wisely focused on writings that were not written by the Manichaeans, but which they adopted and which they obviously revered, namely, the apocryphal writings of the Old and New Testaments. There is no reason, he said, to believe the Catholic standard accusation, according to which Mani had corrupted these writings. There was evidence enough, however, to accuse the Catholics precisely of that crime, as, for instance, when they propagated in late antiquity a belief that various letters had fallen from heaven (I.339). At the onset of his major digression on the apocryphal writings (I.438), Beausobre justified the digression by the fact that his book was written in French, the European lingua franca, rather than in Latin, and for a relatively broad readership: open minds who do not possess a deep theological culture should be made to understand that all these apocryphal writings, while they are undoubtedly "fabuleux," confirm Christian truth rather than endanger it.[61] By that paradoxical statement, Beausobre meant the following: the Church Fathers were right to distinguish between canonical and apocryphal writings. The latter did indeed reflect heretical ideas. But through them, we could reconstruct, at least to some extent, the complex picture of earliest Christianity. The Gospels, according to the Hebrews, the Egyptians, the Nazoreans, or Thomas, were indeed very old writings, which were read by various Christian communities, including the Judaizing Christians, who soon split and formed the Nazareans and the Ebionites, or the Encratites, or again the Docetics (I.460). Beausobre's claim reflected a dramatic transformation of the discourse on religion. Error, too, became a witness to truth, precisely because it permitted a better reconstruction of historical reality. This new discourse was directly related to contemporaneous religious polemics and critique of religion. Beausobre described at length the objection made by "a certain Jew," Orobio de Castro, to the remonstrant theologian Philip van Limborch against the Gospels. De Castro had been shown in Amsterdam, by an Armenian bishop, a *Gospel of Thomas* (translated to Latin from Armenian). According to the bishop's claim, this was the original gospel, still pure of falsification by the Western Christians. To refute this claim, Beausobre referred to the patristic rules for distinguishing between canonical and apocryphal gospels. Although he agreed with these rules, he rejected Richard Simon's argument about the veracity of the biblical text deriving from the Holy Spirit: for Protestants, the Holy Spirit can be invoked in matters of faith, not of facts (I.444). He then continued with a rhetorical argumentation with the Muslims on the authorship and the divinity of the Koran (I.445). The discussion of the apocryphal writings used by the Manichaeans thus considerably broadens the horizons of discourse on religion.

According to Beausobre, then, the *Vorgeschichte* of Manichaeism is to be found first of all in the complex milieus of early Christian sectarians, in which the apocryphal writings were redacted. Already in the first century, the Ebionites were a Judaizing sect. The Gnostics, too, can be identified as Christians coming from a Jewish background (I.367). Beausobre knew that in modern parlance, the appellation "Gnostic" was used as a generic term and retained a serious ambiguity.[62] Such a background explained the close parallels between Gnostic and kabbalistic conceptions, for instance, in the theories of Marcos the Gnostic or those of Basilides. Speaking about the Marcosians, Beausobre referred to their conception of the gigantic dimensions of Christ.[63] The Marcosians, concluded

Beausobre, must have received esoteric traditions *(mystères)* stemming from kabbala, from the Ebionites or from the Essenes (I.386–387). Noting the puzzling chapter in the *Acts of John* describing a mystical dance of Jesus' disciples, he presented an embryonic comparative study of religious dance (I.390).

The discussion of the apocryphal writings implied a perception of Manichaeism as a Christian heresy. This was indeed Beausobre's view, but when dealing with the *Vorgeschichte* of this heresy, he broadened the frame to a considerable extent, by stating that the origin of Manichaeism lies within the system of the Magi on the two principles (I.167). As mentioned above, the extent of dualism in both Zoroastrianism and Manichaeism is a major question to this day.[64] While, at least under monotheistic climates, dualism is a permanent temptation of the mind, in no dualist system do the forces of good and evil seem to be quite parallel, or at least completely equal in power. Beausobre attempted to redeem Mani, as it were, from the cardinal sin of dualism. Mani was a heretic, not an immediate predecessor of Luther. But he should be understood as a legitimate religious thinker, standing at the intersection of various religious traditions and professing complex and nuanced ideas. Establishing himself not only on the major work of Hyde, who had made almost exclusive use of the Arabic and Greek (such as Agathias) sources at his disposal, but also on d'Herbelot and Humphrey Prideaux, Beausobre noted that Zoroaster himself was not a radical dualist, but believed in a single creating principle. "The Persians did not believe in two gods", he stated (I. 172). [65]

The main difference between Zoroaster and Mani lies in the different role they attribute to matter (I.178). For Zoroaster, matter has no creative power. He therefore attributed Ahriman's creation to God. Mani, however, rejected this opinion. For him, matter was alive, possessing both movement and feeling; it was the father of the devil. This, said Beausobre, was the real origin of his error (I.495). Altogether, his heresy was established on a philosophical system, the elements of which he had found in the philosophy of the Magi, and which he tried his best to accommodate to the revelation of Jesus Christ. One can say that in a sense he felt he had a divine vocation for purifying Christianity (I.180). Despite its dualism, clearly affirmed, and in a stronger way than in Zoroastrianism, it is clear that the Manichaeans worshipped only one God.[66]

To better understand the nature of Mani's beliefs, examining Persia is not enough. When discussing the meaning of Mani's conception of God as light, Beausobre referred both to the Brahmans or Indian philosophers, according to whom the word *(la parole)* was identical to God, and to the corporeal. For them, the divinity was enveloped by a luminous body (I.467). The kabbalists or Jewish philosophers also shared with the Manichaeans, the orientals, and various Greek philosophers, a conception of the divinity as a pure and extended light. This great light they called "God's Glory" *(kavod)*. Following Prideaux, Beausobre noted that the *shekhinah* of rabbinic literature, which is fire, is originally a Zoroastrian concept (I.563). This concept, he said, seems also to be supported by the Bible (I.468). For Mani, this divine light is real, by no means metaphorical, similarly to the conception of Gregory Palamas in fourteenth-century Byzantium (I.470). Such conceptions, obviously, entail a corporeal God. Beausobre noted that there was no consensus about a spiritual God in early Christianity, adding that Augustine remained a Manichaean for many years because he possessed a corporeal conception of God (I.477). Far from being a Manichaean idea, anthropomorphic conceptions of the divinity were rather common in early Christianity.[67] Here too, Beausobre showed a keen scholarly sensitivity in recognizing the antiquity and significance of anthropomorphic ideas in early Christianity—a fact the full dimensions of which contemporary research is only beginning to recognize. According to Beausobre, then, the Manichaeans were one heresy among many. In some ways, the early monks, or various Catholic theologians, were no less heretical. The Manichaeans, for instance, were also trinitarians, although they did not think that the three persons of the Trinity were equal in status (I.556). In other words, they might have been heterodox, but certainly not of a particularly shocking kind. Beausobre thus succeeded in de-demonizing Manichaeism.

Since the ultimate root of Manichaeism, the belief in matter as an active principle, stemmed from Iran, it was no wonder that we could find precursors to Mani within Christianity. Only three heresiarchs, however, deserved to be considered as such: Basilides, Marcion, and Bardaisan, each of whom established sects of their own. The beliefs of Simon Magus and his followers Menander, Saturninus, Satornilus or Carpocrates, remained too vaguely understood. Nor did the Valentinians, for their part, qualify as real heretics. In the Valentinians' Achamoth, one could easily recognize the Hebrew Wisdom *(hokhma)*, also one of the ten *sefirot* of kabbalah. Beausobre followed here Johannes Buddeus, a German Hebraist who had argued for a kabbalistic origin of Valentinianism (II.155). Basilides' system, too, showed some clear similarities with the kabbalistic doctrine of creation.[68]

On the Jewish doctrine of *creatio ex nihilo,* Beausobre noted that this doctrine had been predominant for "six or seven centuries," but noted that it was not universally accepted. *Pirke de-Rabbi Eliezer,* Maimonides, Menasseh ben Israel, the Karaites, Philo, the *Sefer Yesira:* all these did not believe in the creation of matter (II.182–204). In this context, Beausobre referred to Huet, the learned bishop of Avranches, who asserted that Plato believed matter was uncreated.[69]

The Manichaeans had also been accused of idolatry, due to their cult of the sun and the moon or rather their belief that the souls redeemed from incarnation would move to these stars. To refute this accusation, Beausobre reviewed various cults offered to the sun. He mentioned the Essenes, Persians, Sabians, Jesideans, Armenians, Chamsi, and other oriental sects, all of whom respected the sun without worshipping it (II.582). Beausobre referred here to biblical criticism: God had prohibited the Israelites practice of not only the cult of the sun and moon but also Baalim, that is the worship of great men, their relics, and their tombs. Beausobre added that some illustrious martyrs had thought that the biblical prohibition of the cult of the sun concerned only the Israelites, while it remained permitted for Gentiles. Moreover, if the cult of the sun and moon was considered idolatrous, this was even truer for the cultic use of images, relics, and tombs of martyrs. Here too, Beausobre rejected the accusation of the idolatry of the Manichaeans by calling attention to idolatrous aspects of Catholicism (II.593–594). About Manichaean cult, he added that Mani retained many Persian practices, just as the early Christians retained various pagan practices, in order to attract pagans more easily (II.599). As demonstrated by Hyde, Zoroastrianism itself did not offer a real worship of the sun as divine (II.609).

This theory represents a new twist of Maimonides' revolutionary version of the theory of accommodation, through which he explained biblical sacrifices.[70] Beausobre wrote here probably with Maimonides in mind, because he moved directly to the Sabians, "ou Idolâtres du Levant" (II.603). The Sabians, as mentioned above, were for the Islamic heresiographers a pagan people of Harran, which Maimonides had transformed into a generic term for idolatry, or cult of the stars. Discussing these Sabians and their name, de Beausobre relied on the authority of such great orientalists as Assemani and Edward Pococke (II.603–604).

An assessment of Beausobre's oeuvre was given by Julien Ries in his historiographical study more than sixty years ago. For Ries, Beausobre could be considered the precursor of nineteenth-century historians of Manichaeism.[71] For Ries, Beausobre's contribution was to show that no solid study of Manichaeism could be established only or mainly on Western sources. After Beausobre, for instance, the story of Scythianus, as recounted by the *Acta Archelai,* was considered legendary, while the value of the *Acta Archelai* became much more dubious. "After Beausobre, scholars will have Manichaeism begin with Mani," he adds.[72] In the 1750s, Mosheim accepted Beausobre's criticism of the *Acta Archelai,* while the Carmelite Cacciari published a Catholic response.[73] A towering intellectual figure, Friedrich Christian Baur, would also accept some of Beausobre's ideas, considering Mani the first great reaction of the spirit against the letter of authoritarian Christianity.[74]

Ries wrote his assessment in the 1950s, long before the discovery and publication of the *Cologne Mani Codex.* It was also written long before the deep impact of the Nag Hammadi discovery of Gnostic codices on our understanding of dualist trends in late antiquity became fully felt. Today, we can be still more appreciative and admire Beausobre's intuitions: he discovered the centrality of Jewish, Gnostic, and Jewish-Christian apocryphal traditions for the *Vorgeschichte* of Manichaeism, and the essential interconnections between these traditions.[75]

VI

From *Mohammedis Imposturae* to the *Three Impostors*:
The Study of Islam and the Enlightenment

Unlike the first students of Zoroastrianism or of Confucianism, early modern scholars interested in Islam could in no way imagine themselves as discoverers of virgin lands of the spirit. From the start, Islam had been felt as a major threat in Christian consciousness. In the words of Albert Hourani, "from the time it first appeared, the religion of Islam was a problem for Christian Europe."[1] Already in the early eighth century, the Byzantine theologian John of Damascus had described Islam as the last and worst of all heresies and could only think of Muhammad through the biblical category of the false prophet.[2] The Arabs would soon show through their vast conquests that Islam should be conceived as a religion in its own right, rather than as a Christian heresy. And yet, throughout the long history of Christian-Islamic polemics, Muhammad has continued to be perceived as an impostor, a manipulator of dubious mores who concocted his own religion while pretending to have received revelation. During the Middle Ages, knowledge and intellectual curiosity about Islam remained minimal in Byzantium and the West despite the translation of the Koran initiated by Peter the Venerable in 1143 and the decision of the Council of Vienna (1311–1312) to establish professorships for teaching Greek, Hebrew, Aramaic ("Chaldee"), and Arabic at the papal court and the universities of Paris, Oxford, Bologna, and Salamanca. It was, however, mainly for polemical and missionary purposes, as well as, to some extent, to learn from the achievements of medieval Arabic science, that Arabic was being taught.

The story of the awkward engagement of medieval Christians with Arabic and Islam has been well told from diverse perspectives.[3] Even during the Renaissance, the interest in Arabic remained limited, and the University of Salamanca, which in 1552 had toyed with the idea of founding a trilingual college patterned after that of Alcala, could not find a place for Arabic in its curriculum and decided to teach rhetoric, next to Greek and Hebrew.[4] And yet, perceptions of Muslims were beginning to change. To give only one instance of how a critical mind could see things, Jean Bodin was able to remark, before the end of the sixteenth century:

> The King of the Turks, who rules over a great part of Europe, safeguards the rites of religion as well as any prince in the world. Yet, he constrains no one, but on the contrary permits everyone to live as his conscience dictates.[5]

The sad story of anti-Islamic prejudice and animus on the part of Christian intellectuals at the dawn of the modern age does not need elaboration. What I wish to underline in this chapter, however, is the odd ways in which this prejudice and animus changed in the course of the seventeenth century. It was the progressive erosion of the traditional stance and gradual emergence of a new, more open attitude that was most significant for the birth of the modern study of Islam. Religious intolerance in Europe, underlined by the violent conflicts between Catholics and Protestants since the sixteenth century, had made it more difficult for open-minded Europeans to retain in good faith the claim of the ethical superiority of Christianity over other religious systems. Although the old derogatory attitudes toward Islam and Muhammad were still alive, a new approach to Islamic societies would progressively assert itself. Moreover, I shall argue that the new status of Islam and of its Prophet had two opposite consequences. On the one hand, the weakening of the traditional negative image of Islam and its Prophet permitted to put them both, to a certain extent, on a par with Christianity and Jesus (or Moses). On the other hand, such a comparison could entail the discrediting of Christianity, as all religions could now be conceived as having been established by similarly false prophets or impostors. If all religions are equally valid, they are also all equally invalid. The study of Islam in the age of reason can no more be disconnected from contemporary intellectual currents than that of other religions. In this case, the leading trends of the Enlightenment would bear directly on the emerging image of Islam, a fact well shown in Jonathan Israel's magisterial study of the Enlightenment.[6] Moreover, the comparative dimension, which is inherent in the study of Islam, had a direct impact on nascent Islamic studies within the history of religions.

The emergence of a new attitude regarding Islam began even before the progress of Arabic philology allowed its crystallization.[7] It was made possible by the contributions of people from different communities: clergy as well as secular scholars, travelers and learned laymen, radical thinkers as well as mainstream followers of the Enlightenment, orientalists and Arabic scholars. Let us start with the detailed accounts by various travelers to Islamic lands, either for business, diplomatic, or religious purposes. These travelers played a major role in the dissemination of knowledge about Islam and Islamic societies, as they were less encumbered by theological prejudices than scholars. They were thus able to appreciate in Islamic societies virtues that were too rarely displayed in Europe. The accumulation of these travel reports offered a solid background for the new scholarly insights into the nature of Islam.

The best known of these early travelers is probably Pietro della Valle (1586–1652), who reached Istanbul in 1614, acquiring there Turkish as well as some Arabic, and then moved on to Cairo, Jerusalem, Aleppo, Baghdad, and Persia, before reaching India, where he remained until 1624. Della Valle wrote a travelogue that was soon translated to different languages and long remained a major source of knowledge about Islam.[8] At the turn of the eighteenth century, Pierre Bayle's knowledge of Islam is still very much indebted to della Valle's book.

Another famous traveler, whose work offered detailed information, in particular on Safavid Persia, was the French Huguenot Jean Chardin (1643–1713). Although he did not question the existence of only one true religion, Chardin spoke admiringly of "Islamic virtues." His first publication, in 1671, was an account of Suleiman's crowning, *Le couronnement de Soleïmaan,* but it is mostly to his *Travels* (originally published in French in Amsterdam in 1711) that he owes his fame. *Travels* provided ethnological descriptions of an Islamic society and introduced European readers to the daily sacraments of Shi'ite society, including purity rituals and almsgiving, as well as marriages, burials, the central role of mullahs, and the "fantastic fervor" during the Ashura festival. These volumes were widely read and admired in French and English throughout the eighteenth century by Enlightenment thinkers such as Montesquieu (who drew most of his knowledge of Persia from Chardin), Rousseau, Voltaire, and Gibbon.[9]

Sir Paul Rycault, who had spent five years in Istanbul and served as British Consul in Smyrna, published in 1668 a work entitled *The Present State of the Ottoman Empire,* in which he dealt with Islam at great length, referring admiringly to its toleration of religious minorities.[10]

A certain Joseph Pitts was taken into captivity in Algiers as a young sailor and spent years as a slave in the Ottoman Empire before he could escape. He was able to describe Islamic rituals, including the hajj to Mecca, from within. For him, nonetheless, Islam was nothing more than "a miscellany of popery, Judaism, and the gentilism of the Arabs."[11] It is mainly through the work of *vulgarisateurs* that knowledge about the Islamic world (i.e., the Ottoman and Safavid empires) entered European consciousness. A good instance is that of the French historiographer Michel Baudier (1589?–1645), who, without possessing any firsthand knowledge of Islamic sources, published in 1625 his *Histoire générale de la religion des Turcs*.[12] In his dedication (to "L'Eglise de Dieu"), Baudier claims that Islam "tries to dethrone God from Heaven." Later, arguing that the Muslims hold a physical conception of God, he reckons that Muhammad, "the false prophet," had borrowed much from "Jewish fables" and that Muhammad's God was of a corporal nature (book 4). And yet, despite his repeating such traditional prejudices about Islam, he also inserted in his work remarks reflecting Montaigne's cultural relativism, his essay "On Cannibals" being a case in point.[13]

A work of traditional scholarship circulating in the latter half of the seventeenth century describes Islam (one of only three religions, with Judaism and Christianity) as having been established by a false prophet and having "poisoned most of the inhabitable world."[14] The work is based on the French translation of a study of Islam by a fifteenth-century Byzantine scholar, Leonius Chalondylas. It is striking that when discussing Islamic theology, the text refers to Maimonides' discussion of idolatry.[15]

The first students of Arabic and Islam in the modern age thus inherited a highly polemical and disparaging attitude toward the religion of Islam. Thanks to the reports of travelers, ambassadors, and missionaries to the Ottoman Empire, however, they also learned to admit the presence of some qualities in Islamic lands, such as religious tolerance, that were patently absent in Christendom. They were caught between two strikingly different approaches, involving both negative and positive attitudes toward Islam. The ensuing tension, which has yet to be completely resolved, impressed on the best scholars the recognition of a cognitive dissonance in their perception of Islam. This recognition, then, permitted the progressive, although limited, disentanglement of Islamic studies from the negative image of Islam inherited from the Middle Ages.

The early orientalists never excluded from their interest the various Eastern Christian communities. This was true even when they defined their field as that of the languages and literatures of Islamic societies— that is, for all practical purposes, Arabic, Turkish, and Persian. The central place of oriental Christianity or, more precisely, of oriental Christians in the project of the early orientalists and in their discourse cannot be over-emphasized.[16] The main work of scholarship on Eastern Christianity from this period is *Oriens christianus,* the monumental work of the Dominican Michel Le Quien.[17]

Christians belonging to the various denominations, Chalcedonian and non-Chalcedonian, were indeed newly discovered as minorities, whose existence, although tolerated by the Ottoman authorities, demanded all possible support from Christian nations.[18] Such a support was offered mainly by diplomats, but these were seconded by missionaries, as both Catholics and Protestants (mainly from the Church of England) were striving to receive pledges of allegiance from the oriental churches. Hence, orientalism was also conceived as a *Hilfswissenschaft,* an ancillary discipline, as it were, for theology. Orientalism permitted the discovery of new versions of the Scriptures in Syriac, Coptic, Armenian, Ge'ez, as well as in Arabic. Moreover, to draw the Eastern Christian communities closer (and avoid their being snatched away by other churches), one sought to understand their traditions, which were often perceived as closer to the earliest times of Christianity than those of the West and thus possibly offered interesting or important liturgical variants. There was also a massive effort to collect, publish, and translate the many Christian manuscripts bought in the East for the major royal libraries of Western Europe, as well as for the Vatican library.[19] A series of learned ecclesiastics from the Levant, in particular Maronite scholars such as Gabriel Sionita and Abraham Echellensis, played an essential role in this chapter of the transmission of knowledge.[20] The intellectual discovery of oriental Christianities, of their traditions, languages, and thriving communities, was indeed perceived as a major part of seventeenth-century orientalism, side by side with the desire to learn about the history of Islam.[21] Moreover, their knowledge of Syriac as well as of Hebrew strengthened their awareness of the Christian and Jewish background of Islam in the late-antique Near East.

It was through the comparison of Islam to both Judaism and Christianity that the early orientalists emphasized what they considered to be its weakness. Paradoxically, this comparison would also show them the way to "rehabilitate" Islam. In other words, the comparative approach did much to hammer in an awareness of the similarities between the three monotheistic faiths, as much as of their differences.

To be sure, the early modern Arabists were unable and unwilling to completely shed prejudice and inherited perceptions of Muhammad and

Islam. This imprisoned the interest in Islam in theological polemics. It did not, however, prevent the development of intellectual curiosity about the civilization of the "Turks," including their religion. It was this intellectual curiosity, rather than the wish to lend support to imperialistic designs, characteristic of a later period, that sustained the remarkable achievements of the early orientalists. They would do much to emend and ultimately transform, the negative view of Islam and its founder.

Guillaume Postel (1510–1581) was offered the first chair of Arabic at the Collège de France. As gifted as he was eccentric, Postel was fascinated by the religions of the Orient, which, he thought, showed the clear superiority of East over West. He published a book on Islam, in which he offered a detailed summary of the Koran.[22] Although serious philological work on Arabic texts would have to wait, Postel taught Joseph Justus Scaliger, who in 1602 would encourage the young van Erpen to take up the study of oriental languages.

The Cambridge-educated William Bedwell (1561–1632), one of the first European-born scholars of Arabic in the modern age, combined a devotion to the study of Arabic with an aversion to Islam.[23] For him, Islam was essentially a religion of violence and lust. In 1615, Bedwell published a polemical tract against Islam, entitled *Mohammedis imposturae; That Is, A Discovery of the Manifold Forgeries, Falsehoods, and Impieties of Mohammed.* The title of his work encapsulates the highly charged character of the study of Islam in the early seventeenth century. There was of course nothing original or particularly radical in Bedwell's attitude, which was rooted in a long anti-Islamic polemical tradition within Christendom. This polemical, disparaging attitude would be shared by a series of scholars throughout the seventeenth century and even in the eighteenth century. For most intellectuals, it was obvious that any comparison between Muhammad and Jesus, of their personalities, precepts, or books, showed Jesus' essential superiority.[24]

Thomas van Erpe, or Erpenius (1584–1624), who had studied with Scaliger in Leiden before his appointment as professor of Arabic there in 1613, might be considered "the first native European to achieve true excellence in Arabic."[25] Like Bedwell before him, however, the *Arabizantium Princeps* Erpenius was interested in language and grammar more than in religion.[26]

The study of Islam in the seventeenth century could hardly have been insulated from the dogmatic arguments among Christians. Thus, Johann-Heinrich Hottinger (1620–1667) explained that he intended in his *Historia*

Orientalis to defend the Protestants against the Catholic accusation of being crypto-Muslims. At the same time, he hoped his work would serve to fight both Islam and the Turks.[27] Hottinger's work dealt with Islam and Muhammad, the religion of pre-Islamic Arabia (that of the Nabateans and the Sabians), and the religious background of Islam (namely, seventh-century Judaism and Christianity).[28] It was widely read and was one of Bayle's main sources on early Islam.

It was only some decades later that, with Edward Pococke, by far the greatest Arabist in seventeenth-century England, a real interest in Islamic theology and Arabic philosophy would appear. Pococke (1604–1691) was interested in the content and context of the Arabic tractates he was editing. Moreover, his knowledge of oriental languages and of Islam was not only bookish. He had been sent to the Ottoman Empire, where he spent some years searching for books and developing ties with oriental Christian communities.[29] In Pococke's eyes, Muhammad was certainly no true prophet. In his *Specimen Historiae Arabum,* he referred to Maimonides' discussion of the false prophet, saying that it can be applied to Muhammad.[30] According to Pococke, Muhammad should nonetheless be considered a remarkable man, who brought moral reform to his people.[31]

In 1671, Pococke published *Philosophus Autodidacticus,* a Latin translation of *Hai Ibn Yakdhan,* a philosophical romance written by the twelfth-century Andalusian philosopher Ibn Tufail.[32] Tufail's philosophical tale tells the story of a child growing up on a desert island and discovering the elements of natural religion, a religion untainted by history and culture.[33] The book intended to show that "the main fundamental truths of religion" were demonstrated "by the light of humane reason and the principles of natural theology." In the preface to his translation, Pococke writes:

> It must be granted indeed, that some very ingenious and learned Men of this latter Age, have endeavoured to demonstrate the main fundamental Truths by the Light of Humane Reason, and the Principles of Natural Theology, which are generally acknowledged by mankind, although much differing in other points.

If such an elevated philosophy could be found in Arabic, it revealed a remarkable trait of Islamic culture. The legend of *Hai Ibn Yaqdhan* would have a powerful impact in the seventeenth and eighteenth centuries.[34] In 1708, Simon Ockley published his own translation of the text, which he dedicated to Edward Pockoke, under the title *The Improvement of Human Reason.*[35] For its modern European Christian readers, the legend may also have implied a certain hidden closeness between Islam itself and natural religion. Here was a text, written in Arabic, that offered a striking solution to contemporary problems. In any case, this mythical story was in tune with the strong naturalist ethos of the eighteenth century— exemplified by Rousseau's *Emile*—and it would resonate for a long time. Pococke was a religious Christian, who did not harbor much sympathy for Islam and who partook of the instinctive deep mistrust of Muhammad.[36] And yet, as an enlightened Christian, he was ready to acknowledge the results of his intellectual enquiries. As such, he had to admit there was much in Islam and its culture that was highly commendable. A similar argument could be made about both Simon Ockley and Adriaan Reland.

One of the real monuments of early orientalism, Barthélemy d'Herbelot's *Bibliothèque orientale, ou dictionnaire universel contenant tout ce qui regarde la connoissance des peuples de l'Orient,* was first published in 1697, two years after its author's death. It would be reprinted a few times, once with additions, before the end of the eighteenth century.[37] Barthélemy d'Herbelot (1625–1695), who had mastered Hebrew and Aramaic before studying Arabic, Turkish, and Persian, served for many years as *Interprète des langues orientales*, although he never traveled to the Orient. Three years before his death, he was appointed to the chair of Syriac at the Collège de France. His *Bibliothèque orientale,* a bulky volume containing a long series of entries on things relating to Islam and the study of the Islamic peoples and languages, may be called the first encyclopedia of Islam. To a great extent, the *Bibliothèque orientale* represents the translation of a contemporary Ottoman source that d'Herbelot's friend Antoine Galland had brought him from Istanbul. The *Kashf al-zunun* of Hadji Khalifa, alias Katip Çelebi, a contemporary scholar from Istanbul, was an encyclopedic work of almost 15,000 entries, in alphabetical order. D'Herbelot's use of Hadji Khalifa's work highlights a striking respect for Islamic scholarship on the part of someone who retained the traditional deprecatory and polemical attitude toward Islam. D'Herbelot also retained a similarly negative perception of its founder. The entry on the Prophet Muhammad starts thus: "This is the famous Impostor Mahomed, Author and Founder of a heresy which called itself Religion, and that we call Mahomedan." Later in the same entry, d'Herbelot adds to the words "Mohammed Aboulcassem" the following explanation: "This name and surname of the false prophet Mahomed."[38]

Antoine Galland (1646–1715), who would become famous as the first Western translator of the *Thousand and One Nights,* took charge of the publication of d'Herbelot's magnum opus.[39] Unlike d'Herbelot, Galland had spent years in the Ottoman Empire. Thanks to his knowledge of Greek, he had been posted in the French Embassy in Istanbul in 1670, and in 1673 had traveled to the Levant, learning Arabic, Turkish, and Persian. In 1709, he was offered the chair of Arabic at the Collège de France. Galland introduced the bulky work with a *Discours pour servir de Préface à la Bibliothèque orientale.* In a sense, this *Discours* can be read as the first manifesto of orientalism, or, more precisely, of the study of the languages, lands, cultures, and history of the Islamic peoples. Of particular interest in the present context is the fact that both the *Bibliothèque orientale* and Galland's *Discours* show religion to be one of the most important categories for the new discipline, orientalism.[40]

The *Discours* starts by listing "oriental languages": Arabic, Persian, and Turkish. The knowledge of these languages was essential if one was "to reach the knowledge of history, customs, mores, religions or sects, Christian as well as Muslim."[41] It was only the knowledge of these languages that could permit those with intellectual curiosity to learn about Muslim beliefs.[42] Indeed, the addition of the study of Turkish and Persian to that of Arabic should be considered one of the main achievements of the seventeenth-century study of Islam.

In 1697, the publication year of the *Bibliothèque orientale,* Humphrey Prideaux published a biography of Muhammad. For all practical purposes, Prideaux (1648–1724), an English divine and scholar, followed the pattern represented by Bedwell at the start of the century. The title of his book clearly stated its ambition and polemical context: *The True Nature of Imposture Fully Display'd in the Life of Mahomet.* Prideaux's work soon became a best seller and was highly influential, beyond the borders of England.[43] According to George Toomer, Prideaux's book bears witness to the decline of Arabic studies in England and tells us much about public taste in eighteenth-century Europe.[44] There is little doubt that the eighteenth century reflects a strong decline in erudition in general, and in the demise of Arabic scholarship in particular.

The most significant change in scholarly outlook and attitudes toward Islam on the part of the early orientalists is highlighted by the work of Adriaan Reland (1676–1718). Reland, who had studied in Leiden and Utrecht, held a professorship in oriental languages in Utrecht since 1701. In his *De religione Mohammedica, libri duo* (Utrecht, 1705), in the dedicatory epistle to his brother Pieter, Reland explained that he intends to fight the repulsive image of Islam as a religion invented by a fanatic (*homo fanaticus*), an epileptic boasting of divine revelations. Such a traditional image cannot explain why a great part of humankind follows the precepts of Islam. Rather than accepting it, argued Reland, one should let Islam speak for itself. In this way, it would reveal a face quite different from the one usually attributed to it. Every religion, he added in his preface, was misrepresented by its antagonists, as we are often misled by passion where religious matters are concerned. Despite the fact that Islam often agrees with natural law, he added, no religion has been more misrepresented. As Reland further declared, he had to defend Islam against false attributions, as he would otherwise have insulted truth by supporting lies and calumnies. He argued that more will be gained for Christianity by friendly behavior than by vicious polemics, adding that in fact, Muslims often put Christians to shame by their behavior.[45] The insistence on both natural law and ethics reflects a decision to move away from theology, a domain where Christian superiority must be constantly reaffirmed. In Jonathan Israel's words, scholars such as Reland "sought to bring Islam (and Judaism) into closer alignment with Christianity."[46] The importance of Reland's work, both in the original Latin and in various vernacular translation, was enormous. Throughout the eighteenth century, much in the changing perception of Islam can be attributed to the influence of *De religione Mohammedica*. This important book would become one of the main sources of knowledge on Islam throughout the new century. It reflects and highlights the drastic transformation in the image of Islam and Muhammad that had occurred during the preceding century.

Toomer's observation that the eighteenth century saw the decline of Arabic studies in Europe is certainly true, but does not tell the whole story.[47] From our perspective, the lack of scholarly dynamism did not have purely negative effects. Indeed, it permitted insights acquired in the preceding period to filter down and become more commonly accepted. Already Paul Hazard was able to detect the evolution from "défaveur" to sympathy with Islam that was beginning to manifest in Europe in the late seventeenth century, and continued through the following century.[48] Similarly, Alastair Hamilton has pointed out that in the eighteenth century, scholars would have the opportunity to study and interpret the material collected in the preceding century.[49]

Regarding Islam, the eighteenth century would be one of popularization. The main scholarly achievements of the previous century would now reach much broader circles. Pierre Bayle's *Dictionnaire historique et critique*, first published in 1696, underwent various editions through the eighteenth century. On Islam, as in so many other fields, Bayle's *Dictionnaire* would be a major source of information for the enlightened elites of Europe.[50] In its various editions, the *Dictionnaire* made good use of contemporary scholarship, duly referred to in marginal notes.

The abstract that opens the entry "Mahomet" defines Muhammad, simply, as "Founder of a religion which soon had, and still has, a very broad scope."[51] Hence, it continued, Islam ("la Religion Mohamétane") is the dominant religion of an area much larger than the one that Christianity rules. Seemingly, Bayle agreed with the Christian traditional perception of Islam as a false religion, one instigated by the devil, who used Muhammad as an instrument for the realization of his plans.[52] "Seemingly," because Bayle then refuted traditional perceptions of Islam and its so-called moral weaknesses. Referring to Hottinger's *Historia Orientalis* and Richard Simon's *Histoire Critique du Levant*, Bayle hailed Islam's high level of moral precepts, as reflected in various Islamic aphorisms and apophthegms. As to the common Christian accusation that Islam was propagated through naked force and violent persuasion, Bayle answered that this reminded him of the Dragons de France in 1685 (when they enforced the Revocation of the Nantes Edict of 1598, brutally expelling all Protestants from the French kingdom). In other words, Muslim armies were only applying Augustine's ruling: "compelle intrare" (678, n. N). As to Muhammad's alleged lewd behavior, Bayle flatly dismissed it as rumor. Indeed, attacks against Islam are usually made on the basis of testimonies coming from Christian rather than Muslim sources. Bayle noted that this was precisely Pococke's claim against Grotius's anti-Islamic theological arguments (683, n. V). Bayle, who continued to compare toleration among Christians and Muslims, commented that Christian iconoclasm seems to have been more violent than similar trends among the Muslims, who, moreover, do not have any cultic statues (as do the Catholics).[53]

As a new religion, early Islam, "the religion of this false doctor," saw the appearance of false prophets, which brought about the creation of different sects. The same phenomenon can be observed in Christianity, both at the time of its birth and during the Reformation (688–689). Such a use of the concept of false prophet has its "neutralization" as an immediate consequence. The concept instantly loses much of its previous subversive value. "False prophet" does not refer only (or mainly) to Muhammad but also to various inspired teachers found in any religion, particularly during its formative period. The recognition of the multiplicity of false prophets does not mean, of course, that Muhammad was not one of them. "Did not his life strongly refute his own imposture?" asked Bayle, referring to a remark of Maimonides that the main characteristic of a prophet-king lies in his rejection of bodily pleasures.[54] Muhammad, then, may well have been a false prophet, but he was only one among many, everywhere, including among Christians, even among the Protestants. Through such a comparative sociological analysis, the concept has lost much of its sting and derogatory meaning. Bayle concluded his article: "This is how half of the world mocks the other half."[55] Bayle, then, did not play the role of the *advocatus diaboli* in favor of Muhammad and his religion. Rather, he sought to show that much of what is condemnable in Islam can also be said about Christianity: the comparative study of the two religions leads to the recognition that they follow the same sociological rules. In other words, the same categories should be applied to Islam as to Christianity.

Like Bayle, the Irish intellectual John Toland's understanding of Islam owes much to Reland. He too rejected Prideaux's anti-Islamic writings. Toland (1670–1722), one of the most original minds of his day, dealt critically with matters of religious history. Following in Bayle's tracks, Toland insisted that a correct understanding of early Islam should place it in its original milieu, a mixture of various Jewish and Christian trends. Like Bayle, he too did not see religious imposture as being a unique phenomenon of nascent Islam, because it was so clearly present in early Christianity.[56] Toland, moreover, was fascinated by early Christian heresies, in particular by the Jewish-Christian Ebionites, and sought to interpret the few Christian apocryphal texts known at the time, such as the *Gospel of Barnabas,* in this light. It was only thanks to such texts that one could understand "the original plan of Christianity" and realize that Jesus did not intend to abolish the Laws of Moses.

Among the *vulgarisateurs* having carried the new perception of Muhammad to broad circles, the most significant is certainly Henri, Comte de Boulainvilliers (1658–1722), a French historian and political thinker. Boulainvilliers was strongly influenced by Spinoza, whose *Ethics* he translated, and on whose *Tractatus theologico-politicus* he wrote an essay. His *Vie de Mahomet* was published posthumously in London in 1730.[57] It would be immediately translated to English (and in 1747 to German), and would prove highly influential in its different versions. Boulainvilliers was no Arabist; his knowledge came from secondary literature rather than

from original sources. Among his sources, however, Reland was of paramount importance.[58]

In his view, as summarized in the *Avertissement,* the Arabs, in contradistinction to other "barbarians," in particular those from Northern
countries, were, among other qualities, "spiritual, generous, disinterested,
courageous, careful." The main goal of Islam was in keeping with these
inherent qualities of the Arabs, and Muhammad's religious thought was
wholly "conforme aux lumières de la raison."[59] For Boulainvilliers, then,
Muhammad is no impostor, or false prophet. He is called, rather, the legislator of the Arabs, an Arab Moses, who promulgated a highly rational
religion for his people.[60] While Islam could not be said to represent the
most perfect possible example of true or natural religion, it comes close
to this ideal. Due in great part to the influence exerted by Boulainvilliers,
the expression "legislator of the Arabs" in reference to Muhammad
would come to replace that of "impostor" in the latter half of the eighteenth century. *La vie de Mahomet* would be echoed in various Enlightenment views of Muhammad and Islam.[61]

Such a radical transformation of the image of Muhammad and Islam
was, naturally, received with strong opposition. The old view of Muhammad as the arch-impostor in the religious history of humanity, power-
fully expressed by Prideaux, could still attract followers. The Arabist
scholar Jean Gagnier, for instance, published in 1732 a *Life of Muhammad* that described Muhammad as "the greatest villain of mankind, and
the most mortal enemy of God."[62] Such a perception, however, clearly
belonged to the past and had lost the power it once had. Despite such
attempts, during the eighteenth century, the figure of Muhammad gradually liberated itself from its traditional demonic shades to become histo-
ricized, as that of one founder of religion among others.

One should fully appreciate the true value of the progressive "neutralization" of Muhammad, his becoming more "banal" in the age of reason.
As the traditional demonized image of Muhammad was losing some of
its power, the study of Islam could be conducted on a more rational, less
polemical ground. The new, more benign, image of Muhammad had indeed a profound impact on Islamic studies. The full impact of its transformation, however, had a wider effect on the perception of both Judaism and Christianity, as on the comparison between Moses, Jesus, and
Muhammad (a comparison always implicit, and often explicit), which
now placed the founders of the three religions on the same footing. Moreover, most Arabists did not belong to the radical Enlightenment, and

most radicals did not know Arabic, but a dialectical relationship between these two groups sometimes permitted a vision of Islam as either a rational religion or a political device—in any case, as a more rational religion than Christianity.

To be sure, Muhammad did not become instantly and unambiguously a cultural hero of the Enlightenment. The negative aspects of his figure were never quite erased. On the one hand, Muhammad now started to be perceived as a Legislator, a founder of religion, like Moses and Jesus. On the other hand, Moses and also Jesus now started to be seen as sharing some of Muhammad's traditional qualities and could well have been, like him, religious impostors. While the animus against Muhammad was weakening, that against the Church was steadily growing, and anticlerical writers started describing Jesus in terms until then attributed only to Muhammad. In chapter 2, we saw how an equilibrium was obtained in the seventeenth century between Homer and the Bible, as Homer was gaining in status and the Bible was simultaneously losing its superior status as revealed text. This precarious equilibrium, putting the two literary bodies on the same level, permitted, for a while, their comparison. Similarly, it seems that for a while in the eighteenth century, Moses, Jesus, and Muhammad were perceived to be on a par. This entailed new insights regarding the nature of the three Abrahamic religions and their relationship. The new image of Muhammad, then, beyond its transformation of the perception of Islam, can be said to have had a broader cultural impact on Enlightenment views of religious history and religion.

Since 1719 an anonymous pamphlet delivering an explosive message, *La vie et l'esprit de Mr. Benoit de Spinosa*, started circulating in Europe. It would fast become better known as *Le traité des trois imposteurs*, the title with which it appeared for the first time in 1721, although its original form dates from the late 1670s or early 1680s.[63] This curious book was quite different from its Latin homonym, *De tribus impostoribus*, also anonymous, which had already been circulating in Europe for about a century.[64] Throughout the eighteenth century, the *Traité des trois imposteurs* remained a disturbing book. "Chimerical book, about which all speak, and which no one has seen," wrote Prosper Marchand in his *Dictionnaire historique*.[65]

The *Traité des trois imposteurs* is a mixture of Spinozism and radical antireligious polemics. According to the author, all religions are established on fear and ignorance, which are commonly found among all peoples.[66] Everywhere in the ancient world, founders of religions, deceiving their people, managed to procure various material benefits for their priests. Be it in Delos, Delphi, or Rome (with the Sybilline books), some madmen have pretended to talk with the gods, while others have claimed to speak with the dead, or to decipher the future in animal entrails.[67] The most ambitious among them, however, gave laws to their peoples, claiming that these laws had a divine origin, as they had received them from a god or a goddess.[68] In the ancient world, indeed, there was no general, unified system of pagan religion. Rather, each *polis* had its own religious laws and conceptions.[69] The most famous among these legislators came from Asia: Moses, Jesus, and Muhammad.[70]

Moses, to whom chapter III.10 is devoted, was the grandson of an Egyptian magician, while the Hebrews were the most ignorant people in Egypt. The longest chapter is devoted to Jesus, as the main goal of the tractate is directed against Christian clericalism. Chapters 12–21 (74–102) are devoted to the politics and morals of Jesus Christ. Chapter 22 deals with Muhammad, whose imposture appeared some time after that of Jesus. Just as Jesus had sought to replace the law of Moses with his own, so did Muhammad seek to replace the law of Jesus, while using tricks similar to the ones used earlier by Moses to convince people he was a prophet sent by God. Among these tricks, he would have an acolyte, hidden in a well, claim he was God, then order his stoning in order to erase any traces of the imposture. It would remain to radical freethinkers to directly compare Muhammad with Moses and Jesus. A variant on chapter III.9 of the *Traité des trois imposteurs* adds Numa Pompilius to Moses, Jesus, and Muhammad.[71]

Much ink has been spilled in the search for the sources of the *Traité des trois imposteurs*. Where does the idea of religious imposture, so prominent in the *Three Impostors,* stem from? Throughout the seventeenth century, and in particular in the second half of the century, the idea of religious imposture was a strikingly recurrent one, a fact duly noted by Silvia Berti.[72] In England, especially during its troubled mid-seventeenth century, imposture seems to have been commonly attributed to both religious and political leaders. Roman Catholic priests, in particular, were obviously labeled impostors.[73] Not surprisingly, some of the earliest uses of the term *imposture* in English, during the first half of the seventeenth century, refer to Muhammad.[74] The point that interests us here is the parallelism between Muhammad and Jesus.

Ernest Renan argued that the comparison of the three *Religionsstifter* entailed the very idea of comparative religion, and that such an idea could be born only in a time when at least some vague notions about the nature of the different religions of the world had been established. More precisely, Renan argued that it emanated from the court of Emperor Friedrich II (1194–1250), and reflected his predilection for the Arabs and their philosophy.[75] Hence stem, according to Renan, the traditions which mention Averroes and his circle as standing at the root of the malevolent comparison between the three religious leaders. As the supposedly Averroist dictum would have it: *Lex Moysi, lex puerorum, lex Christi, lex impossibilum, lex Mahumeti, lex porcorum.*[76]

Louis Massignon has shown quite convincingly, however, that it was only in the Islamic world that some kind of equal status between Moses, Jesus, and Muhammad could have developed.[77] More precisely, Massignon called attention to a document dating from 1080 at the latest. According to this text, Abu Tahir, the leader of the Qarmatian heretics from Bahrein, who conquered Mekka and desacrated the Ka'abah in 312/924, is reportedly said that of the three individuals who corrupted humankind, namely the shepherd (Moses), the medicine man (Jesus), and the camel driver (Muhammad), the third was the worst trickster and magician.[78]

Whatever the medieval origins of the comparison of religious impostors, however, early modern intellectuals were quite aware of the ancient roots of the idea of religious imposture. Joseph Scaliger, for instance, referred to Apollonius of Tyana, the neo-Pythagorean teacher of the first century C.E., as to "un franc imposteur." In antiquity, Apollonius had often been accused of magic or religious imposture, an accusation related to his voyages to the East in search of the wisdom of the magi and the gymnosophists, or *brachmanoi*. Charles Blount, the deist thinker, had implicitly compared Jesus with Apollonius in his *Life of Apollonius.*[79] Around the mid-seventeenth century, the case of Sabbatai Zevi from Smyrna, who had proclaimed himself as the Messiah, had brought among the Jewish communities throughout Europe a wave of intense messianic expectations. No wonder, under such circumstances, that Bar Kochba, the famous false messiah of the second century C.E. is also called an impostor in seventeenth-century texts.[80]

An interesting book in this respect is *Apology for All the Great Men Who Have Been Accused of Magic*, written by Cardinal Mazarin's librarian, Gabriel Naudé (1600–1653). Naudé stated that throughout history, a series of great men, wrongly accused of being magicians, were actually lawgivers, who had used tricks to convince people to obey their laws. Naudé's list of lawgivers who claimed to have received their laws from divinities includes Trismegistus (from Mercury), Zalmoxis (from Saturnus), Minos (from Jupiter), Lycurgus (from Apollo), Numa (from the nymph Egeria), and Mohamet (from the angel Gabriel).[81]

In the biblical tradition, however, the obvious impostors are the false prophets, and among the Jews the false messiahs. Here again, early modern Christian Hebraists found in Maimonides' writings some texts of capital importance. When John Selden dealt with religious impostors in antiquity in two chapters of his *De Diis Syris* (chapters 12–13), his main reference was Maimonides' *Epistle to the Yemen*.[82] In this *Epistle*, written in 1172 to fight a messianic surge in the Yemenite Jewish community, Maimonides had referred at length to false prophets and false messiahs, singling out Jesus, Paul, and Muhammad. Maimonides argued that the tenets of other religions that resemble those of Scripture were clearly counterfeit, false imitations, referring to "the signs of the impostors" *(badim)* in Isaiah 44: 25.[83] As we have seen in an earlier chapter, the *De Diis Syris,* written by the young Selden, would exert a powerful influence, directly or indirectly, throughout the seventeenth century. Gerardus Vossius, in his 1642 *Theologia Gentilis,* would also, in Selden's footsteps, discuss religious impostors using Maimonidean categories. Vossius's work was read widely, and it is no surprise if we find the deist thinker Herbert of Cherbury also dealing with religious imposture in the same terms.[84]

In *Leviathan,* Hobbes argued that the "first founders and legislators" of pagan nations had made false claims about the divine origin of their laws, in order to convince their peoples to live peacefully in obedience of these laws. Thus, Hobbes compared Muhammad with both Numa and Pachacuti, the Inca king (of whom he had read in the works of Las Casas):

> so Numa Pompilius pretended to receive the ceremonies he instituted amongst the Romans from the nymph Egeria and the first king and founder of the kingdom of Peru pretended himself and his wife to be the children of the sun; and Mahomet, to set up his new religion, pretended to have conferences with the Holy Ghost in form of a dove.[85]

For Hobbes, the trio Numa, Pachacuti, and Muhammad, was parallel to that of Abraham, Moses, and Jesus. Unlike revealed religion, civil religion was manmade, while natural religion was neither revealed nor manmade, but immanent. In Hobbes's text, Muhammad is not put on a par with the divine lawgivers. On the other hand, neither Numa nor Pachacuti are considered to be false prophets or impostors (a category reserved to insiders to the tradition of divine revelation). It can be said, then, that Hobbes did not consider Muhammad as an impostor. For him, he was no more a trickster than other lawgivers and *Religionsstifter*. This text, then, reflects what one could perhaps call the "banalization" of Muhammad (as opposed to his previous demonization) among seventeenth-century thinkers.

This new attitude toward Muhammad was commonly accepted in the eighteenth century. Thus Rousseau considered Muhammad to have established civil religion (i.e., in opposition to barbarian rule) among the Arabs, just like Numa had established it among the Romans, in order to tame their savage instincts and to civilize them, as Livy told us (*Contrat Social*, ch. 2, 7). Another example of this view of Muhammad as a *héros civilisateur* is offered by the sequel to the *Cérémonies et coutumes de tous les peuples,* which described Muhammad as "having busied himself with so much ardor to civilize his compatriots."[86]

The presence of Numa side by side with the three impostors demands explanation. Numa Pompilius, the mythical first king of Rome, and founder of its religious law, had been a paradigmatic figure in Roman and Hellenistic historiography. In the first century B.C.E. Varro had devoted much attention to him, as the true creator of Roman religion and of its relationship with the state. Livy (ch. 1, 9–21) depicted Numa Pompilius as someone who had to inculcate fear of heaven in the uncouth *(rudem)* Roman populace. For Livy, the establishment of the *sacra* and the role of the priests were meant to induce piety and reduce violence, but had little to do with truth. It was significant that false, "marvelous" stories, such as Numa's nightly meeting with the goddess Egeria, were needed to justify Numa's achievements. Numa, however, was not considered to have been an impostor, but rather a manipulator or a trickster, who had used a stratagem to establish religion and civilize the uncouth Romans—a highly laudable goal. Numa the trickster, then, was the positive version of the impostor. Throughout the Middle Ages and up to the modern age, the figure of Numa would incarnate the idea of civil religion, as Mark Silk has shown.[87]

In Hellenistic Jewish literature, Moses, the *nomothetēs* (legislator) of the Jews, had already been compared with ancient lawgivers such as Solon, Lycurgus, and Zaleucus Locrensis, who were perceived as political leaders using religion to strengthen the social fabric of their societies.[88] The Jewish comparison of Moses with Lycurgus would soon be picked up and broadened by early Christian theologians, who added Numa to the list of pagan lawgivers. In the late second century, Clement of Alexandria espoused this tradition, which he sought to reinterpret from his own peculiar viewpoint. For him, Numa was a Pythagorean philosopher, who was strongly influenced by Mosaic conceptions, while Pythagoras himself was a disciple of Zarathustra.[89] The clearest trace of this influence is the aniconic character of Numa's religion. During the first 170 years of Rome, indeed, Roman temples were devoid of any painting or sculpture.[90] This perception of Numa as having been influenced by Moses is remarkable on various counts: it assumes that Roman archaic religion, or at least some of its aspects, came from the East; it insists on the apolitical side of this religion and on its aniconism; and it emphasizes the comparison between Numa and Moses.

In the mind of the enlightened *philosophes,* civil religion was indeed more appropriate than Christianity, whose revealed character could not convince everyone. Moreover, Numa's conception of religion as the most effective cement of society is the best example of the Enlightenment idea of civil religion.[91]

As we have seen, a long tradition presented Numa as a lawgiver, in parallel to Moses. Now Muhammad was in the process of joining the list of these respected lawgivers who had acted as tricksters to establish religious laws among their respective peoples. Equating Muhammad with Moses would then be a natural step; and as Jesus had been a second Moses, so could Muhammad join the two of them, in the list of the three monotheistic lawgivers.

The dissemination of the legend of the three impostors in the eighteenth century reflects the growing sentiment that religions were to be considered as aspects of societies and could be compared with one another, just as societies could. The old model, of monotheistic revelation, had entailed the uniqueness of truth versus multiple examples of idolatrous error. According to the new model, all religions had been established by tricksters and had no intrinsic truth-value. This, however, did not necessarily imply that they were all completely wrong or morally bad. On the contrary: like the religion imposed on Rome by Numa, they all had a real value as legitimate expressions of the need for societies to have fundamental rules. In other words, religions could be justified as representing the closest possible human imitation of natural law.

The rejection of revelation by radical Enlightenment thinkers legitimized an identical approach to all religions as purely human phenomena and the application of identical principles to their study. It also permitted a new approach to religious toleration: as all religions were now considered to be equally devoid of divine content, and as their different pretensions to truth, based on divine revelation, had been reduced to naught, none could claim a unique superiority. In other words, toleration no longer meant a generous but condescending attitude toward some religious minorities, as was the case in Islamic societies toward believers of other prophetic religions (or religions of the book [*ahl al-kitab*], that is, usually, Jews, Christians, and Zoroastrians). Rather, the new idea of toleration was predicated on a general recognition of agnosticism: as no religion has any ontological truth-value, or rather, as human beings are unable to recognize ultimate truth, no religion may have any predominance and all have to be judged solely by their social effects.

The most pregnant image of this new toleration is probably Gotthold Ephraim Lessing's presentation of the legend of the three rings. Lessing's last work, *Nathan der Weise,* published in 1779, a short decade before the French Revolution, was publicly staged for the first time in Berlin in 1783. According to the tale, which Lessing had borrowed from Boccaccio's *Decameron* (ch. 1, 3), there is only one true ring, but its two copies are so perfectly done that the true ring cannot be recognized. Boccaccio was not, however, the inventor of the tale, a variant of which is already found in an Eastern Christian text from the eighth century.[92] Like the idea of the three impostors, the idea of the three rings seems to have its roots in the religious polemics between Jews, Christians, and Muslims of medieval Islamic societies. From our perspective, it is noteworthy that religious relativism underlines them both, in different ways. The legend of the three rings and that of the three impostors, in a sense, appear to be the reverse side of one another: if no religion is divine, or if one cannot distinguish that which has a divine origin from the others, all must be dealt with in the same way.[93]

The first steps of the modern study of Islam (and of Arabic) reflected to a great extent the traditional animosity toward the impostor's heresy. As we have seen, the gradual, although limited, liberation of Muhammad from his medieval demonic figure, along with the budding ethnological observation of Islamic societies, permitted the emergence of modern orientalism. Moreover, the early modern study of Islam, with its constant explicit or implicit comparison of Islam with Christianity, had a major impact on the formulation of the new, comparative study of religions. We can see, therefore, how a culture of erudition permitted cultural transfer from the Near East to Europe in the early modern age and how the image of Islam was transformed in an era of comparison. Eventually, the radical Enlightenment would appreciate Islam, in strong contradistinction with Christianity, as a rational religion.

In *Orientalism,* a book first published in 1978, and which would soon become a huge success, Edward Said presented a vastly different view of things. *Orientalism* sought to reveal the vast and devastating effects of deeply anchored prejudices on the perception of Arabs and Islam in the days of European imperialism, since the Napoleonic invasion of Egypt. Said's book has had a series of profound consequences, some of them highly unfortunate, for the academic world and beyond the world of Arabic and Islamic studies. Among these has been a now commonly shared perception of orientalism[94] as the intellectual tool of imperialist ambitions on the Near East, and of orientalists as its henchmen. Such a perception does great injustice to the field and its scholars, certainly those of the seventeenth century, before the bloom of French and English imperialism, who remained outside the frame of Said's investigations.

VII

From China to Rome:

The Discovery of Civil Religion

1. Chinese Atheism and the *Querelle des Rites*

As we saw in chapter I, the Jesuits had sought to find deep religious feelings even in the weirdest and wildest pagan rituals and beliefs of the native peoples of America. As we shall see here, their brethren who embarked on a mission to evangelize China developed a highly different approach. They soon found themselves arguing that the rituals of the Chinese elites, of which they thought highly, and which they sought to respect, reflected all but true religiosity. The Chinese rituals, according to them, rather reflected deep morality and political sense. There is a paradox here that demands explaining: it was precisely the high level of culture shown by the Chinese, a culture that the Jesuits found comparable to that of Europe, that brought them to deny the Chinese, or at least their intellectual elites, any real religiosity.

Before Matteo Ricci, who first set foot in China in 1582, died in Beijing in 1610, he and his five comrades had established a very significant Jesuit mission.[1] They had introduced themselves as "Western monks," using a term reserved for Buddhist monks that implied a parallelism between Buddhism and Christianity. But they soon realized that Buddhism had bad press among the Confucian intellectual and political elites and decided to meet the Chinese literati on their own turf, as Christian intellectuals. The Jesuits immediately invested many efforts in learning Chinese. They wanted to approach the emperor on his own terms, to seduce him and his court with their knowledge of the country's language and customs. They reasoned that convincing the emperor of Christian truth would prove easier than converting the whole Chinese people: once convinced of the truth of Christianity, the emperor could then convert his people himself. The Jesuits did everything in their power to impress the emperor with their wisdom and scientific (particularly mathematical) knowledge. To achieve this, they had to appear at court in a convincing manner, that is, like mandarins. Their adoption of Chinese customs and behavioral patterns is traditionally called accommodation.[2] Accommodation meant, first, adequate linguistic abilities. Mastering Chinese had another obvious advantage, as it could permit translating the Scriptures, or at least part of them.[3]

Like the few other early modern travelers to East Asia, the Jesuits were strongly impressed by various aspects of Chinese culture and civilization. According to Charles Le Gobien (1698), the Chinese were "the most civilized and sophisticated *(spirituels)* of all Asian peoples."[4] "Spirituels," in this context, probably has intellectual rather than religious connotations. The Jesuits were puzzled by the status of religion in China and sought to understand the nature and function of the different "sects" in the Chinese empire.

From the start, their perception of the religious identity of the Chinese was that of three main "sects" and their *convivencia* (to use a term traditionally referring to the so-called symbiosis between Jews, Christians, and Muslims in medieval Spain, traditionally referred to as San Jiao): the literati, who ruled the kingdom, side by side with the Buddhists ("Foe"), and the Taoist (or disciples of "Lanzu," i.e., Lao Tzu). The Buddhists, who worshipped images of the Buddha, were usually identified as idolaters, and the Buddha himself could be described, like Muhammad, as an "impostor,"[5] while the Taoists were dubbed as "magicians," representing popular religion. Athanasius Kircher would amend this religious tripartite classification in his *China Monumentis* (1667), arguing that the Buddhists corresponded to the Egyptian philosophers, while the Taoists, the true representatives of Chinese idolatry, partook of views originating in the West, more precisely in Egypt, which had conquered "Tartary," China and Japan by way of Persia and India.[6] Whether the Buddhists or the Taoists were perceived as real idolaters, both groups were identified as representing essentially popular religion. By choice as much as by necessity, the Jesuits were more interested in the Confucian elites. The real question was the nature of the cult offered to Confucius. The Jesuits argued that one should speak, rather than of a cult, of "the honors" given to Confucius, the emblematic figure of Chinese civil religion. These honors, they claimed, were not of a religious nature, and hence could not be classified as pagan.[7] The Jesuits were making use of Stoic categories that have come to us, in particular, through Varro's discussion of *theologia tripertita.*[8] Varro spoke of three kinds of theologies: *theologia naturalis, theologia fabulosa,* and *theologia civilis,* respectively handed down by philosophers, poets, and statesmen. Civil theology is not meant to express truth about the divine but rather to offer a moral code for the people that is grounded in religious principles. The Jesuits, therefore, could speak of the *Sinorum scientia politico-moralis.*

If the Chinese educated elite, or literati, sought to base public morality on religious principles, one might then consider them to be, essentially, atheists, who manipulated religious concepts only for the public good. As the Jesuit Philippe Couplet pointed out in his preface to the Latin translation of Confucius's *Analects,* the Chinese elites could not be considered idol worshippers, since they had no false gods and no images.[9] Even if sacrifices were offered to angels, these were less respected than the Sovereign Lord of the universe, and the emperor built a temple to God. Confucius stopped superstition and idolatry. His morality, moreover, was so elevated that it might have been said to proceed from the school of Jesus Christ. Such a claim reminds one of Tertullian's reference in the late second century to *Seneca noster.* It was on the basis of such perceptions that Joachim Bouvet expressed the hope, in his *Histoire de l'empereur de Chine,* that the Chinese emperor would soon eradicate idolatry in his dominion.[10] In seeking to convince the emperor's son of the truth of Christianity, Bouvet had told him that as Chinese religion was identical to natural religion, it was rather close, in its principles, to Christianity, which was the perfection of natural law.[11]

Hence, Nicolas Longobardi, who replaced Ricci as the head of the mission, referred to most Chinese as atheists, since they did not believe in the "Buddhist pagodas."[12] In his monograph on Chinese religion, he recalled the fundamental distinction, known in ancient schools of thought and religious traditions, between esoteric and exoteric doctrines, in order to explain the different teachings of the three Chinese sects.[13] Esoteric doctrines were true and referred to religious cult. Exoteric doctrines, on the other hand, were patently false and referred to "civil" and "fabulous" cult. Their only virtue lay in leading the people toward the good and making them turn away from evil. Longobardi's vocabulary highlighted his application of Varro's *theologia tripertita* to the three Chinese "sects," although one could not speak of a clear parallelism between literati *(lettrés),* idolaters, and sorcerers on the one hand, and philosophers, poets, and statesmen on the other. Among the Chinese, religious cult was only attributed to visible things. The literati, therefore, only simulated religious behavior, which remained "toute extérieure."[14] In a deeper sense, one should consider them to be atheists.[15] What is surprising here is that it was precisely this atheism of Confucian intellectuals that enhanced, for the Jesuits of the China mission, the literati's estrangement from the pagan customs of their land and hence their inner closeness to Christianity. The explanation for this is that the Jesuits were convinced that China, despite its obviously non-monotheistic religious system, represented a very high level of civilization. To neutralize China's major differences from Christian Europe, they devised arguments that "neutralized" Chinese religion, or at least that of the elites. Another Jesuit Father, Nicolas Trigault, who spent thirty-eight years in China, considered the Chinese to be "the least pagan people" as they worshipped the supreme deity, the King of Heaven.[16] He also called attention to the fact that the Jews whom the Jesuits met in China also worshipped the idols, in order to be considered as mandarins.

Such a perception of things, as is not difficult to imagine, could not be to everyone's taste. Throughout the seventeenth century, a widespread sensitivity to "idolatry" among Roman Catholics reflected the standard Protestant accusations against Catholic rituals. The Jesuits' efforts to assimilate Chinese manners and culture would soon ignite a powerful reaction within the Catholic Church, in particular among their direct missionary competitors, the Dominicans. The main argument against the Jesuits' behavior was that by accommodating the Chinese, they were actually flirting with idolatry and accommodating nothing less than pagan mores and rituals. In their irresistible drive to behave according to Chinese mores, the Jesuit Fathers had too easily sacrificed the traditional Christian radical opposition to idolatry. For the Dominicans, the Jesuit arguments for accommodation did not hold water. Confucius's cult to the spirits could not be convincingly presented as reflecting civil religion. It was patently religious in nature. That entailed the idolatrous nature of Confucianism, a religion rather similar to those of Greece or of Rome. This would be the position of the Dominican enemies of the Jesuits, such as Father Noël Alexandre, who argued at length that although some of the Chinese rituals might be understood as civil, most were clearly religious or superstitious, reflecting the essentially idolatrous nature of Confucian religion. To buttress his argument, Alexandre pointed out that the Chinese Muslims also spoke of idolatry in reference to Confucianism.[17] Hence, he insisted that authorizing the Chinese ceremonies, or rituals, would be tantamount to destroying the foundations of Christianity.[18] Even if the Chinese literati could be considered atheists, argues Alexandre, the Confucian cult of spirits is certainly more religious than civil.[19] The Jesuits, then, in their attempt to blur obvious facts, were acting as impostors, and their attempts at accommodation should be condemned in terms as strong and emphatic as possible.[20]

The polemic known as "la Querelle des Rites" reached its peak in 1700 in the Sorbonne with the condemnation of the Jesuits' efforts at accommodation and Rome's confirmation of that condemnation.[21] It became one of the most significant affairs in the modern history of the Catholic Church. The enemies of the Jesuits seemingly won the day within the Church. But in a deeper sense, the Jesuits prevailed, as they had launched, much beyond the Catholic hierarchy, the deep and long-standing attraction to all *chinoiseries* among European intellectuals that would be so evident throughout the eighteenth century and would lead to the birth of sinology.[22]

As we have seen, the Jesuits were ultimately unable to decide between two rather different perceptions of the nature of Confucian rituals. While they usually viewed the rituals as reflecting the civil religion of atheistic elites, rather than idol worship, some argued that these rituals reflected a form of natural religion. In either case, however, the rituals showed that a high culture was in no need of divine revelation to prosper and command respect. In this, the Sinophile Jesuits were adding a powerful argument for the cause of natural religion and against the continued prevalence of Christianity in European consciousness. The impact of the Jesuits on the early development of modern Chinese studies was all the more powerful as it would be only in the nineteenth century that Chinese would be taught in universities. Until then, the Jesuits held the key to all things Chinese: the study of Chinese language.

2. Enlightenment Perceptions of Roman Religion

In many ways, Johann Adam Hartung's epoch-making *Die Religion der Römer* (Erlangen, 1836) represents the first serious attempt to study Roman religion on its own terms rather than as an offspring of Greek religion. Pantheon, cult, priesthood, relationship between "Church" and state, legends, as well as the historical evolution of these various topics would all be studied for themselves from now on, independently of

parallels, similarities, and differences in Greek institutions or conceptions. From Hartung, a direct line leads to the analyses of Theodor Mommsen, Georg Wissowa, and Kurt Latte, to mention only some of the leading German students of Roman religion. This story is well known and is
summarized in various epistemological studies.[23] What is less known is
the prehistory, as it were, of the modern study of Roman religion. More
precisely, there has been little analysis of the perceptions of this religion
among early modern intellectuals and scholars, in the three centuries between Machiavelli and Hartung, and, in particular, toward the end of the
Enlightenment. Such early studies are quite neglected today and are not
perceived to be part of the history of scholarship. Yet, despite their obviously dated approach, some of these works, at least, can shed light on the
significance of Roman religion for European intellectual history, and thus
on those aspects of Roman religion that were of particular importance
for intellectuals at the time of the French Revolution.

While the Roman heritage was quite central to the formation of European identity since the Middle-Ages, this heritage did not include religion, certainly not in a prominent fashion. Of all aspects of Roman civilization, its religion seems to have been traditionally perceived by European
thinkers since the Renaissance as perhaps the least relevant, interesting,
and respectable. Its polytheist nature was not the only cause of the almost instinctive lack of interest in Roman religion. Here, the difference
between Greek and Roman religion was remarkable. The Greek gods
and goddesses succeeded in retaining a powerful attraction for Christian
European minds. But they were the heroes of a fascinating mythology,
while the Roman gods, although their names and figures were familiar,
had no *hieroi logoi* of their own. Hence, even Theodor Mommsen could
perceive Roman religion as *geistlos,* and reflecting, as it were, a lack of
myths and a hypertrophy of cult. In more than one sense, then, Roman
religion showed no interest in truth. Roman religion lacked a truth-
dimension not only because the Christian single true God was opposed
to the falseness of idols but also because of the lack of a serious Roman
mythology (as myths deal, in their own way, with metaphysical problems). All this goes a long way in explaining the meager scholarly interest
in Roman religion before Hartung. And yet, it seems that this very pecu-
liarity of Roman religion also fostered a certain interest among some
early modern European intellectuals, even at a time when myth and mythology were becoming central to the understanding of ancient religions,
literatures, and cultures. In a sense, Roman religion appeared to some,

just like Confucianism to the Jesuits, as a negative version of other religions, and hence as a more rational sort of religion, radically different from Christianity, and better fitted for statehood.

At least since the time of Boccaccio, there had been in European culture a continuous interest in the figures of the Roman gods. But this interest seems to have focused only on the gods' figures, which were seen as parallel to those of the Greek gods, not in any way on the nature and functioning of Roman religion. Among the major Renaissance mythographic works, Lilio Gregorio Giraldi's *De deis gentium* (Basel, 1548) was the most scholarly, while Vincenzo Cartari's *Le imagine dei Dei de gli Antichi* (Venice, 1571), whose purpose was to help artists in their renderings of ancient deities, remained by far the most popular.[24]

One of the few significant scholarly works from the sixteenth century dealing specifically with Roman religion seems to have been Albricius Philosophus's *De imaginibus deorum* (published in Florence after 1487), which, despite its general title, treats only Roman religion, and in particular its various religious functions, such as that of the Arval brothers, the *Flamen dialis*, the Vestals, the Pontifical College, or the augurs.[25]

It was Guillaume Du Choul (1496–1560), however, who would open in earnest the era of the study of Roman religion itself, in his *Discours de la religion des anciens Romains* (Lyon, 1556). Du Choul's work, which soon achieved notoriety and appeared in Italian translation in 1589, made much use of figurative sources. In particular, Du Choul analyzed coins, many of which had been brought to him by peasants working on his estates. Du Choul himself was a man of means, who had visited Italy, and an accomplished numismatist.[26] He devoted the first chapter of his book to the various Roman temples, comparing the Temple of Peace to that of Solomon.[27] He then discussed different Roman religious institutions, priestly functions, and festivals, and concludes with the remark that in many ways the ordinances of the Christian religion are similar to those of the ancient Egyptian and Roman religions.

At this early stage, the comparative perspective on the Roman gods was rather common and was often used by Christian missionaries turned anthropologists, in Central and South America and in China. For the Spanish Jesuits and Dominicans in New Spain and Peru, Roman religion was the obvious paganism with which they could compare the new and often-strange rituals they were witnessing. The Jesuits in China, on their side, naturally compared the explicit behavior and implicit values of Confucianism with those of the ancient Romans. They noted in particular, among

Chinese and Romans, the central place of both family and state in religious ritual. Comparing the importance of public and state rituals in China with Roman civil religion permitted the legitimation of Confucian cult, thus offering a justification for the Jesuits' acculturation to Chinese mores.[28]

As is well known, Niccolo Machiavelli, in Book 1, chapter 11 of his *Discourses on Livy*, sang the praises of the religion established by Numa Pompilius, arguing that this religion was among the main reasons for Rome's good fortune. Indeed, he said, it was observance of divine cult that permitted republics to prosper.[29] For Machiavelli, however, Christianity represented a different kind of religion, one from which the political dimension was absent. This absence was central to the explanations of the political miseries and rivalries among the contemporary Italian cities. Machiavelli thought that the Christian religion was particularly ill-suited to the good functioning of the state. What has been called "the Machiavellian moment" in early modern intellectual history would pick up Machiavelli's perception of the public and political dimension of ancient Roman religion. It would also insist on the necessity of a civil, or rather civic, religion in the state. Christianity, as it was mainly focusing on the salvation of the individual, could not really provide such a dimension.[30]

As we have seen, the concept of "civil religion," whose roots political scientists find in Rousseau's *Contrat social*, was actually quite commonly used in the seventeenth and eighteenth century and is an obvious inheritance from Varro's *theologia tripertita*.[31] Both the modern concepts of civil religion and of political theology descend from the early modern reinterpretation of Varro's conceptions. It is, however, to Machiavelli's *Discourses on Livy* that we probably owe the modern recognition of the place of religion in the ancient state.

After such pioneering works, the seventeenth century witnessed some consolidation and diffusion of this understanding of Roman civil religion.[32] The major synthesis that reflects the progress in the understanding of Roman religion achieved at the end of the seventeenth century is Bernard de Montfaucon's *L'Antiquité expliquée et représentée en figures*.[33] The magnum opus of the great Benedictine scholar begins with a detailed analysis of the different classes of gods and with rituals among Greeks and Romans. Montfaucon's work represented a perfect example of antiquarian scholarship and owed a great deal to its author's study trips to Italy. Such a concrete contact with the physical remains of the ancient world, which helped transform the study of Roman civilization in the early modern age, would not be available with respect to Greece until much later. Another typical instance of the same tradition is *Romae Antiquae Notitia; or, The Antiquities of Rome,* written by Basil Kennett, from Corpus Christi College, Oxford, which was reprinted many times during the eighteenth century.[34] Kennett devoted a whole book (part 2, book 2) to the religion of the Romans. Chapter 1 of that book, entitled "Of the Religion and Morality of the Romans in General," begins in the following way: "That religion is absolutely necessary for the establishing of Civil Government, is a Truth." Kennett goes on to quote Machiavelli's *Discourse on Livy* (I. 11). The twelve chapters of Kennett's book dealt in succession with the various religious functions, such as the Luperci and Arval brothers, Augurs, Haruspices and Pontifices, Flamiens and Rex Sacrorum, Duumviri, Keepers of the Sybilline writings, sacrifices, calendar, and the festivals.

It is not only to the antiquarians but also to thinkers preoccupied more broadly with the role of religion within the state that we owe the recognition of the inherently political dimension of Roman religion. The thinkers of the French Enlightenment would be among the first to develop the implications of Machiavelli's perception of the political advantages of Roman religion. The new interest in Roman religion among the *philosophes* was directly connected to their own interest in the changing relationship between religion and political power.[35] Hence, the dramatic transformation of the interest in Roman religion seems to have been directly connected to the Enlightenment, as would become apparent throughout the eighteenth century. In 1716, the young Charles-Louis de Secondat, better known as Montesquieu, read at the Bordeaux Academy a dissertation entitled *Politique des Romains dans la religion.* This text, which was published posthumously, deals *in nuce* with some of the themes that Montesquieu would develop in his major works, *Considérations sur les causes de la grandeur des Romains et de leur décadence* (1734) and *De l'Esprit des lois* (1748). For the mature Montesquieu, the goal of religion is the same as that of civil law: to make people good citizens.[36] To be sure, the view of religion's role in society developed by Montesquieu in his later works was more complex than that reflected in the *Considérations.* He did not think about religion only in the utilitarian or Erastian mode, in its strengthening function in society, through balancing the deficiencies of secular law. Montesquieu's early dissertation, however, reflects quite clearly this new interest in Roman religion. He begins by opposing Roman religious legislators to those of all other peoples: while the Roman lawgivers established religion for the state, those of all other peoples established the state for religion.[37]

This perception of the role of religion in Roman society and its dia-metrical opposition to what obtained in other societies offers a striking counterpart to the argument developed by Josephus Flavius on the spe-cific character of the religion of Moses in his polemical work against Ap-ion. Josephus claimed that the relationship between religion and the virtues developed by Moses ran counter to that common in his day.[38] According to Josephus, religion was not subservient to society's well-being. Rather, the various virtues, including harmony within society, were for Moses aspects of religion. It should be noted that to develop his perception of Moses' achievement, Josephus (who was writing in Rome) compared him with other ancient legislators, such as Lycurgus and Solon. This under-standing of Josephus provides the background for his invention of the term *theokratia*—almost a hapax legomenon in ancient literature, but whose rediscovery in the early modern age would have dramatic signifi-cance for the discourse on the relationship between state and religion.[39]

For Montesquieu, who follows the Roman historians, and Livy in par-ticular, Romulus, Tatius, and Numa, "the wisest king in secular history," (le plus sage prince dont l'histoire profane ait jamais parlé) and hence a counterpart to Moses, had invented Roman religion, a religion for politi-cal expediency, rather than established the political world as ancillary to religion.[40] The cult and ceremonies they established were perceived to be so wise that they were retained even when the kingdom became a repub-lic. Roman religion, for those who established it, did not have anything to do with true ethics, but was only meant to inspire a fear of the gods in the people. The political leaders could then use this fear to lead the people according to the leaders' will. Montesquieu, then, perceives the advantages of Roman religion over religions like Christianity, where truth and belief are ultimate values, and for which God is the truly legitimate leader of soci-ety. Later, the Romans refused to accept reforms to the religion established by Numa, even when such reforms would have made sense, as the magis-trates knew that any reform would weaken the authority of religion.

The lack of a truth-dimension and of the necessity to believe *true* statements in Roman religion led such wise men as Scaevola and Varro to consider it necessary for the people to remain ignorant of various true things and to believe in many false statements. These enlightened Roman intellectuals, who encouraged the cult of the gods, were certainly no polytheists themselves, but believed in one supreme god, of which the other gods were only parts.[41] It was this theism—or even pantheism—of the elites, as in the case of the Stoic Balbus in Cicero's *De natura deorum,* that was at the origin of the tolerant and irenic spirit of the pagan world.[42] The Roman world knew religious persecution even less than Greece, accepted all theologies, and heresies and religious wars were unknown in it. As long as a citizen participated in the temple ritual, he was the High Pontiff in his own family. The only religion traditionally proscribed in Rome was the Egyptian religion, and that stemmed from its own intolerant nature. If Jews and Christians also suffered from some hatred, spite, or even persecution by the Romans, this was because the Romans thought the Jews were Egyptians, and the Christians Jews.

One characteristic of Roman religion that exactly contradicted Egyptian religion was that in Rome priesthood was a civil office while in Egypt priests formed a separate class.[43] The Roman priests were senators and therefore did not develop interests of their own. They did not use superstition to oppress the republic, but rather to serve it. In Rome, then, there was an inherent religious dimension to the state, most clearly reflected in the religious duties of the king.[44] The religious dimension of Roman politics also meant a political dimension to religion, and this dimension grew along with Roman military victories. Rather than destroying the temples of conquered peoples and imposing Roman gods on them, the Romans were wise enough to adopt the gods of the vanquished. In this way, Rome came to be perceived by these peoples as the guardian of religion rather than the master of the world.[45] This syncretistic attitude also had another justification: like the Greeks, the Romans identified foreign deities with their own gods, to avoid an unnecessary multiplication of divine beings.[46] In the last paragraph of his *Considérations,* Montesquieu acknowledges the Roman lack of precision in their mythology. This carelessness, however, remained without consequences, as popular credulity is always stronger than any "logical" mythology. Actually, the Romans really did not care for religion, as their only divinity was the genius of the republic.[47]

This text shows that for the young Montesquieu, religion has no intrinsic truth-value. What counts is only the correct and peaceful ruling of society. The best religion, in this perception, is that which is useful for the political leaders to keep the people obedient. Its rituals, therefore, are more of a civil than of a sacred character.[48] Roman religion was the best-known example of such a religion in the ancient world and should become a model for modern societies seeking to free themselves from the yoke of Christianity.

Montesquieu's views on Roman religion are clearly his own, but his emphasis on its rationality, as it were, and on usefulness to the state as its main characteristic, reflects a widespread attitude among Enlightenment intellectuals. Thus, the entry "Religion" in the *Encyclopédie,* for instance, insisting that Greek and Roman religion are basically the same and that the second is the daughter of the first. The entry follows a certain Abbé Coyer (1707–1782) in enumerating four points where Roman religion was able to perfect Greek religion: its gods were more respectable, its dogmas more reasonable, its *merveilleux* less fanatical, and its cult wiser.[49] In other words, the reform and transformation of religion from the Greek to the Roman world reflects, to use Weberian terms, its rationalization. This religious reform is a known characteristic of what one can call "secondary" religions, or religions founded on older, established ones. Hence the Romans rejected various gods, too weak or vicious for their taste, and deified concord, peace, salvation, and liberty. Cult underwent a similar rationalization: for instance, no phenomena of religious enthusiasm, no bacchanalia, no sacred prostitution, no lamenting women were allowed in the various Roman festivals, described by Dionysius of Halicarnassus in his *Roman Antiquities* as otherwise fundamentally similar to the Greek ones. The Roman gods are active, but the gods' intervention is only meant to improve ethical dimensions. It seems that for enlightened intellectuals, the implicit model for the relationship between Greek and Roman religion is the relationship between Judaism and Christianity. Hence, when the author says that Romulus rejected Greek fables (myths) because of their "corporeality," he seems to draw an implicit parallel with the traditional Christian view of the Jewish reading of Scripture. Romulus had not invented Roman religion, but had brought it back from Alba. Neither did Numa invent it; rather, he only gave it a stable and enduring form.

This conception of Roman religion as a rationalist reform of Greek religion reflects some of Montesquieu's ideas: the Romans had transformed religion into a docile instrument of social peace. A similar echo of Montesquieu, focusing on the political dimension of religion, can be found in a book published anonymously around the time of the French Revolution, and which seems to fairly represent the common view of things. In Rome, we read, in opposition to almost all other peoples of the earth, no priestly class was established. Roman priests were indifferently asked to administer civilian as well as religious affairs.[50]

Another, somewhat eccentric, example of eighteenth-century scholarly perceptions of Roman religion is provided by Nicolas-Antoine Boulanger, who, seeking a general explanatory principle for ancient religion, analyzes from a comparative perspective what he calls the solar festivals of the Romans.[51] For him, Mexican festivals help understand the festivals of both the Romans and the Jews. Like the religion of Israel, that of Rome is to some extent part and parcel of the cultural background of educated persons and can be used to compare and better understand the religious systems of the New World in America and Asia. Thus, both Charles de Brosses, in his seminal *Du culte des dieux fétiches,* and the Dominican Noël Alexandre, offer a parallel between Chinese and Roman religions.[52]

One of the last serious treatments of Roman religion before Hartung is that of the Swiss writer Benjamin Constant. Constant had close relations with many German intellectuals, such as Schleiermacher, Schelling, and Herder, as well as with scholars like Görres and Creuzer. Much of what he writes about Roman religion reflects the views of the ancient historian Niebuhr, whose *Römische Geschichte* had been published in 1811. Constant's *De la religion* was published in 1821. Two of the main themes of the book were reflections on the nature of polytheism and the essence of sacrifice.[53] The scholarly progress accomplished in the understanding of Roman religion is reflected in Constant's complex perception of the joint influences of Etruscan and Greek elements (and the final victory of the second over the first) in the formation of Roman religion. Constant's discussion is intelligent and well informed. But his concerns reflect those of his times: the Enlightenment has given place to romanticism, and with it has gone the focus on the political dimensions of religion, that is, the function of religion in the life of the republic. The Machiavellian moment from the sixteenth century had given birth to an Erastian trajectory in modern European thought. This trajectory highlighted the advantages of Roman religion for the functioning of the republic. It had run its course and was replaced by the romantic interest in the individual and in the nation as a metaphorical person. With its decline a central dimension of Roman religion was lost, and with it a major insight on the nature of ancient religion. For Theodor Mommsen, for instance, one of the main virtues of Roman religion would be its usefulness in the crystallization and strengthening of a national identity. Twentieth-century scholarship would be slow in rediscovering the properly political dimension of Roman religion.

At the start of his manifesto "On the gods of Greece, Italy, and India," published in 1784, Sir William Jones mentions the "tale" of Cadmus (Kadmos). Jones points out that the tale (i.e., myth) "learnedly" traced by Samuel Bochart, referred to the perversion of historical or natural phenomena, which is the first of the "four principal forces of all mythology." The second of these forces, the "wild admiration of the heavenly bodies," is reflected in the myths and religions of Egyptians, Greeks, Sabians (from Arabia), Persians, Chinese, and Indians. Indeed, for Jones, there is beyond any doubt a "great similarity" between the religion and popular worship not only of Greece, Italy, and India but also between them and those of "Egypt, China, Persia, Phrygia, Phoenice, Syria, America and those of the Goths of northern Europe." He adds that all these various myths are "almost the same in another dress with an embroidery of images apparently Asiatick."[1]

Before the rediscovery of Sanskrit by William Jones, knowledge about India consisted mainly of ethnographical observations. Jesuit missionaries, in particular, contributed much to the discovery of Indian religions and mores. But few among them followed in the footsteps of Roberto Nobili (1577–1656) and learned Sanskrit and South Indian languages, or in those of Roa, who had learned Sanskrit in Agra, where he had been a missionary, and who eventually taught Athanasius Kircher in Rome—a fact made clear in the latter's *China illustrata*.[2] Thanks to Jones's intellectual prowess, European scholars were finally able to start deciphering the great literature of India and to study its religious traditions. In striking contradistinction with Confucianism, however, Brahmanism was only perceived as paganism, and as such its religious tradition was despised. Thus, in 1616, the Jesuit Fernandes Trancoso describes the beliefs of the Brahmans as "absurdities, infamies, lies."[3] None of these efforts to understand

Indian religions in depth, however, went very far, and most knowledge on Indian myths and religious practices remained that reported by travelers. Francois Bernier (1620–1688), for instance, who acquired his nickname "Mogul" from his ten-year stay on the Indian subcontinent, knows of the Brahmans' four great books of law, or Beths, as well as about naked fakirs, long pilgrimages, or widows sacrificing themselves on their husbands' funeral pyres (a practice the Muslim rulers try to prevent).[4] Bernier mentions the Indians' belief in metempsychosis, as well as the three daily prayers. If the Great Mogul, who is a Muslim, allows such old superstitions to go on among the pagans (*Gentils*), he adds, this is due to his tolerance, and to the fact that their religious praxis does not shock him.[5]

As with other strange and unknown religious cultures, the simplest stratagem to understand Indian religion was to compare it with familiar traditions. Here too, the comparison with the religion of the Jews appeared an obvious possibility. In 1704, the Marquis de la Créquinière published *The Agreement of the Customs of the East-Indians with those of the Jews*.[6] In his preface, the author states that he applied himself to studying the religion of the Indians, whose customs are precious remains from antiquity and can be best understood when compared with those of that ancient people, the Jews.[7] Similarly, Philip Buttmann, in his *Älteste Erdfunde des Morgenländes: ein biblisch-philologischer Versuch* (Berlin, 1803) proposes that India is the birthplace of humankind that is alluded to in the Hebrew tradition. The author already knows of a relationship between the peoples of South Asia and those of Europe. From now on, there would be no need to seek biblical proof texts for the new Aryan paradise. A new chapter would now begin in the history of the history of religions, in which not only antediluvian history but even Noah's Flood and his sons would be either forgotten or actively eradicated. Another interesting work in the same vein, dating from the late eighteenth century, is *Comparison of the Institutions of Moses with Those of the Hindoos and Other Ancient Nations*. The author, Joseph Priestley (1733–1804), was an English natural philosopher and radical theologian, who advocated religious toleration and eventually had to flee to the United States.[8] Priestley knows the works of Anquetil Duperron and Jones, as well as the earlier, and less-trustworthy works of travelers such as Tavernier, La Croze, Bouchet, and Lord. He remarks that "the Hindoos have preserved the knowledge of the Supreme Being, when the Greeks, and other more polished nations in the western part of the world, had lost sight of him ... their attention being engrossed by inferior objects of worship," referring here to the Laws of Manu. He also points out the great similarities between the Mosaic description of the Flood and a similar "unequivocal tradition of an universal deluge" in Indian literature, while other similarities between the Bible and India deal with the idea of paradise and that of an expiatory goat (the sacrificial horse in India).[9]

In the nineteenth century, however, the continuing degradation of the status of the Bible would dramatically weaken interest in the biblical story, even as an epistemological device—except of course among theologians.[10] For many, this story became irrelevant, or almost irrelevant, as a document reflecting, even partially, the early stages of world history. As the old myth was discarded, new myths took its place, however, that would accompany some of the most ominous transformations of intellectual conceptions in modern European patterns of thought.[11] The new interest in comparative mythology during the Enlightenment, and the "discovery" of Avestan by Anquetil Duperron and of Sanskrit by Sir William "Oriental" Jones would soon bring about a dramatic change of attitudes, terms, and options.[12] With romanticism, a moving away from the "Oriental mirage" will be detected in particular in Germany—the expression was coined by the French (Jewish) historian of religion Salomon Reinach (1858–1932) to explain the "Greek miracle." Early Greek culture will then be denied any real Near Eastern roots. The discovery of the Indo-European (or Aryan) family of languages will lead to the replacement of the old model by a new one, focusing on Indian parallels to the biblical story of the Flood. Rather than the end of the "Oriental mirage," we should then probably speak of the discovery of new horizons of the Orient with the passage to India. In contradistinction to the seventeenth-century attempts to contextualize the biblical myth, this new trend would offer a real "re-mythologization," by denying the cultural and historical context of the biblical text any deep significance and looking instead for structural and phenomenological parallels.

One of the most influential works of comparative religion to be written in the eighteenth century is Charles de Brosses's *Du culte des dieux fétiches*.[13] By Gallicizing *fetisso,* a Portuguese word used by merchants to refer to small ritual statues they encountered on the Senegal coast, President de Brosses (1709–1777) created the word *fetish*. His method, seeking to interpret newly discovered religious practices through comparison with those of the ancient past, is traditional. What is of particular interest in this case, however, is the decision to compare the present with the past in the same geographical area: Africa, a continent practically ignored in most studies on the religions of humankind at the time. Another highly influential work seeking to offer a general, encompassing theory of religious history was *L'antiquité dévoilée par ses usages, ou Examen critique des principales opinions, cérémonies et institutions religieuses et politiques des différens peuples de la terre,* by Nicolas-Antoine Boulanger (1722–1759), which sought to explain all cults as responses to the original flood.[14] Boulanger, a versatile spirit who had in his youth learned oriental languages, followed Vico in arguing for the religious origin of politics.[15] In such a scheme, all religions echoed one another. To give only one example, the "secular feasts" of the Mexicans served Boulanger to explain similar customs of Romans and Jews, who ignored the reason of their own behavior in various circumstances.[16]

Comparing Hinduism to Israelite religion, Priestley refers to the recently published theories of Charles François Dupuis (1742–1809). Like Priestley, Dupuis was an intellectual and a scientist endowed with many gifts and interests. Although he had expressed deep concern over the bloodbath in revolutionary France, he was elected to the National Convention and was eventually appointed to a professorship at the Collège de France. He had started as an astronomer and soon searched for connections between astronomy and mythology. His quest found its full expression in the twelve volumes of his *Origine de tous les cultes, ou la Religion universelle,* published in 1795.[17] In this work of encyclopedic dimensions, Dupuis sought to explain all religions, past and present, as avatars of an original cult of the sun. Similar attempts to find one single source for all forms of religion and mythology had already taken place in the eighteenth century.

The interest in mythology was not quite new. As we have seen, the word itself had been used since the early years of the eighteenth century. Both Bernard Fontenelle's *Sur l'origine des fables* and Giambattista Vico's *Scienza nuova* were major stages in the growing interest in myths and mythology.[18] The entry "Mythologie" in d'Alembert's *Grande Encyclopédie* was written by the polymath Nicolas Fréret.[19] For Fontenelle, myths *(les fables)* represented the history of human error. For Nicolas Fréret, mythology has a very broad meaning. It not only refers to the "histoire fabuleuse" of gods, semi-gods and heroes of antiquity but also to

> everything relating to pagan religion, i.e., the various systems and
> dogmas of theology, successively established in the different ages

of paganism, mysteries and cultic ceremonies honoring the so-called divinities, oracles.[20]

Fréret goes on to state that mythology, thus conceived, represents the largest branch of humanistic studies.[21] He explains this last statement by the fact that a full comprehension of Greek and Latin literature cannot be achieved without a deep knowledge of pagan mysteries and religious customs. He adds that even non-scholarly minds need to learn "Mythology," as it is now a fashionable topic, often mentioned in conversation. Moreover, painters, sculptors, and poets have an imperious need to learn it for the very practice of their craft. "Mythology," then, refers here to the whole study of ancient polytheistic systems, such as that of Phoenicians, Egyptians, Syrians, Celts, Germans, and Swedes. Incidentally, it is thanks to their inherently tolerant nature that ancient polytheisms permitted the introduction of foreign cults and the consequent transformations of religion.

Since Guillaume Postel and Joseph Justus Scaliger, scholars had retained a particular interest in ancient Phoenician mythology, which was supposed, in particular, to have had a powerful influence on Hebrew religion. More precisely, the figure of Sankhuniaton, the Phoenician author from the ninth century B.C.E. whose quotations by Philo of Byblos have been preserved for us by Eusebius of Caesarea, exerted a real fascination on scholars up to the end of the eighteenth century.[22] Throughout the passage from idolatry to mythology, Sankhuniaton was perceived as holding the key to ancient religious history. Selden, Kircher, and Grotius refer to him, as does the Dominican friar Gregorio Garcia, who proposed to find the origin of the American peoples in the Phoenicians and in the lost ten tribes of Israel.[23] Bochart, likewise, made systematic use of Sankhuniaton.[24] Various works were even explicitly devoted to Sankhuniaton, such as Henry Dodwell's *A Discourse Concerning Sanchoniaton's Phoenician History* (1691), or Richard Cumberland's *Sanchoniato's Phoenician History* (1720). Indeed, with the new wave of explicit interest in mythology, that is, the comparative history of ancient polytheist religions, Sankhuniaton was thought by the encyclopedists to offer the solution to the origin of the gods. This is, for instance, the argument that Etienne Fourmont (1683–1745), an early sinologist and a leading scholar of his time, presents in his comparative study of ancient peoples.[25] In the early seventeenth century, fables were understood as the record of the ancient pagans' false religious conceptions. At the end of the eighteenth century, the myths of ancient polytheism were perceived as reflecting the deep truth in religion. The old conception of one true religion versus the multiplicity of false religions was gone. One learned to consider all religions—the ancient polytheistic systems as well as the newly discovered ones, such as that of India—as so many reflections of truth. A univalent conception of truth, then, which may be the clearest characteristic of the age of reason, succeeded the symbolic mind of the Renaissance. With the loss of multiple hermeneutics, symbols could no longer be understood. It is only toward the end of our period, with the new equivalence of religious and mythological systems, that a new era in the polyvalent and symbolic understanding of reality could start. This symbolic understanding would soon find its fullest expression in Schelling's philosophy of mythology.

Our story ends with the new interest in myth and mythology that arose toward the end of the eighteenth century and flourished in the early nineteenth century.[26] As we have seen, the fascination with Sankhuniaton and his mythology, which grew through the eighteenth century, also represented a wish to look elsewhere than in the Bible for the religious origins of humankind. Contemporary with Dupuis' all-encompassing comparative theory of religion, and far from revolutionary France, August Christian Wolf was publishing his *Prolegomena ad Homerum*.[27] Wolf's insight permitted him to apply to the text of Homer the methods newly developed by his theologian colleagues in Göttingen for the text of the Hebrew Bible. Here, it seemed, was a potentially fruitful model for future scholarship. This, alas, was not to happen, and the disciplines, at the same time, were departing from one another. Classical philologists were turning their back on orientalists and theologians, and the West was now learning to despise (and exploit) the East. The progressive estrangement of theology and classics, in the nineteenth century, also reflects the strong disenchantment, or *Entzauberung* to use a Weberian term, with anything having to do with the old biblical source of authority: its text, its language, its people. Martin Bernal has shown how nineteenth-century Hellenic studies, in particular in Germany, were imbued with the new expression, radicalized, de-Christianized, and racialized, of the old aversion to Israel.[28] This new anti-Semitism cannot quite be disentangled from the romantic search for the roots of European languages, cultures, and religions further East than the land of ancient Israel. India would now become the goal of those who saw themselves as the inheritors of the ancient Greeks and cousins of the ancient Aryans.[29]

Hence, the nineteenth century, which could have witnessed the full blossoming of the groping efforts we have sought to follow in this book, would be deprived of the insights of previous generations of often-brilliant scholarship. The paradigm shift to which this book has been devoted, and which permitted the discovery of religions as cultures across the ages and continents, had run its course. With the formation of modern scholarly disciplines, the study of religions, as we have followed it through a series of idiosyncratic and brilliant minds, could not retain its essentially interdisciplinary character. In the domain of the comparative history of religion, in particular, it seems that methods and theories would have to be invented all over again, this time in the context of European imperialism and colonial encounters at their peak.[30]

We cannot go any further in what must remain an unfinished story. The most important single fact to be remembered, perhaps, from the early history of the modern history of religions is the dialectics between a field of knowledge, cultural transfer, and religious change. If the history of religions is a field particularly fraught with ambiguity and ideological overtones, this seems inevitable in a modern Europe learning at once to discover the cultures of the world and to exploit exotic countries, all while engaged in constant and violent struggles with its own religious and national identities.

Instead of a conclusion, we might be permitted to throw a brief, prospective look at the aftermath of our story. We will do this using a specific example of two approaches of East and West among historians of religions in the late nineteenth century and at the dawn of the twentieth—about a hundred years ago. When Franz Cumont published, in 1906, *Les Religions orientales dans le paganisme romain,* he was consciously embarking on a new and long journey in search of previously uncharted lands. The book, based on a set of lectures he had delivered at the Collège de France the preceding year, was proposing a strikingly new understanding of late antique religious history. Cumont's main claim was that only the development of the "oriental religions" in the Roman Empire could explain the eventual end of ancient polytheism and the success of Christianity. Cumont spoke of "oriental religions," rather than, as was traditionally thought and repeated, of the Jewish, monotheistic roots of Christianity. He was of course fully aware of the immense task awaiting scholarship.[31]

As a phenomenon, the seduction of the Orient has had a long history, and its roots go back to Greek antiquity. At the turn of the twentieth century, in the world of German scholarship, the case of Richard Reitzenstein offers a clear parallel to that of Cumont. "Le mirage de l'orient," as Salomon Reinach has named it, in contradistinction to "le miracle grec," was indeed quite powerful at the time. But it was, usually, a different kind of East than the one Cumont was referring to. The global success of Edward Said's *Orientalism,* a book first published in 1978, has brought with it some unfortunate attitudes. It has led us to forget that in the late nineteenth century, while orientalism as a whole encompassed the study of the languages, cultures, and history of all Asian nations, in the field of religion it referred mainly to South and East Asia—rather than to the Near East. The First World Congress of orientalists had taken place in Paris in 1873. Max Müller, in his address to the Ninth Congress (London, 1893), opposed the military conquest of Eastern nations in favor of the real "conquest," that of orientalist scholarship. But Müller, a Sanskritist by training, was mainly interested in the religious literatures of India and further East. His most-lasting contribution to knowledge probably comes from his editorship of the Sacred Books of the East. The religious cultures of the Near East play a relatively minor role in the new Eastern fad. Raymond Schwab has studied this major cultural phenomenon in his magisterial "la renaissance orientale."[32] To give one example among many: a book published in 1891, under the title *Oriental Religions and Christianity,* that originated in a series of lectures at the Union Theological Seminary in New York, deals with Hinduism, Buddhism, and what was then called Mohammedanism, and compares the New Testament with the Bhagavad-Gita. It does not however refer, even in cursory fashion, to the "oriental religions" of the early Christian centuries studied by Cumont.[33]

In the French-speaking world, the major orientalist figure in the generation before Cumont was Ernest Renan (1823–1892). In a sense, Cumont's attitude toward the Orient was diametrically opposed to Renan's. Where Cumont admired and respected, Renan despised and rejected.[34] Isis, Sarapis, Mithra: the heroes of Cumont's book, under their "exotic dress" represent here the superstitions of the Orient, conquering the very heart of Europe, "shaking hands" with the worst in Western religiosity. For Cumont, the time was not yet ripe for a scholarly handshake across the same landscapes.

From Renan to Cumont, we can follow the transformation of a negative perception of the Orient and oriental religions into a positive one. Actually, Renan does not consistently refer to the concept of "oriental religions." For him, as for Müller, the classification of religions still follows the neat taxonomy of languages, Indo-European versus Semitic. For Renan, Judaism is the best expression of Semitic religiosity (and religion is, famously, the only field of culture in which the Semites were able to express real creativity, namely, their invention of monotheism). For Cumont, on the other hand—and this is quite typical of traditional scholarly perceptions—Judaism was too similar, in the public formality of its ritualism, to Roman religion, to have offered any significant spiritual challenge to religious men and women in the empire. "Oriental religions," which dealt with man as a whole,[35] were another story altogether.

Cumont, then, is also the inheritor of Renan's perception of Judaism. While the latter allotted to the Semites, in the field of religion—and there only—cultural superiority, Cumont shows no interest in that ominous slip from linguistic categories to racial taxonomy so common in the late nineteenth century, and so clearly reflected in Max Müller and Ernest Renan. The discovery of the Indo-European and Semitic families of languages had soon lead to the double assumption—not always explicit—that these linguistic families also reflected different groups of peoples, or of races, and that the religions of these peoples shared family resemblances. While Indo-European religions were rich in myths, those of the Semites (i.e., for all practical purposes, Judaism and Islam) reflected a striking poverty of imagination. Such was, indeed, the viewpoint of Max Müller, and such was that of Ernest Renan.[36]

Although it stands to reason to see Cumont as deeply indebted to Renan's intellectual heritage, one should call attention to a major transformation in the discourse. Cumont, indeed, avoids being ensnared in Renan's identification of the Orient with a hypostasized Semitic world. For him, this is a false concept, born from the amalgam of a category mistake and the modern avatar of old religious prejudices.

Cumont broadens Renan's concept of Semitic creativity in matters of religion (and only in those matters) to "the Orient." For him, indeed, the East is superior to the West, in particular in matters of religion. Hence, what Gibbon had described as the "Decline and Fall of the Roman Empire" should be emended. In the religious sphere, writes Cumont, one must speak of progress, rather than of decadence, in late antiquity. This progress, in its turn, finds for him its ultimate expression in the victory of Christianity. In a sense, this scheme represents a return to the categories of traditional Christian historiography, but with a major twist: this victory was prepared not so much by Judaism as by the "oriental religions."

Where does Cumont's idea of the spiritual superiority of "oriental religions" come from and can we search for its roots? The very idea of oriental religions could not appear before the birth of orientalism itself, or more precisely, of the concept of orientalism. Although "orientalism" and "orientalist," are documented, in French as well as in English, in the eighteenth century, these words become more common only during the first half of the nineteenth century. A direct consequence of such concepts was of course the reification of an "Eastern" identity, in religion as well as in language or culture and the opposition between East and West. The concept of "oriental Religions" appeared in scholarly discourse only after the paradigm change that occurred with the establishment of orientalism as a field of study of languages, cultures, and religions clearly standing outside the realm of the intellectual and religious heritage of Europe. In speaking of "oriental religions," Cumont was seeking to recreate the link, then forgotten, but obvious to scholars of earlier times, whose works have occupied us throughout this book, between the religious cultures of the Mediterranean and the Near East. After a century of scholarship that has reflected his intellectual inheritance, the extent of his success in this matter remains a moot point.

INTRODUCTION

1. *Heptaplomeres* Part V. I quote the translation of Marion L. D. Kuntz, Jean Bodin, *Colloquium of the Seven about the Secrets of the Sublime* (Princeton: Princeton University Press, 1975), 266.

2. See Caterina Volpi, *Le immagini degli dei di Vincenzo Cartari* (Roma: De Luca, 1996).

3. See K. A. Vogel, "Cultural Variety in a Renaissance Perspective: Johannes Boemus on 'The Manners, Laws, and Customs of All People' (1520)," in *Shifting Cultures: Interaction and Discourse in the Expansion of Europe*, eds. Henriette Bugge and Joan Pau Rubiés (Periplus Parerga, Bd. 4; Münster: LIT, 1995), 17–34. Voegel deals with the reasons for Boemus's omission of reports on New World cultures and religions.

4. Las Casas's *Brevissima relacion de la destruccion de las Indias* was published in 1552, while D'Acosta's *De procuranda Indorum salute* appeared in 1596. See in particular Louis Hanke, *All Mankind Is One: A Study of the Disputation between Bartolomé de Las Casas and Juan Ginés de Sepúlveda in 1550 on the Intellectual and Religious Capacity of the American Indians* (De Kalb: Northern Illinois University Press, 1974); Anthony Pagden, *Natural Man: The American Indian and the Origins of Comparative Ethnology* (Cambridge: Cambridge University Press, 1981); Carmen Bernand and Serge Gruzinski, *De l'idolâtrie: une archéologie des sciences religieuses* (Paris: Seuil, 1988). On the birth of early modern ethnology, see the seminal study of Margaret T. Hodgen, *Early Anthropology in the Sixteenth and Seventeenth Centuries* (Philadelphia: University of Pennsylvania Press, 1964).

5. See Sabine MacCormack, *Religion in the Andes* (Princeton: Princeton University Press, 1991).

6. On the early comparative method in the history of religions, see Michel de Certeau, "Histoire et anthropologie chez Lafitau," in *Le lieu de l'autre: histoire religieuse et mystique*, ed. Luce Giard (Paris: Le Seuil, 2005), esp. "Une technique: la comparaison," 96–97.

7. *Cérémonies et coutumes religieuses de tous le peuples du monde, représentés par des figures dessinées de la main de Bernard Picart, avec un explication historique, et quelques dissertations curieuses* (Amsterdam: Chez J. F. Bernard, 1723–1743 (Six volumes). See Silvia Berti, "Bernard Picart e Jean-Frédéric Bernard

dalla religione riformata al deismo. Un incontro con il mondo ebraico nell'Amsterdam del primo settecento," *Rivista Storica Italiana* 117 (2005): 974–1001. Berti offers a detailed picture of the publication and its context. Picart's engravings have been recently studied in Paola von Wyss-Giacosa's splendid monograph, *Religionsbilder der frühen Aufklärung: Bernard Picarts Tafeln für die Cérémonies et coutumes religieuses de tous les peuples du monde* (Wabern; Bern: Benteli Verlag, 2006).

8. "Alors que le XVIIe et le XIXe siècles inventent, le XVIIIe illustre, accumule et prépare." Pierre Chaunu, quoted by Alastair Hamilton, "The Study of Islam in Early Modern Europe," *Archiv für Religionsgeschichte* 3 (2001): 182.

9. I quote *La scienza nuova* in the 1744 edition. Giambattista Vico, with an introduction by Paolo Rossi, *La scienza nuova* (Milan: Biblioteca Universale Rizzoli, 1977). Bernard Fontenelle's *De l'origine des fables* was written before the end of the seventeenth century but was not published until 1724. On Fontenelle's significance for the modern study of religion, see James S. Preus, *Explaining Religion: Criticism and Theory from Bodin to Freud* (New Haven, London: Yale University Press, 1987), ch. 3, 40–55. Despite its importance and fame, Joseph-François Lafitau's masterpiece, *Les moeurs des sauvages ameriquains comparées aux moeurs des premiers temps* (Paris, 1724), has not been recently fully reprinted. A new edition, by Edna Hindie Lemay (Paris: F. Maspero, 1983, 2 vols.), oddly omits precisely the entire section on religion. See, however, a full English translation, by W. N. Fenton and E. L. Moore, *Customs of the American Indians Compared with the Customs of Primitive Times*, 2 vols. (Toronto: Champlain Society, 1974–1977).

10. Paolo Rossi, *The Dark Abyss of Time: The History of the Earth and the History of Nations from Hooke to Vico* (Chicago; London: Chicago University Press, 1984), x. Cf. Vico, *Scienza nuova*, Part 1, 28.

11. See Frances Yates, *Giordano Bruno and the Hermetic Traditions* (Chicago: University of Chicago Press, 1964). See further Anthony Grafton, "Protestant versus Prophet: Isaac Casaubon on Hermes Trismegistus," in his *Defenders of the Text: The Traditions of Scholarship in an Age of Science, 1450–1800* (Cambridge, Mass.; London: Harvard University Press, 1991), 145–161.

12. Charles F. Dupuis, *Origine de tous les cultes, ou Religion universelle*, 4 vols. (Paris: Agasse [1794]). Cf. Frank Edward Manuel, *The Eighteenth Century Confronts the Gods* (Cambridge, Mass.: Harvard University Press, 1959), 259–270.

13. For an excellent study of the birth of modern psychology in the same period, see Fernando Vidal, *Les sciences de l'âme, XVIe-XVIIIe siècle* (Paris: Champion, 2006). I should like to thank Saskia Brown for calling my attention to this work, which she translated into English (to be published by Harvard University Press). Vidal insists from the start, as I do here, that the birth of a scientific or scholarly discipline can predate the establishment of university chairs and departments that occurred in the last third of the nineteenth century

14. Charles Taylor, *A Secular Age* (Cambridge, Mass.: Harvard University Press, 2007).

15. Paul Hazard, *La crise de la conscience européenne, 1680–1715* (Paris: Boivin, 1935). English ed.: *The European Mind: The Critical Years, 1680–1715* (New Haven: Yale University Press, 1953).

16. See Jonathan I. Israel, *Radical Enlightenment: Philosophy and the Making of Modernity, 1650–1750* (Oxford: Oxford University Press, 2001), 14–20, where Israel argues that Hazard "starts the crisis, unacceptably late, around 1680" and that to encompass its full scope, one should go back to at least the 1650s. For Israel, the crisis started with the profound impact of Cartesianism on radical thinkers. This crisis had been prepared by the "libertinisme érudit" since the start of the century, and by the decline of belief in hell.

17. Edmund Husserl's *Krisis in den europäischen Wissenschaften und die transcendentale phänomenologische Philosophie* was published in *Philosophia* 1 (1936): 77–176.

18. Paul Hazard, *The European Mind, 1680–1715* (Hammondsworth, Eng: Penguin Books, 1964).

19. An English edition appeared in 1970; Michel Foucault, *The Order of Things: An Archaeology of the Human Sciences* (New York: Vintage Books).

20. See Serge Gruzinski, *Les quatre parties du monde: histoire d'une mondialisation* (Paris: La Martinière, 2004), 255. The idea of idolatry was one of the major preoccupations, if not obsessions, of early modern students of religion, starting with the Spanish missionaries in America. See Serge Gruzinsky and Carmen Bernand, *De l'idolâtrie: une archéologie des sciences religieuses* (Paris: Seuil, 1988). See further the recent issue of *Journal of the History of Ideas* 67 (2006) devoted to the topic, with an introduction by Jonathan Sheehan, "Thinking about Idols in Early Modern Europe": 561–569, and with articles by Joan-Pau Rubiés, Carina L. Johnson, Sabine MacCormack, and Peter N. Miller. To a striking extent, Maimonides offered for seventeenth-century Christian scholars and thinkers the best intellectual frame for understanding the phenomenon of idolatry. See ch. IV.2 below.

21. Wilfred Cantwell Smith, *The Meaning and End of Religion: A New Approach* (New York: Macmillan, 1963), for instance, 37–44. On the history of the term "religion" itself, see Ernst Feil, *Religio, die Geschichte eines neuzeitlichen Grundbegriffs*, 3 vols. (Göttingen: Vandenhoeck & Ruprecht, 1986–2001). For the most sustained and rigorous analysis of the semantic transformation of "religion" in the early modern times, see Peter Harrison, *"Religion" and the religions in the English Enlightenment* (Cambridge: Cambridge University Press, 1990). See further Jonathan Z. Smith, "Religion, Religions, Religious," in Mark C. Taylor, ed., *Critical Terms for Religious Studies* (Chicago, London: University of Chicago Press, 1998), 269–284.

22. Guy G. Stroumsa, *The End of Sacrifice: The Religious Transformations of Late Antiquity* (Chicago: Chicago University Press, 2009). This book was originally published as *La fin du sacrifice: les mutations religieuses de l'antiquité tardive* (Paris: Odile Jacob, 2005).

23. For a recent reinterpretation of Jaspers's concept, see Shmuel Noah Eisenstadt, ed., *The Origins and Diversity of the Axial Age Civilizations* (Albany: State University of New York Press, 1986).

24. As far as I can see, the arguments used by freethinkers were first submitted by less radically oriented scholars.

25. Max Müller, *Lectures on the Science of Religion* (London: 1893), 29. The lectures were delivered in 1870 and first printed in 1873. I owe this reference to

Simon Cook. Cf. Lourens P. van den Bosch, *Friedrich Max Müller: A Life Devoted to the Humanities* (Leiden: Brill, 2002), ch. 3, "Mythology in comparative perspective," 243–292. To be sure, a parallel case could be made for Islam, and indeed, medieval Islamicate civilizations showed some extremely impressive intellectual efforts to understand the history of religions from a comparative perspective. It is in this context that Maimonides should be understood. See Sarah Stroumsa, *Maimonides in His World: Portrait of a Mediterranean Thinker* (Princeton: Princeton University Press, 2009), ch. 4.

26. For a recent study of the discipline of the modern study of religion and its development in the late nineteenth century, see Hans Georg Kippenberg, *Die Entdeckung der Religionsgeschichte: Religionswissenschaft und Moderne* (Munich: Beck, 1997). English translation: *Discovering Religious History in the Modern Age* (Princeton: Princeton University Press, 2002).

27. Richard Popkin speaks of the "budding development of comparative religion" in the second half of the seventeenth century. See James E. Force and Richard H. Popkin, eds., *Essays on the Context, Nature, and Influence of Isaac Newton's Theology* (Dordrecht; Boston: Kluwer Academic Publishers, 1990), 9. While it is true that the latter part of the seventeenth century would see a plethora of works on "comparative religion," it seems to me that the real watershed separating the Renaissance from the modern world happened in the early part of the century.

28. Martin Mulsow has insisted on the dramatic intellectual changes that made the modern history of religions possible. See in particular his "Antiquarianism and Idolatry: The *Historia* of Religions in the Seventeenth Century," in *Historia: Empiricism and Erudition in Early Modern Europe*, eds. Gianna Pomata and Nancy G. Siraisi (Cambridge, Mass.; London: MIT Press, 2005), 181–209.

29. Edward W. Said, *Orientalism* (New York: Pantheon, 1978 [2nd. ed. 1994]). One should note that Said discusses a period later than the one dealt with here.

1. PARADIGM SHIFT

1. Cristóbal Colón, *Diario del decrubrimento,* ed. Manuel Alvar (Cabildo Insular de Gran Canaria, 1976), t. 2, 51–53: "Y creo que ligeramente se harían cristianos, que me carecio que ninguna secta tenían . . . Non tienen secta ninguna ni non son idólatras."

2. Alain Milhou, "El indio americano y el mito de la religión naturál," in *La imagen del indio en la Europa moderna* (Seville: Consejo Superior de Investigaciones Científicas, 1990), 171–196, see 183.

3. See Anthony Pagden, *The Fall of Natural Man: The American Indian and the Origins of Comparative Ethnology* (Cambridge: Cambridge University Press, 1982), and Louis Hanke, *All Mankind Is One: A Study of the Disputation between Bartolomé de las Casas and Juan Ginès de Sepúlveda in 1550 on the Intellectual and Religious Capacity of the American Indians* (DeKalb, Ill.: Northern Illinois University Press 1979) (see preface, n. 4). In contradistinction to the theologians, both the Crown and the Vatican declared the Indians to be human, so that they could become free vassals of the king soon after the discovery of America, before the end of the fifteenth century.

4. Serge Gruzinski, *Les quatre parties du monde: histoire d'une mondialisation* (Paris: Martinière, 2004).

5. See, for instance, the classical work of Margaret T. Hodgen, *Early Anthropology in the Sixteenth and Seventeenth Centuries* (Philadelphia: University of Pennsylvania Press, 1964). See further Fernando Vidal, *Les sciences de l'âme, XVIe-XVIIIe siècle* (Paris: Champion, 2006).

6. Sabine MacCormack, *Religion in the Andes: Vision and Imagination in Early Colonial Peru* (Princeton: Princeton University Press, 1992), 240.

7. I quote from Pedro de Cieza de León, *La crónica del Peru,* ed. M. Ballesteros (Madrid: Historia 16, 1984), 117; cf. the better edition published by the Pontificia Universidad Catolica del Peru (7 vols.; Lima, 1984–1994).

8. Marcel Bataillon, "La herejia de fray Francisco de la Cruz y la reacción anti-lascasiana," in his *Estudios sobre Bartolomé de las Casas* (Barcelona: Peninsula, 1976), 353–365, see esp. 256.

9. José de Acosta, *Historia naturál y moral de las Indias,* ed. Barbara G. Beddall (Valencia: Hispaniae Scientia, 1977). Acosta redacted the first two books of his work (of six) in Latin, the others in Castillan.

10. MacCormack, *Religion in the Andes,* 281.

11. Acosta, *Historia naturál,* 301, 311.

12. Ibid., 311, ". . . el demonio ha tenido de engañar a los Indios, es el mismo con que engaño a los Griegos, y Romanos, y otros Gentiles antiguos."

13. Ibid., ch. 14, 335.

14. Ibid., ch. 16, 344.

15. Ibid., ch. 26, 373.

16. Ibid., ch. 27, 376–379.

17. Thus J. J. R. Villarías Robles, *El sistema económico del imperio inca: Historia crítica de una controversia* (Madrid: Consejo Superiór de Investigaciones Científicas, 1998), 103.

18. The classical work presenting this theory on the origin of the American Indians' is Gregorio García, O. P., *Orígen de los Indios del Nuevo Mundo,* published in Valencia in 1607. See the critical edition of Franklin Pease (Mexico: Fondo de cultura economica, 1981). The same approach is taken in the *Antiquitates Iudaicae* of Arias Montano, the great Spanish intellectual of the *siglo d'oro.*

19. Acosta, *Historia naturál,* 310.

20. Elsewhere, Acosta lumps together Chinese, Mexicans, Peruvians, and Japanese as peoples without script; for him, script is essentially identified with an alphabet.

21. References in MacCormack, *Religion in the Andes,* 206.

22. For sophisticated discussions of the concept of idolatry, including tentative new definitions, among sixteenth-century missionaries to the Americas, such as Bartolome de Las Casas and José de Acosta, see MacCormack, *Religion in the Andes,* 265–266. On the centrality of the concept of idolatry in early modern scholarship, see ch. IV.2 below.

23. Bartolomé Alvarez, *De las costumbres y conversión de los Indios del Perú; Memorial a Felipe II,* ed. Maria del Carmen Martín Rubio (Madrid: Polifemo, 1998), ch. 125ff., 69ff. The manuscript, redacted in a Bolivian village in 1587–1588, was discovered in 1991 by a Madrid book dealer.

24. Inca Garcilaso de la Vega, *Commentarios reales,* ed. Mercedes Serna (Madrid: Clasicos Castalia, 2000), 130, n. 39. Garcilaso is also the translator of the *Dialoghi d'amore,* a Platonic text written by Leone Ebreo. Sabine Hyland has devoted a book to a sixteenth-century Jesuit, son of an Incan mother and Spanish father, who believed that the Incan culture, religion, and language were equal to their Christian counterpart. See S. Hyland, *The Jesuit and the Incas: The Extraordinary Life of Padre Blas, Valera, S. J.* (Ann Arbor: University of Michigan Press, 2003).

25. This point is noted by MacCormack, *Religion in the Andes,* 377.

26. During his trip to Brazil in May 2007, Benedict XVI claimed that "the annoucement of Jesus and of his Gospel did at no moment entail the alienation of Precolumbian cultures and did not impose a foreign culture" (*Le Monde,* May 13, 2007). Contrary to this statement, the Church had established a complex system to "extirpate idolatry" in New Spain and Peru. See, for instance, Pablo Joseph de Arriaga, S. J. *La extirpación de la idolátria en el Perú* (Lima, 1621). Cf. Pierre Duviols, *La lutte contre les religions autochtones dans le Pérou colonial; l'extirpation de l'idolâtrie entre 1532 et 1660* (Lima: Institut Français d'Etudes Andines, 1971), id., *Cultura andina y represion: procesos y visitas de idolatrias y hechicerias, Cajatambo, siglo XVII* (Cusco: Centro de estudios rurales andinos "Bartolomé de las Casas, 1986), and K. Mills, *Idolatry and Its Enemies: Colonial Andean Religion and Extirpation, 1640–1750* (Princeton: Princeton University Press, 1997).

27. See especially John H. Elliott, *The Old World and the New, 1492–1650* (Cambridge: Cambridge University Press, 1970).

28. On the representation of Islam in the European mind, see ch. VI.6 below. On the importance of the identification with Rome in Spanish consciousness, see Sabine MacCormack, *On the Wings of Time: Rome, the Incas, Spain, and Peru* (Princeton: Princeton University Press, 2007).

29. See in particular Carmen Bernand et Serge Gruzinski, *De l'idolâtrie: une archéologie des sciences religieuses* (Paris: Le Seuil, 1988). Cf. S. MacCormack, "Gods, Demons, and Idols in the Andes," *Journal of the History of Ideas* 67 (2006): 623–647.

30. Thus, for instance, Las Casas's *Brevissima relación de la destruyción de las Indias,* published in Valencia in 1542. Cf. Bartolomé de Las Casas, *Obra indigenista,* éd. José Alcina Franch (Madrid: Alianza Editorial, 1983).

31. See Jonathan Sheehan, "Introduction: Thinking about Idols in Early Modern Europe," *Journal of the History of Ideas* 67 (2006): 561–569.

32. The first edition of Joseph-François Lafitau, *Mœurs des sauvages ameriquains, comparées aux mœurs des premiers temps,* dates from 1724. In 1983, Edna Hindie Lemay published an edited version of *Mœurs des sauvages américains* (Paris: Maspero). Lafitau, particularly in the French-speaking world, is considered the father of modern anthropology. Oddly enough, the some 350 pages dedicated by the author to the Iroquois religion have disappeared from the new edition.

33. MacCormack, *Religion in the Andes,* 240.

34. This accommodation, of which the "Querelle des rites," around 1700, represents the acme, reflects the patristic idea, later picked up by Maimonides, of a "divine ruse" (a pious fraud, *tallatuf* in Arabic, *engaño* in Spanish) that had tolerated

animal sacrifices to permit the Israelites, "paganized" by their long sojourn in Egypt, to express their religious feelings. Hegel's famous "ruse of reason" (*List der Vernunft*) might well stem from this old tradition, which was rediscovered by Christian Hebraists in the early seventeenth century. Cf. Ch. IV.2 below.

35. This broadening of the concept of religion has been noted, but not really explained, by Wilfred Cantwell Smith, *The Meaning and End of Religion: A New Approach* (New York: Macmillan, 1963).

36. See ch. IV.1 below.

37. See Max Müller, *Lectures on the Science of Religion* (London: 1893), 29. quoted in introduction, n. 25, above.

38. On the birth and limits of ethnological curiosity among late-antique Christian intellectuals, see Guy G. Stroumsa, *Barbarian Philosophy: The Religious Revolution of Early Christianity* (Tübingen: Mohr Siebeck, 1999), 56–84.

39. On the idea of accommodation, see ch. VII.1, below.

40. In a sense, this transformation of the concept of religion is parallel to that which occurred in late antiquity, and which I have sought to describe in *The End of Sacrifice.*

41. See Claude Lévi-Strauss, *Anthropologie Structurale II* (Paris: Plon, 1973).

42. So Octavio Paz, *Sor Juana Inés de la Cruz, o Las trampas de la fé* (Barcelona: Seix Barral, 1982), for instance, 224.

43. See Sabine MacCormack, "Ethnography in South America," in *Cambridge History of the Native Peoples of the Americas,* eds. F. Salomon and S. Schwartz (Cambridge: Cambridge University Press, 1999), 96–187. See further Giuliano Gliozzi, *Adamo e il nuovo mondo: la nascita dell' antropologia come ideologia coloniale: dale genealogie bibliche alle teorie razziali (1500–1700)* (Florence: Nuova Italia, 1976).

44. MacCormack, *Religion in the Andes,* 405.

45. See n. 32 above.

46. Montaigne's knowledge on the Indians of Peru came from Francisco Lopez de Gómara, *Historia general de las Indias* (Saragossa, 1552), which appeared in French, in Martin Fumée's translation, in 1578 in Paris. In his *Essays*, III. 6 ("Des coches"), Montaigne quotes entire pages from this work. See in Montaigne, *Les Essais,* eds. Jean Balsamo, Michel Magnien, and Catherine Magnien-Simonin (La Pléiade; Paris: Gallimard, 2007), 1768, n. 1 to p. 956. The editors note that Lopez de Gómara, in his turn, had been influenced by the *Suma de Geografia* (1519) of Martín Fernandez de Enciso, conquistador of Cenú.

47. See Jacques Le Brun, "Critique biblique et esprit moderne à la fin du XVIIᵉ siècle, sens et portée du retour aux origines," in *L'histoire aujourd'hui: nouveaux objets, nouvelles méthodes* (Université de Liège, "Faculté ouverte" Série B; Liège, 1988), XXX.

48. John H. Elliott, *The Old World and the New, 1492–1650* (Cambridge: Cambridge University Press, 1970), 17.

49. See especially David E. Mungello, *Curious Land: Jesuit Accommodation and the Origins of Sinology* (Honolulu: University of Hawaii Press, 1985).

50. The bibliography on Christian Hebraism and on Christian Kabbalah is quite large. See, for instance, J. Friedman, "The Myth of Jewish Antiquity: New

Christians and Christian Hebrews in Early Modern Europe," in *Jewish Christians and Christian Jews from the Renaissance to the Enlightenment*, eds. Richard H. Popkin and Gordon M. Weiner (Archives d'histoire des idées; Dordrecht; Boston; London, 1994), 35–55.

51. See Stephen G. Burnett, *From Christian Hebraism to Jewish Studies: Johannes Buxtorf (1564–1629) and Hebrew Learning in the Seventeenth Century* (Leiden; New York: Brill, 1996).

52. See Frank E. Manuel, *The Eighteenth Century Confronts the Gods* (New York: Atheneum, 1967), 9.

53. See in particular Anthony Pagden, *The Fall of Natural Man: The American Indian and the Origins of Comparative Ethnology* (Cambridge, New York: Cambridge University Press, 1986).

54. This point is made, in particular, by Wilfred Cantwell Smith, *The Meaning and End of Religion*.

55. For an impressive collection of recent studies on early scholarship on early Christian literature, see Emmanuel Bury and Bernard Meunier, eds., *Les Pères de l'Eglise au XVIIe siècle* (Paris: Cerf, 1993).

56. For an important analysis of Pietro della Valle and of other travelers' reports from south India, see Joan Pau Rubiés, *Travel and Ethnology in the Renaissance: South India through European Eyes, 1250–1625* (Cambridge: Cambridge University Press, 2000). The intellectual discovery of India, however, is a case *sui generis*, since the study of Sanskrit would not start in earnest in Europe before Sir William Jones, near the end of the eighteenth century. See Epilogue below.

57. See Anne-Marie Lecoq, ed., *La Querelle des Anciens et des Modernes* (Paris: Gallimard, 2001); cf. ch. II.2 below.

58. See, for instance, Anthony Grafton, *Defenders of the Text: The Traditions of Scholarship in an Age of Science* (Cambridge, Mass.: Harvard University Press, 1991), 104–144.

59. The full title reads: *Purchas His Pilgrimage; or, Relations of the World and the Religions Observed in All Ages and Places Discovered, from the Creation unto the Present* (London, 1613). On Purchas's training at Saint John's College, Cambridge, see William T. Costello, S. J., *The Scholastic Curriculum at Early Seventeenth Century Cambridge* (Cambridge, Mass.: Harvard University Press, 1958), 104–106.

60. Brerewood's book appeared in French translation in 1640. An "ecumenical" plan to republish it in Geneva, together with additions by the Catholic Richard Simon, never materialized. Simon's text was discovered and published only recently; see Jacques Le Brun and John D. Woodbridge, eds., Richard Simon, *Additions aux recherches curieuses d'Edward Brerewood sur la diversité des langues et religions* (Paris: Presses Universitaires de France, 1983).

61. Alexander Ross, *Pansebeia; or, A View of All Religions in the World*, 2nd ed. (London, 1653).

62. See M. T. Larsen, "The 'Babel/Bible' Controversy and Its Aftermath," in *The Civilizations of the Ancient Near East*, vol. 1, ed. Jack M. Sasson (New York: Scribner, 1995), 95–106.

63. On Kircher, see, for instance, John Fletcher, ed., *Athanasius Kircher und seine Beziehungen zum Gelehrten Europas seiner Zeit* (Wolfenbüttler Arbeiten zum Barockforschung, 17; Wiesbaden: Harrassowitz, 1988).

64. Gerardus Vossius, *De theologia gentili et physiologia christiana, sive de origine ac progressu idololatriae* (Amsterdam, 1641; reprint, New York: Garland, 1976), 3 vols. On Vossius, see C. S. M. Rademaker, *The Life and Works of Gerardus Johannes Vossius (1577–1649)* (Assen: Van Gorcum, 1981).

65. See Aharon Katchen, *Christian Hebraists and Dutch Rabbis: Seventeenth-Century Apologetics and the Study of Maimonides' Mishneh Torah* (Cambridge, Mass.: Harvard University Press, 1984), 288. John Selden's *De Diis Syris* (London, 1617) had been reprinted in Leiden in 1627.

66. Edward Herbert's *De Religione Gentium* was published posthumously in Amsterdam in 1663, but his *De veritate* appeared in Paris in 1624, and a French translation was published in 1639. This work was never translated to English.

67. This is the view not only of the English theologian Humphrey Prideaux, *The True Nature of Imposture* (London, 1697), but also that of the excellent Arabist Adriaan Reland, *De religione Mohammedica* (Utrecht, 1705).

68. See ch. VI below.

69. Charles Blount, *Great Is Diana of the Ephesians; or, The Original of Idolatry, Together with the Politick Institution of the Gentile Sacrifices* (London, 1680).

70. The dissertation is inserted in the fifth volume of Dom Augustin Calmet's *Commentaire littéral sur tous les livres de l'Ancien et du Nouveau Testament*, vol. 5, (Paris, 1726), 130–136.

71. On the Sabians, see chs. IV.2 and V.1 below.

72. On the opposition between Western, Christian civilization and other cultures, which is at the bottom of Samuel P. Huntington's search for the "clash of civilizations," see K. Mahbubani, "The West and the Rest," *The National Interest* (Summer 1992): 3–13. I owe this reference to Philippe Borgeaud, "Une rumeur bien entretenue: le retour de(s) Dieu(x)," *Critique* 704–705 (2006): 60 (59–68). On the early modern study of early Christianity and the stakes for Catholics and Protestant scholars, see in particular Jonathan Z. Smith, *Drugery Divine: On the Comparison of Early Christianities and the Religions of Late Antiquity* (Chicago: Chicago University Press, 1990).

II. RESPUBLICA HEBRAEORUM

1. On Scaliger and his work, see Anthony Grafton's monumental study: *Joseph Scaliger: A Study in the History of Classical Scholarship*, 2 vols. (Oxford: Clarendon Press, 1983–1993).

2. *Antiquitatum Iudaicarum Libri IX, in quis, praeter Iudaeae, Hierosolymorum, et Templi Salomonis accuratam delineationem, praecipui sacri ac profani gentis ritus describuntur* (Leiden, 1593). His important philological study on Hebrew lexicography, *De arcano sermone*, which had gotten him into some trouble, was not reprinted in this volume. On Arias Montano, see Ben Rekers, *Benito Arias Montano (1527–1598)* (London; Leiden: Warburg; Brill, 1972). On an early instance of his philological acumen, see D. Cabanelas, O.F.M., "Arias Montano y los

libros plumbeos de Granada," in *Miscelanea de estudios arabes y hebraicos* 18–19 (1969–1970), 7–41.

3. See the *Prolegomena* to Bishop Brian Walton's *Biblia Sacra Polyglotta* (London, 1654–57; reprint Graz, 1965) for a history of research in the half century following Arias Montano. Cf. Peter N. Miller, *Peiresc's Europe: Learning and Virtue in the Seventeenth Century* (New Haven and London: Yale University Press, 2000), 81.

4. See Jacques Le Brun and Guy G. Stroumsa, *Les juifs présentés aux chrétiens* (Paris: Les Belles Lettres, 1998), introduction.

5. On Leone Modena and Richard Simon, see ch. III below.

6. See Anthony Grafton, "Scaliger's Chronology: Philology, Astronomy, World History," in his *Defenders of the Text: The Traditions of Scholarship in an Age of Science* (Cambridge, Mass.: Harvard University Press, 1991), 104–144; cf. n. 11 in the introduction above.

7. See below, pt. 2, in this chapter.

8. "All religions come from the East." The claim about the Eastern origin of all religion is traditional, and goes back at least to late antiquity: see, for instance, Eusebius of Caesarea, *Vita Constantini,* II. 67.

9. See, for instance, Mark Silk, "Numa Pompilius and the Idea of Civil Religion in the West," *Journal of the American Academy of Religion* 72 (2004): 863–896. See further Guy G. Stroumsa, "Moses the Lawgiver and the Idea of Civil Religion in Patristic Thought," in *Teologie politiche: modelli a confronto,* ed. Giovanni Filoramo (Brescia: Morcelliana, 2005), 135–148. Cf. ch. VII, n. 8, below.

10. For Maimonides in England, see R. H. Popkin, "Some Further Comments on Newton and Maimonides," in *Essays on the Context, Nature, and Influence of Isaac Newton's Theology,* eds. J. E. Force and R. H. Popkin (Archives Internationales d'Histoire des Idées, 129; Boston; London: Kluwer, 1990), 1–7; S. Levy, "English Students of Maimonides," *Miscellanies of the Jewish Historical Society of England* 4 (1942): 61–77; J. L. Teicher, "Maimonides and England," *Transactions of the Jewish Historical Society of England* 16 (1951): 97–100. Cf. ch. IV.2 below.

11. Despite Selden's towering figure in both legal and intellectual history, almost no attention seems to have been devoted to his pioneering work as a historian of religion. Except for a partial English translation of the *De Diis Syris,* entitled *The Fabulous Gods Denounced in the Bible* (Philadelphia: Lippincott, 1880), this work does not seem to have been analyzed. For Selden's interest in Jewish law, see J. R. Ziskind, trans., *John Selden on Jewish Marriage Law: The Uxor Hebraica* (Leiden: Brill, 1991), and in particular Jason P. Rosenblatt, *Renaissance England's Chief Rabbi: John Selden* (Oxford: Oxford University Press, 2006). Selden's *De iure naturali et gentium, iuxta disciplinam ebraeorum libri septem* (London, 1640) is a remarkable attempt to identify natural law and the seven Noahide commandments from the Jewish tradition. This, too, seems to have escaped scholarly attention. I. Herzog, "John Selden and Jewish Law," *Journal of Comparative Legislation and International Law,* Third Series, 12 (1931): 236–245, does not grant this work any particular attention. G. J. Toomer, *John Selden: A Life in Scholarship* (Oxford and New York: Oxford University Press, 2009), 2 vols., appeared too late for me to take it into account.

12. On whom, see Albert I. Baumgarten, *The Phoenician History of Philo of Byblos: A Commentary* (EPROER 89; Leiden: Brill, 1981). See Epilogue below.

13. It remains unclear to me whether this is the first modern discussion of the Noahide commandments by a gentile author.

14. I quote according to the edition published in Leipzig in 1695. The identification of the Noahide Laws with natural law is the central claim of the work.

15. Petrus Cunaeus, *De republica Hebraeorum* (Leiden, 1617; second ed., 1732).

16. P. N. Miller, *Peiresc's Europe*, 81.

17. *Theokratia* (*a hapax* in Greek) had been coined by Josephus in his *Contra Apionem* to describe the regime presented by the Law of Moses; cf. Cunaeus's reference to *theokratia* in Josephus, *Antiquities of the Jews*. I. 4. See François Laplanche, "Christian Erudition in the Sixteenth and Seventeenth Centuries and the Hebrew State," *Hebraic Political Studies* 3 (2008): 5–18, esp. 14–18.

18. For other examples of Maimonides' application of the Farabian abstract model to a concrete religion, see, for instance, Lawrence V. Berman, "Maimonides, Disciple of Al-Farabi," *Israel Oriental Studies* 4 (1974): 154–178, esp. 155, and Sarah Stroumsa, *Maimonides in His World: Portrait of a Mediterranean Thinker* (Princeton: Princeton University Press, 2009), chapter 4.

19. Maimonides, *Mishneh Torah*; see, for instance, book I, chs. 1 and 9. On his discussion of the Noahide Laws, see book I, ch. 3.

20. I am unable to demonstrate that Spinoza's seven dogmas of universal faith do come from the seven Noahide Laws, but this is a tantalizing possibility. I read the text in the new edition of Fokke Akkerman, in Spinoza, *Oeuvres, III, Tractatus Theologico-Politicus, Traité théologico-politique* (Paris: Presses Universitaires de France, 1984). The list of seven dogmas of the universal faith are on pp. 474–476. The literature on Spinoza's *Tractatus* is, of course, immense. See in particular Freidrich Niewöhner, "Die Religion Noah's bei Uriel da Costa und Baruch de Spinoza. Eine historische Miniatur zur Genese des Deismus," in *Spinoza's Political and Theological Thought*, ed. C. de Deugd (Amsterdam and New York: North Holland, 1984), 143–149.

21. See Rémi Brague, *La voie romaine* (Paris: Criterion, 1994).

22. See Robin Lane Fox, *Pagans and Christians* (Hammonworth: Penguin, 1987), 377. Cf. Guy G. Stroumsa, *Barbarian Philosophy: The Religious Revolution of Early Christianity* (Tübingen: Mohr Siebeck, 1999), 214.

23. See Menahem Stern, *Greek and Roman Authors on Jews and Judaism*, vol. 2 (Jerusalem: Israel Academy of Sciences and Humanities, 1980), 206–216. For a discussion of the problem and essential references, see Hugo Rahner, *Griechische Mythen in christlicher Deutung* (Freiburg; Basel; Vienna: Herder, 1992 [first ed. Zurich: Rhein-Verlag, 1945]), 242–243. For a classical study of possible contacts between Hebrew and Greek thought in antiquity, see Thorleif Borman, *Hebrew Thought Compared with Greek* (Philadelphia: Westminster, 1960).

24. See Martin Bernal, *Black Athena: The Afroasiatic Roots of Classical Civilization*, vol 1, *The Fabrication of Ancient Greece, 1785–1985* (New Brunswick: Rutgers University Press, 1987), esp. 335–366.

25. See, for instance, Walter Burkert, *The Orientalizing Revolution: Near Eastern Influence on Greek Culture in the Early Archaic Age* (Cambridge, Mass.: Harvard

University Press, 1992) as well as "Oriental and Greek Mythology: The Meeting of Parallels," in *Interpetations of Greek Mythology*, ed. Jan N. Bremmer (London: Routledge,1987), 10–40.

26. On the polemics around the biblical canon, see, for instance, François Laplanche, "Le canon de l'Ancien Testament dans la controverse entre catholiques et protestants au XVIIe. siècle. Le point de vue de Grotius," in *La formation des canons scripturaires*, ed. Michel Tardieu (Paris: Cerf, 1993), 107–122. See further his *La Bible en France entre mythe et critique, XVIe-XIXe siècle* (Paris: Albin Michel, 1994).

27. Stroumsa, *Barbarian Philosophy,* 27–43.

28. For an instance of a pedagogical book on this topic written by a priest, see P. L. Thomassin, *Méthode d'étudier les lettres humaines et les Écritures* (Paris, 1681), where one learns to detect the traces of Scripture in Homer. Cf., later, G. de Lavau, *Histoire de la fable conférée avec l'histoire sainte* (1730). On Thomassin, see Bruno Neveu, *Erudition et religion aux XVIIe et XVIIIe siècles* (Paris: Albin Michel, 1994), 371–373.

29. See Bruno Neveu, "L'érudition ecclésiastique du XVIIe siècle et la nostalgie de l'Antiquité chrétienne," in his *Erudition et religion aux XVIIe et XVIIIe siècle,* 334–363.

30. On Spencer, see chapter IV.2 below.

31. See Grafton, "Scaliger's Chronology: Philology, Astronomy, World History," in Grafton, *Defenders of the Text,* 104–144 and notes.

32. See Richard Simon's text in Le Brun and Stroumsa, *Les juifs présentés aux chrétiens.*

33. For a classical example, see Bernard de Fontenelle, *De l'origine des fables* (a work published in 1724, but written in the last decade of the seventeenth century). On Fontenelle's book, see James S. Preus, *Explaining Religion* (New Haven and London: Yale University Press, 1987), 40–55. On "fable" as the equivalent of "myth" in the seventeenth century, see Laplanche, *La Bible en France entre mythe et critique, XVIe-XIXe siècle,* 137. Cf. Jean Starobinski, "Fable et mythologie aux 17e et 18e siècles," in *Dictionnaire des mythologies*, ed. Yves Bonnefoy (Paris: Flammarion, 1981), 390–400. See also Peter G. Bietenholz, *Historia and Fabula: Myths and Legends in Historical Thought from Antiquity to the Modern Age* (Brill's Studies in Intellectual History; Leiden; New York; Köln: Brill, 1994), 222–232 (on Richard Simon).

34. The entry "Mythologie" in Diderot and D'Alembert's *Encyclopédie* (Paris, 1751–1765) is based on a text written by the polymath Nicolas Fréret (1688–1749), and adapted by Jaucourt; as an adolescent, Fréret had already begun the redaction of a *Dictionnaire mythologique*. On eighteenth-century discussions of mythology, see further Burton Feldman and Robert D. Richardson, Jr., *The Rise of Modern Mythology* (Bloomington, IN: Indiana University Press, 2000).

35. So, also, Charles de Brosses, *Du culte des dieux fétiches* (Geneva, 1760), where the author compares primitive religion ("la religion sauvage") as described in ethnological observation to Egyptian or Israelite religion. See Frank E. Manuel, *The Eighteenth Century Confronts the Gods* (Cambridge, Mass.: Harvard University Press, 1959), 184–209. Cf. Epilogue, n. 6, below.

36. In his preface, the author writes: "Phoeniciae enimverro originis esse grae-corum nationem, linguam, ritus, plerosque et caeremonias." In the eighteenth century, Robert Wood maintained that *Delphi Phoenicizantes* was plagiarized from a manuscript found at Merton College in Oxford, according to George J. Toomer, *Eastern Wisedome and Learning: The Study of Arabic in Seventeenth-Century England* (Oxford: Clarendon Press, 1996), 67.

37. Full title: *Homeros Hebraios, sive Historia Hebraeorum ab Homero Hebraicis nominibus ac sententiis conscripta in Odyssea et Iliade* (Dordrecht, 1704).

38. In his *Historia Ecclesiastica Veteri Testamenti*, published in 1715, the German Church historian Johannes Buddeus, compares the sacrifice of Isaac to that of Iphigenia. Similarly, the Protestant Hebraist Louis Cappel identified Iphigenia and Jiphtigenia (Jephtah's daughter), while for Petau the siege of Troy had happened under Yair, a few years before Jephtah. See P. Jurieu, *Histoire critique des dogmes et des cultes* . . . (Amsterdam, 1704), 202.

39. "Explication d'un Passage d'Homère; où l'on éclaircit en même temps quelques endroits de l'Écriture Sainte," *Histoire Critique de la République des Lettres*, IV (1713), pp. 150–164.

40. *Histoire Critique de la République des Lettres* V (1714), p. 258.

41. This reference is given by Wilfred Cantwell Smith, *What Is Scripture? A Comparative Approach* (Minneapolis: Fortress, 1993), 193.

42. I quote according to the second edition Guérin du Rocher, *Hérodote historien du people hébreu sans le savoir* (Liège, 1790).

43. François Laplanche, *La Bible en France: entre mythe et critique, XVIe-XIXe siècle*, 35–38.

44. Ernest Renan, *Revue des deux mondes* (November 1865): 239; quoted by Georges Gusdorf, *La révolution galiléenne [Les sciences humaines et la pensée occidentale, III], II* (Paris: Payot, 1969), 364.

45. Full title: *De dispertione gentium et terrarum divisione facta in aedificatione turris Babel)* and *Canaan (De coloniis et sermone Phoenicium* . . .), which first appeared together in 1682. *Phaleg* had already been published in 1645.

46. Victor Bérard, *Les phéniciens et l'Odyssée* I (Paris: Armand Colin, 1902), 119–120, quoted by Noémi Hepp, *Homère en France au XVIIe siècle* (Paris: Klincksieck, 1968), 307.

47. *Memoirs; or, The Life of Pierre Daniel Huet,* trans. from Latin (2 vols., London, 1810), 32.

48. Alphonse Dupront, *Pierre-Daniel Huet et l'exégèse comparatiste au XVIIe siècle* (Paris: Leroux, 1930), 45. On Huet, see now April G. Shelford, *Transforming the Republic of Letters: Pierre-Daniel Huet and European Intellectual Life, 1650–1720* (Rochester, N.Y.: Rochester University Press, 2007), *non vidi.*

49. Dupront, *Pierre-Daniel Huet*, 254.

50. Pierre-Daniel Huet, *Lettre-traité sur les origines du roman* (ed. du tricentenaire; Paris, 1971), 51. For further discussion on Huet, see below, ch. IV.1.

51. Claude Fleury, *Moeurs des Israélites*, 8–9.

52. Ibid., 1.

53. This text appeared only in *Les Oeuvres d'Homère, traduites en français par Mme. Dacier, avec supplément,* 7 vols. (Amsterdam, 1731). Cf. Noémi Hepp, *Deux*

amis d'Homère au XVIIe. siècle; textes inédits de Paul Pélisson et de Claude Fleury (Paris: Klincksieck, 1970).

54. In this, he is very different from Richard Simon, as noted by Jacques Le Brun, "Richard Simon," *Supplément au Dictionnaire de la Bible* XII (Paris: Letouzey et Ané, 1996), 1353–1383.

55. Ibid., 1359–1363.

56. Fénelon, *Oeuvres, I,* Introduction, XVIII (La Pléiade: NRF; Paris: Gallimard, 1983).

57. See Francois Gaquère, *La vie et les oeuvres de Claude Fleury (1640–1723)* (Paris: Gigord, 1925), 354. See also Raymond E. Wanner, *Claude Fleury (1640–1723) as an Educational Historiographer and Thinker* (Archives Internationales d'Histoire des Idées 76; La Haye: Nijhoff, 1975).

58. Texts quoted by D. M. Foerster, *Homer in English Criticism* (New Haven: Yale University Press, 1947), 20.

59. See also her pamphlet, Anne Dacier, *Des causes de la corruption du goût* (1714), published as a reaction to the modernized translation of Homer published the same year by Houard de la Motte.

60. Preface to *L'Iliade d'Homère,* XLVII (I quote according to *Iliade, traduite en français par Madame Dacier* [Paris, 1756]).

61. See Hepp, *Homère en France au XVIIe siècle,* 645; for various other examples, see ibid., 306–334.

62. See Gustavo Costa, *La critica Omerica di Thomas Blackwell (1701–1757)* (Florence: Sansoni, 1959), 36.

63. Thomas Blackwell, *An Enquiry into the Life and Writings of Homer* (London, 1735), section I.3.

64. Ibid., 84.

65. Ibid., 219–220.

66. See below, ch. IV.1.

67. Thomas Blackwell, *Letters Concerning Mythology* (London, 1748), letter 18.

68. See K. Simonsuuri, *Homer's Original Genius: Eighteenth-Century Notions of the Early Greek Epic (1688–1798)* (Cambridge: Cambridge University Press, 1979), 114.

69. Robert Wood, *Essay on the Original Genius and Writings of Homer, with a comparative view on the ancient and present state of the Troade* (London, 1775), 7, 46, 130, 156.

70. Donald M. Foerster, *Homer in English Criticism: The Historical Approach in the Eighteenth Century* (Yale Studies in English, 105; New Haven: Yale University Press, 1947), 108.

71. See Anthony Grafton, "Prolegomena to Friedrich August Wolf," in Grafton, *Defenders of the Text,* 214–243 and notes.

72. Ibid., 112. On Heyne, see Axel E.-A. Horstmann, "Mythologie und Altertumswissenschaft: der Mythosbegriff bei Christian Gottlob Heyne," *Archiv für Begriffsgeschichte* 16 (1972), 60–85.

73. See Ch. Hartlich and W. Sachs, *Der Ursprung des Mythosbegriffes in den modernen Bibelwissenschaft* (Tübingen: Mohr, 1952). On the origins of biblical

criticism, see H.-J. Kraus, *Geschichte der historisch-kritischen Erforschung des Alten Testaments* (Neukirchen, Vluyn: Neukirchner Verlag, 1982 [first ed. 1956]). Hartlich and Sachs note that Lowth's study of biblical poetry prepared the way for the concept of myth in biblical criticism.

III. FROM BIBLICAL PHILOLOGY TO THE STUDY OF JUDAISM

1. That such a project seemed threatening, even to theological scholars, is reflected in the title of a work by Johannes Buxtorf junior, the *Anticritica* (published in 1648), in which he defended a literal understanding of the notion of inspiration for the Old Testament text, vowels included.

2. Ernest Renan in the *Revue des Deux Mondes* (November 1865): 240. Cf. also Georges Gusdorf, *La révolution galiléenne,* vol. 2 (Paris: Payot, 1969), who compares Simon not only to Spinoza but also to Erasmus.

3. See Jacques Le Brun, "Richard Simon," *Supplément au Dictionnaire de la Bible* XII (Paris: Letouzey et Ané, 1996), 1370.

4. On Brerewood, see chapter I.2 above.

5. See chapter I, n. 60, above.

6. In Richard Simon's preface to Jerome Dandini's *Voyage au Mont Liban.* (Paris, 1675); quoted by Le Brun, "Richard Simon," 1370.

7. "Nous sommes dans un temps où l'on s'applique à la réunion des religions."

8. It is also in the context of this intense Catholic interest for oriental Christianities that one should understand his claim: "Les Catholiques sont plus habiles dans les langues orientales et dans la Critique que les Protestants." R. Simon [Le Prieur de Bolleville], *Réponse au livre intitulé Sentimens de quelques théologiens de Hollande sur l'Histoire Critique du Vieux Testament* (Rotterdam, 1686), 18. It is a fact that neither the Renaissance nor the Reformation showed much interest in the cults and cultures of the newly discovered worlds.

9. Girolamo Dandini, *Missione apostolica al Patriarcha e Maroniti del Monte Libano . . . e la sua pellagrinazione a Gierusalemme* (Cesena, 1656). Cf. the French translation, *Voyage au Mont Liban . . . avec des remarques sur la théologie des chrétiens du Levant, et sur celle des Mahométans* (par R. S. P. [Richard Simon] (Paris, 1675).

10. Ibid., ch. 12, 60.

11. Jérome Dandini, *Voyage au Mont Liban* (Paris, 1675).

12. "Comme le Mohammetisme est un mélange de la Religion juive et de la Religion chrétienne, l'on ne doit point être surpris de voir parmy les Turcs plusieurs choses qui s'observent parmy nous. Ceux qui ont une connaissance parfaite de ces deux religions peuvent montrer facilement l'origine de la plupart des cérémonies Mahometanes." Simon writes this key sentence in the "remarks" that follow his translation of Dandini's book.

13. Richard Simon, *Additions aux Recherches curieuses sur la diversité des langues et des religions d'Edward Brerewood,* ed. Jacques Le Brun and John D. Woodbridge (Paris: Presses Universitaires de France, 1983), 76–78.

14. This is clearly a rendering of the Qur'anic *al-amr bi'l-ma'rûf wa'l-nahy 'an al-munkar.* On this fundamental concept of Islamic ethics, see Michael A. Cook,

Commanding Right and Forbidding Wrong in Islamic Thought (Cambridge: Cambridge University Press, 2000).

15. Ibid., 80–81.

16. Ibid., 82, and n. 47.

17. See C. S. M. Rademaker, *The Life and Works of Gerardus Ioannes Vossius (1577–1649)* (Aassen: van Gorcum, 1981). On Vossius, see above, ch. I.2.

18. "Réponse au live intitulé Sentimens de quelques théologiens de Hollande," in Richard Simon, *De l'inspiration des livres sacrés* (Paris, 1686), 201.

19. In the preface to the *Histoire critique du Vieux Testament*, Simon had accused Vossius and the Protestants in general of ignorance of Hebraica, as well as of being "demi-juifs."

20. Incidentally, the study of the Jewish parallels to the New Testament had begun already at the beginning of the century, following a polemic in Germany and Holland about the language of the New Testament. Should one apply to the language of the New Testament aesthetic criteria similar to those used for pagan Greek literature? The argument that this would be mistaken was supported by the identification of Hebraisms in New Testament Greek, as in, for instance, Johann Vorstius's *Philologia sacra seu commentatio de hebraismo Novi Testamenti* (Leiden, 1658). See Gottschalk E. Guhrauer, *Joachim Jungius und sein Zeitalter* (Stuttgart, Tübingen, 1850), 112–121. By far the most important opus remains John Lightfoot's *Horae hebraicae et talmudicae* (Cambridge, 1674).

21. *Histoire critique du Vieux Testament* (Paris, 1680), ch. 17.

22. "l'un des pères de la méthode ethnologique." See Arnold van Gennep, "Nouvelles recherches sur l'histoire en France de la méthode ethnographique, Claude Guichard, Richard Simon, Claude Fleury," *Revue de l'Histoire des Religions* 82 (1920): 139–162. *Les rites de passage* was first published in Paris in 1909.

23. In the *Histoire critique du texte du Nouveau Testament.* (Paris, 1689).

24. See ch. II.1 above.

25. See in particular Mark R. Cohen, trans., ed., *The Autobiography of a Seventeenth-Century Rabbi: Leon Modena's Life of Judah* (Princeton: Princeton University Press, 1988).

26. A reprint of the 1678 Venice edition was published in Bologna in 1979. On the book and its context, see M. R. Cohen, "Leone da Modena's *Riti*: Seventeenth-Century Plea for Social Toleration of Jews," *Jewish Social Studies* 34 (1972): 287–319.

27. In addition to Simon's translation, it appeared in two English translations, in Dutch, in Latin, and later in Russian. See Le Brun and Stroumsa, *Les juifs présentés aux chrétiens* (Paris: Les Belles Lettres, 1998), introduction.

28. See préface générale, *Cérémonies et coutumes religieuses de tous les peuples du monde*, 3.

29. I quote here according to the original edition. See the new edition of both Modena's *Riti* (in Simon's French translation) and Simon's *Cérémonies* by Le Brun and Stroumsa, *Les juifs présentés aux chrétiens*. In the first and second editions, Simon's essay is printed on more than two hundred pages.

30. For the best introduction to Simon, see Le Brun, "Richard Simon." See also Le Brun in *Grundriss der Geschichte de Philosophie, Die Philosophie des 17.*

Jahrhundert, Band 2: Frankreich und Niederlande, ed. Jean-Pierre Schobinger (Basel: Schwabe, 1993), 1013–1018.

31. See P. M. Beaude, "Richard Simon: critique et théologie," in *Kecharitoménè: Mélanges René Laurentin* (Paris: Desclée, 1990), 71–84, esp. 81: "Simon inaugure un regard de type 'ethnologique' et non plus 'théologique' " on Jewish culture.

32. On the relationships between Simon, Isaac de la Peyrère, and Spinoza, see Paul Auvray, *Richard Simon (1638–1712): Etude bio-bibliographique avec des textes inédits* (Paris: Presses Universitaires de France, 1974), 62–64. On Diderot and Lessing, see J. D. Woodbridge, "German Responses to the Biblical Critic Richard Simon: From Leibniz to J. S. Semler," in *Wolfenbütteler Forschungen* 41 (1988): 65–87, esp. 68–71. On Voltaire's knowledge of Simon, see Miriam Yardeni, "La vision des juifs et du judaïsme," *Revue des Etudes Juives* 129 (1970): 179, n. 4.

33. Le Brun, "Richard Simon," 1380.

34. On points of biography, see Jean Steinmann, *Richard Simon et les origines de la critique biblique* (Paris: Desclée de Brouwer, 1960).

35. See Karl-Heinz Kohl, *Entzauberter Blick: das Bild vom Guten Wilden und die Erfahrung der Zivilisation* (Berlin: Medusa, 1981), 43ff.

36. See, for instance, Francis Schmidt, "Arzareth en Amérique: l'autorité du *Quatrième Livre d'Esdras* dans la discussion sur la parenté des Juifs et des Indiens (1540–1729)," in *Moïse géographe: Recherches sur les représentations juives et chrétiennes de l'espace,* eds. Alain Desreumaux and Francis Schmidt (Paris, 1988), 155–201.

37. For Simon's great interest in the Christian Orient, see his *Additions aux Recherches curieuses,* where eleven chapters are devoted to the various Eastern Churches. See J. Le Brun and J. Woodbridge, *Additions aux Recherches curieuses d'Edward Brerewood.*

38. The "Querelle des Rites" is discussed at length in ch. VII.1 below.

39. Cf. ch. II.2.

40. "espèce de mythologie comme parmi les paiens," 20; I quote according to the second edition, Paris 1684.

41. See François Laplanche, *La Bible en France entre mythe et critique, XVIe-XIXe siècle* (Paris: Albin Michel, 1994), 38–40.

42. R. Simon, *Comparaison des Cérémonies des Juifs et de la discipline de l'Eglise* (Paris, 1681), 105. On the myths invented by the pagan poets, see 22–23.

43. Ibid., 22–23.

44. On Simon's concept of revelation, see William McKane, *Selected Christian Hebraists* (Cambridge: Cambridge University Press, 1989).

45. "Ce fut la raison qui obligea nôtre Seigneur d'attaquer non seulement les Saducéens qui détrusaient la meilleure partie de la Religion Juive, en rejettant toutes les Traditions, mais aussi les Pharisiens qui avaient rendu ridicule la religion de leurs Pères, en multipliant ces mêmes traditions par des subtilitez trop éloignées du Texte de la Loy. Voila à mon avis l'origine de toutes ces fables, et de ces vaines allégories qui se trouvent aujourd'hui dans les Livres du Talmud." R. Simon, *Comparaison,* 111. On p. 105, he says about the Gemara that "elle est remplie d'une infinité de questions inutiles et d'histoires, ou plûtot de contes faits à plaisir . . ."

46. "Notre Seigneur imita le Rite Juif," ibid., 80.

47. Ibid., 72.

48. Ibid., 121.

49. Ibid., 90.

50. "Ils ne peuvent examiner ces rêveries sans tomber dans l'hérésie des Cara-ïtes," ibid., 106.

51. See Giuliano Tamani, "Il caraismo nella cultura europea del seicento e del settecento," *Annali della facolta' di lingue e letterature straniere di Ca' Foscari,* 16 (1977): Serie orientale 8, 1–17.

52. On Simon's work on the Hebrew Bible and on his combination of philological boldness and Catholic conservatism, see McKane, *Selected Christian Hebraists,* 111–150.

53. Steinman, *Richard Simon,* 215–221. On Simon's attitude toward Karaism, see ibid., 58, 74–75. See further Joseph Kaplan, "'Karaites' in Early Eighteenth-Century Amsterdam," in *Sceptics, Millenarians, and Jews,* eds. David S. Katz and Jonathan I Israel (Brill's Studies in Intellectual History 17; Leiden; Köln; New York: Brill, 1990), 196–236, esp. 221–229.

54. "Comme la Religion Chrétienne ne diffère point en substance de celle des Juifs . . ." Ibid., 87.

55. Ibid., 87.

56. "une science chimérique sans aucun fondement," ibid., 22–23.

57. Ibid., 39.

58. Ibid., 20.

59. "les merveilles de la Cabale pratique," ibid., 137.

60. Ibid., 24–28, 31.

61. "Il n'y en a pas un de bon sens," ibid., 129–130.

62. Yardeni, "La vision des juifs et du judaïsme," 199.

63. Ibid., 123–124.

64. "Richard Simon mérite notre attention pour avoir été un des premiers à comprendre quelle serait dans le monde moderne la situation des religions du livre." This is the concluding sentence of his "Sens et portée du retour aux origines dans l'oeuvre de Richard Simon," *XVIIe Siècle* 33 (1981): 185–198.

65. Gusdorf, *La révolution galiléenne,* 364.

IV. BIBLICAL MYTH, RELIGIOUS HISTORY, AND IDOLATRY

1. See Jean Baruzi, *Leibniz et l'organisation religieuse de la terre* (Paris: Alcan, 1907).

2. On intellectual approaches to the origins of humankind, see Claudine Poulouin, *Le temps des origines: l'Eden, le Déluge et "les temps reculés" de Pascal à l'Encyclopédie* (Paris: Champion, 1998). See further Jacques Solé, "Newton et les fils de Noé: la théologie des gentils vue par les chrétiens (1670–1680)," in *Les religions du paganisme antique dans l'Europe chrétienne, XVI-XVIIIs* (Paris: Presses de l'Université de Paris-Sorbonne, 1988), 75–80. See further Martin Mulsow and Jan Assmann, eds., *Sintflut und Gedächtnis: Erinnern und Vergessen des Ursprungs* (Munich: Wilhelm Fink Verlag, 2006).

3. See the classical monograph of Don Cameron Allen, *The Legend of Noah: Renaissance Rationalism in Art, Science, and Letters* (Urbana, Ill., 1949). On another central myth of Genesis and its place in the history of Western culture, see Arno Borst, *Der Turmbau von Babel*, 4 vols. (Stuttgart: Hiersemann, 1957–1963).

4. On the history of the concept of nature and its relationship with truth, see Pierre Hadot, *Le voile d'Isis: Essai sur l'idée de nature* (Paris: Gallimard, 2004), passim. English trans., *The Veil of Isis: An Essay on the History of the Idea of Nature* (Cambridge, Mass.: Harvard University Press, 2006).

5. See in particular Gregorio Garcia, O.P., *Origen de los Indios de el Nuevo Mundo, e Indias Occidentales* (Valencia, 1607). See further Fay Luis de León, *Escritos sobre America* (Clássicos del pensiamento 141; Madrid: Tecnos, 1999), with an introductory essay by Andres Moreno Mengibar and Juan Martos Fernández, esp. "Nuevo mundo y exégesis bíblica," ix–xviii.

6. On Ophir and the history of its identification in early modern scholarship, see Dom Augustin Calmet, *Comentaire littéral sur l'Ancien et le Nouveau Testament*, vol. 1, (Genèse) (Paris, 1707), "Dissertation sur le Pays d'Ophir," 32–41.

7. See also Thomas Thorowgood, *Iewes in America, or Probabilities that the Americans Are of that Race* (London, 1650), and George Hornius, *De originibus Americanis libri quatuor* (1652). A Jewish intellectual of the stature of Menasseh Ben Israel shared that approach.

8. Hugo Grotius, *De veritate religionis christianae, Opera Omnia Theologica*, vol. 3 (Basel, 1732), 18–20.

9. Bossuet, *Discours sur l'histoire universelle* (Paris, 1681), 11.

10. Their monographs were republished by Biagio Ugolini, *Thesaurus Antiquitatum Sacrarum*, vol. VII (Venice, 1747). On Ugolini, see A. Vivian, "Biagio Ugolini et son *Thesaurus Antiquitatum Sacrarum*: Bilan des études juives au milieu du XVIIIe siècle," in *La République des Lettres et l'histoire du judaïsme antique (XVIe.– XVIIIe. S)*, eds. Christine Grell and François Laplanche (Paris: Presses de l'Université de Paris-Sorbonne, 1992), 115–147. Zur Shalev has discovered some unpublished drafts of Bochart's treatise on paradise, both in French and Latin, and intends to publish them.

11. On comparative chronology, see in particular Anthony Grafton, "Scaliger's Chronology: Philology, Astronomy, World History," in his *Defenders of the Text: The Taditions of Scholarship in an Age of Science, 1450–1800* (Cambridge, Mass.: Harvard University Press, 1991), 104–144. Cf. ch. II.1 above.

12. See below, pt. 2, in this chapter.

13. *La saincte géographie* bears the following subtitle: *c'est-à-dire, exacte description de la terre, et véritable démonstration du paradis terrestre, depuis la création du Monde jusques à maintenant: selon le sens littéral de la saincte Ecriture, et selon la doctrine des Saincts Pères et Docteurs de l'Eglise*. On this work, see Solé, *Les mythes chrétiens de la Renaissance aux Lumières*, 117–118, and Poulouin, *Le temps des origines*, 237–244.

14. In his "The Phoenicians Are Coming!" (see n. 22 below) Zur Shalev points out that Bochart does not mention d'Auzoles's work, taking this as "a mark of distaste for this kind of scholarship."

15. On Selden's work, see ch. II. 1, above.

16. Also in the mid-seventeenth century, Alexander Ross, who demonstrates his broad anthropological knowledge on all known religions of Asia, Africa, and the Americas, remains unable to go beyond a phenomenological description of the different cults in his *Pansebeia; or, A View of All Religions in the World*. See ch. I. 2 above.

17. On Bochart and his work, see Poulouin, *Le temps des origines*, 106–128.

18. Bernard Hemmerdinger, "Pour un nouveau Bochart," *Parole de l'Orient* 5 (1974): 395–399.

19. François Laplanche, *La Bible en France entre mythe et critique* (16e.-19e. s.) (Paris, 1994), 35–38.

20. Ernest Renan, "L'exégèse biblique et l'esprit français," *Revue des Deux Mondes* (November 1865): 239.

21. On Bochart's importance for the history of linguistics, see Daniel Droixhe, *La linguistique et l'appel de l'histoire (1600–1800)* (Genève, 1978), 38–39, 46–47.

22. Zur Shalev, "Orientalism, Geography, and Biblical Antiquity in Seventeenth-Century Protestant Scholarship: The Case of Samuel Bochart's *Geographia sacra* (1646)," forthcoming. See also the chapter on Bochart in his doctoral dissertation, *Geographia Sacra: Cartography, Religion, and Scholarship in the Sixteenth and Seventeenth Centuries* (Princeton University, 2003), which adds much to our understanding of the circumstances of the redaction and publication of Bochart's book, and of its reception.

23. I have read Huet's autobiography in the English translation, *Memoirs of the Life of Peter Daniel Huet, Written by Himself* (2 vols., London, 1810), vol. 1, 36ff.

24. "Mosem esse Theut Aegyptium, conditamque ab eo Hermopolin urbem . . . Theuth autem ille, sive Thoth, is ipse est Phoenicum Tautates Gallorum, Theuth sive Wodan Germanorum, Tiis Danorum, Teves Anglorum."

25. See Alphonse Dupront, *Pierre-Daniel Huet et l'exégèse comparatiste au XVIIe siècle* (Paris: Leroux, 1930), 61. On Huet, see further Elena Rapetti, *Pierre-Daniel Huet: Erudizione, filologia, apologetica* (Milan: Vita e pensiero, 1999) *(non vidi)*.

26. See Dupront, *Pierre-Daniel Huet*, 159–164.

27. On Acosta's work, see ch. I.1, above.

28. Dupront, *Pierre-Daniel Huet*, 167–170.

29. See Klaus Müller, *Tora für die Völker: Die noachidischen Gebote und Ansätze zu ihrer Rezeption im Christentum* (Studien zu Kirche und Israel, 15; Berlin: Institut Kirche und Judentum, 1994), 219–237. See further Steven S. Schwartzschild, "Do Noachites Have to Believe in Revelation?" *Jewish Quarterly Review* (1962): 297–308, and (1963): 30–65. On Selden, see Richard Tuck, *Natural Rights Theories: Their Origin and Development* (Cambridge: Cambridge University Press, 1979), 35.

30. N. A. Pluche, *Histoire du ciel, considéré selon les idées des poëtes, des philosophes, et de Moïse,* 2 vols. (Paris, 1739).

31. See ch. I.1, above. Some sophisticated discussions of the concept of idolatry, including attempts at new definitions, occur already among sixteenth-century missionaries to the Americas, such as Bartolomé de Las Casas and José de Acosta. See

Sabine MacCormack, *Religion in the Andes: Vision and Imagination in Early Colonial Peru* (Princeton: Princeton University Press, 1992), 265–266.

32. Oddly enough, "idolatry" does not appear in the index of the excellent anthology of Burton Feldman and Robert D. Richardson, Jr., *The Rise of Modern Mythology* (Bloomington, IN: Indiana University Press, 2000). Moshe Halbertal and Avishai Margalit, *Idolatry* (Cambridge, Mass.: Harvard University Press, 1992), does not deal with this issue.

33. See, for instance, Thomas Tenison, *On Idolatry: A Discourse* (London, 1678). Like John Spencer, Tenison was a Fellow of Corpus Christi College, Cambridge. Another example is that of Etienne Fourmont (1683–1745), a versatile scholar who became professor of Arabic at the Collège de France. On Fourmont, see, for instance, Feldman and Richardson Jr., *The Rise of Modern Mythology*, 83–85. On the notion of idolatry in seventeenth-century scholarship, see, for instance, H. Pinard de la Boullaye, *L'étude comparée des religions*, vol. 1 (Paris: Beauchesne, 1929), 168–175. On "idolatry," more specifically, in the English context, see Peter Harrison, *"Religion" and the Religions in the English Enlightenment* (Cambridge: Cambridge University Press, 1990), 45–58.

34. William Robertson Smith, *The Religion of the Semites: The Fundamental Institutions* (New York: Schocken, 1972 [1st ed. 1888–1891]), preface to the 1st ed., xiii; cf. ix, and also *Dictionary of National Biography*, xviii, 767, s.v. Spencer.

35. Aharon Katchen, *Christian Hebraists and Dutch Rabbis: Seventeenth-Century Apologetics and the Study of Maimonides'* Mishneh Torah (Cambridge, Mass.: Harvard University Press, 1979), 24.

36. The term (in Greek) appears in John Selden, *De Diis Syris* (London, 1617).

37. On the importance of Fontenelle's work for the study of religion, see James S. Preus, *Explaining Religion* (New Haven and London: Yale University Press, 1987), 40–55.

38. This trait of Protestant anti-Catholic polemics would however become weakened toward the end of the seventeenth century, as reflected, for instance, in the words of the Huguenot theologian Pierre Jurieu: "Autrefois, quand on nous attaquait, nous attaquions à notre tour. Si l'on nous accusait de schisme et d'hérésie, nous accusions nos accusateurs d'idolâtrie et de superstition; mais ce règne est passé il y a longtemps." *Préjugés légitimes contre le papisme* (2 vols.; Amsterdam, 1685), preface, 1.

39. The dissertation is inserted in the fifth volume of Augustin Calmet's *Commentaire littéral sur tous les livres de l'Ancien et du Nouveau Testament*, vol. 5 (Paris, 1726), 130–136. On "idolatry," see Jonathan Sheehan, "Sacred and Profane: Idolatry, Antiquarianism, and the Polemics of Distinction in the Seventeenth Century," *Past and Present* 192 (2006): 35–66.

40. See Grotius, *Opera omnia theologica*; London, 1689, 3 vols.; *avodah zarah*, 1, 39–43; on Exodus 20: 4–5.

41. See Avital Wohlman, *Maïmonide et Thomas d'Aquin: un dialogue exemplaire* (Paris: Cerf, 1988), and J. Schwarz, *Meister Eckhart reads Maimonides* (Tel Aviv: Alma, 2002), in Hebrew. See further Görge K. Hasselhoff, *Dicit Rabbi Moyses: Studien zum Bild von Moses Maimonides im lateinischen Western vom 13. bis zum 15. Jahrhundert* (Würzburg: Königshausen & Neumann, 2004), and G. K. Hasselhoff

and Ottfried Fraisse, *Moses Maimonides (1138–2004): His Religious, Scientific, and Philosophical* Wirkungsgeschichte *in Different Cultural Contexts* (Würzburg: Ergon, 2004).

42. "Scito igitur, plures mihi ejus librum quam si *isometron chryson* misisti." Joseph Justus Scaliger, *Epistolae omnes* (Frankfurt, 1628), Epistola LXII, 177–180. Cf. M. Kayserling, "Les hébraïsants chrétiens du XVIIe siècle," *Revue des Etudes Juives* 20 (1890): 261–268, referring to *Epistolae,* 465.

43. Peter T. van Rooden, *Theology, Biblical Scholarship, and Rabbinical Studies in the Seventeenth Century: Constantijn L'Empereur (1591–1648), Professor of Hebrew at Leiden* (Leiden; New York: Brill, 1987).

44. See François Dreyfus, "La condescendance divine *(synkatabasis)* comme principe herméneutique de l'Ancien Testament dans la tradition juive et dans la tradition chrétienne," Suppl. to *Vetus Testamentum* 36 (19): 96–107. On Maimonides' "gracious ruse," see below.

45. On possible links between Maimonides and the patristic tradition via Arabic Christian texts, see Shlomo Pines, "Some Traits of Christian Theological Writing in Relation to Moslem Kalam and to Jewish Thought," *Proceedings of the Israel Academy of Sciences,* vol. 4 (1973), 4–6. Dreyfus ("La condescendance") finds Pines's suggestions unconvincing, but with rather weak arguments, and he does not suggest any other channel of influence, thinking rather that the similarities stem from the same interpretative problems and methods.

46. On the Sabians, see Tamara M. Green, *The City of the Moon God: Religious Traditions of Harran* (Religions of the Greco-Roman World 114; Leiden; Brill, 1992). See further Sarah Stroumsa, *Maimonides in His World,* 84–105.

47. On Ibn Waḥshiyya, see Toufic Fahd, in *Encyclopedia of Islam,* vol. 3, 963–965.

48. Reflecting the Hebrew translation *avodah mitsrit* (Egyptian agriculture) by the twelfth-century Abraham Ibn Ezra. The slip from "Nabathean" to "Egyptian" has been explained long ago by Moritz Steinschneider as stemming from the graphic similarity between *nabatiyya* (Nabatean) and *qubtiyya* (Egyptian) in Arabic script.

49. *Answer to the Jewish Part of Mr. Selden's History of Tithes* (Oxford, 1625), 46–47.

50. The Maimonidean moment in seventeenth-century thought, however, is underlined by Amos Funkenstein, *Theology and Scientific Imagination from the Middle Ages to the Seventeenth Century* (Princeton: Princeton University Press, 1981), which I quote according to the French translation, *Théologie et imagination scientifique* (Paris: Presses Universitaires de France, 1995), 274: "it was in the seventeenth century, rather than in the Middle Ages, that Maimonides' theory had the most powerful influence." For further aspects of Maimonides' influence in the seventeenth century, see ch. II.1, above.

51. R. H. Popkin, "Some Further Comments on Newton and Maimonides," in *Essays on the Context, Nature, and Influence of Isaac Newton's Theology,* eds. J. E. Force and R. H. Popkin (Archives Internationales d'Histoire des Idées, 129; Boston; London: Kluwer, 1990), 1.

52. Although this major text achieved a significant circulation in early modern Europe, it would not be published before the late nineteenth century.

53. G. Lloyd Jones, *The Discovery of Hebrew in Tudor England: A Third Language* (Manchester: Manchester University Press, 1983), 181, 214.

54. On Spencer, see *Dictionary of National Biography*, vol. 18, 766–768.

55. I am quoting from the third and better edition, John Spencer, *De legibus Hebraeorum ritualibus* (Tübingen, 1732). In this edition, the text is introduced by C. M. Pfaff's detailed Latin study of the international controversy aroused by Spencer's book.

56. Steven D. Benin, "The 'Cunning of God' and Divine Accommodation," *Journal of the History of Ideas* 45 (1984): 179–191.

57. Henning Graf Reventlow, *The Authority of the Bible and the Rise of the Modern World* (London, SCM, 1984), 568–569, n. 31, refers to G. V. Lechler, *Geschichte des englischen Deismus* (Stuttgart, 1841), 137–139, as the first in modern times to draw attention to Spencer's *De legibus hebraeorum ritualibus*.

58. François Laplanche, *L'Ecriture, le sacré et l'histoire: érudits et politiques protestants devant la Bible en France au dix-septième siècle* (Amsterdam; Maarssen: Holland University Press, 1986), 615.

59. See Funkenstein, *Théologie et imagination scientifique*, 276.

60. Francis Schmidt, "Des inepties tolérables: la raison des rites de John Spencer (1685) à W. Robertson Smith (1889)," *Archives de Sciences Sociales des Religions* 85 (1994): 121–136. Jan Assmann, *Moses the Egyptian: The Memory of Egypt in Western Monotheism* (Cambridge, Mass.: Harvard University Press, 1997), ch. 5, "Before the Law," 55–90.

61. See I. Abrahams, "The Purchase of Hebrew Books by the English Parliament in 1647," *The Jewish Historical Society of England, Transactions*, vol. 7 (1915–1917), 62–77.

62. On this literature, see Jacob Heinemann, *The Reasons of the Commandments in Jewish Literature* (2 vols.; Jerusalem, 1956; in Hebrew). Cf. Alexander Altmann, "Commandments, Reasons for," *Encyclopedia Judaica*, vol. 5, 783–792.

63. Pinard de la Boullaye, *L'étude comparée des religions*, vol. 1, 180–181.

64. See Sarah Stroumsa, *Maimonides in His World*, ch. 4.

65. W. Robertson Smith, *Religion of the Semites*, preface, vi, quoted in *Dictionary of National Biography*, vol. 18, 767, s.v. Spencer.

66. Justin Champion, *The Pillars of Priesthood Shaken: The Church of England and Its Enemies, 1660–1730* (Cambridge, 1992), 155; see 155–157 for the (mainly hostile) reception of Spencer in England.

67. Laplanche, *L'Ecriture*, 615, 677.

V. IRANIAN RELIGIONS AND THE IDEA OF DUALISM

1. See J. Duchesne-Guillemin, "The Pre-History of Iranian Studies," in *The Western Response to Zoroaster* (Ratanbai Katrak Lectures 1956; Oxford: Oxford University Press, 1958), ch. 1, 1–19. See also Duchesne-Guillemin, "Histoire des

études," in *La religion de l'Iran ancien* (Paris: Presses Universitaires de France, 1962), ch. 6, 384–399.

2. "un épisode singulier dans la bataille idéologique qui emplit le dix-huitième siècle." R. Schwab, *Vie d'Anquetil Duperron, suivie des Usages civils et religieux des Parses, par Anquetil-Dupperron* (Paris: E. Leroux, 1934), 9.

3. On the quarrel of the Ancients and the Moderns, see ch. II.2 above, on the quarrel over ritual, ch. VII.1 below.

4. Huet's *Demonstratio evangelica* (Amsterdam, 1679) claims that the religious leaders of the ancient world were all imitations of Moses. As Dupront argues in his *Pierre-Daniel Huet et l'exégèse comparatiste au XVIIe siècle*, Huet might have been contesting various views that followed John Marsham's rejection of the chronological primacy of Israel in the ancient world. On Huet and his *Demonstratio Evangelica*, see ch. IV.1 above.

5. "Relation abrégée du voyage que M. Anquetil du Perron a fait dans l'Inde pour la Recherche et la Traduction des ouvrages attribués à Zoroastre," *Journal des Sçavans* 2 (June 1762): 1–27.

6. "le sçavant Docteur Hyde . . . ce livre rempli d'une immense érudition orientale. . . . Quoi qu'il en soit, les Perses n'ont guères été connus jusqu'ici que par les recherches du Docteur Hyde," ibid., 2.

7. "Mémoire dans lequel on établit que les livres Zends déposés à la bibliothèque du Roi, le 15 Mars 1762, sont les propres ouvrages de Zoroastre, ou que du moins ils sont aussi anciens que ce Législateur," *Journal des Scavans* (May 1769): 270-ff., esp. 336 ff. Abraham Hyacinthe Anquetil-Duperron published his *Zend-Avesta* in Paris, 1771.

8. Michael Stausberg, *Fascinazion Zarathustra: Zoroaster und die europäische Religionsgeschichte der frühen Neuzeit*, 2 vols. (Religionsgeschichtliche Versuche und Vorarbeiten 42; Berlin; New York: De Gruyter, 1998). See my review in *Revue de l'Histoire des Religions* 216 (1999): 481–483.

9. See Duchesne-Guillemin, "The Pre-History of Iranian Studies," 8–9. The argument in the same chapter (11–12) that what Paul Hazard called "la crise de la conscience européenne" separates Hyde from Anquetil-Duperron is mistaken. Rather, Hyde's work should be seen as a typical product of this crisis.

10. Julien Ries has referred to the "véritable début de l'orientalisme" with Hyde. Reference in Stausberg, *Fascinazion Zarathustra*, vol. 2, 681.

11. See George J. Toomer, *Eastern Wisdome and Learning: The Study of Arabic in Seventeenth-Century England* (Oxford: Clarendon Press, 1996), 249. See also 295–298 on Hyde's later career. For the basic biographical facts, see *Dictionary of National Biography*, vol. 10, 401–402, s.v. Thomas Hyde.

12. See Thomas Hyde, *Syntagma Dissertationum*, 2 vols. (Oxford, 1767), [a posthumous collection of his essays], vol. 2, 433 ff.

13. See Timothy H. Barrett, *Singular Listlessness: A Short History of Chinese Books and British Scholars* (London: Wellsweep, 1989), 37–38. See further Jonathan D. Spence, *The Chan's Great Continent: China in Western Minds* (New York; London: W. W. Norton, 1998), 65, and Toomer, *Eastern Wisdome and Learning*, 249.

14. I was unable to find a discussion of the *Sad dar* in Ilya Gershevitch et al. *Iranistik, Literatur* (Lieferung 1) (*Handbuch der Orientalistik*; Leiden; Köln: Brill, 1968).

15. *Guide of the Perplexed*, III. 47; Pines's translation, (Chicago: Chicago University Press, 1964), 594–595. For one among many references to Maimonides in Hyde's book, see *Historia religionis veterum Persarum*, 126. Together with Pocock and Spencer, Hyde remained throughout the eighteenth century a *locus classicus* for discussion on the Sabians. See, for instance, Jacob Brucker, *Historia Critica Philosophiae*, 6 vols. (Leipzig, 1742–1757), vol. 1, *De Philosophia Barbarica*, passim.

16. Hyde refers here to a book of Ibn Shana; see *Historia religionis veterum Persarum*, 126.

17. As we saw above (chs. I.1 and IV.1), the comparison between the newly discovered peoples of the Americas and peoples known from antiquity was common in the seventeenth and eighteenth centuries. The former were often considered to be sons of Noah, or offspring of the ten lost tribes of Israel. Abraham Hyacinthe Anquetil-Duperron himself wrote a work entitled *Considérations philosophiques, historiques, et géographiques sur les deux mondes (1780–1804)*; this work has been published only recently, by Guido Abbatista, (Pisa: Scuola Normale Superiore, 1993). Anquetil-Duperron notes that Brucker, in his *History of Philosophy*, bases his idea that Mancocapac, the Peruvian legislator, was a Zoroastrian who had fled the Muslims, on the work of Hyde (24). On the Noahide traditions, see Don Cameron Allen, *The Legend of Noah: Renaissance Rationalism in Art, Science and Letters* (Urbana: University of Illinois Press, 1949).

18. See, for instance, Sarah Stroumsa, "The Barāhima in Early Kalam," *Jerusalem Studies in Arabic and Islam* 6 (1985): 233, n. 15. See also Barthélemi d'Herbelot, *Bibliothèque Orientale* (Paris, 1697), 930–331, *s.v.* Zerdascht. D'Herbelot refers to various Islamic sources according to which "Les Mages de Perse, pour authoriser leurs doctrines, confondent . . . leur Zoroastre avec le Patriarche Abraham." He adds that the origin of this confusion stems from a rabbinic Midrash on Ur, Abraham's original city (*ur* is the Aramaic word for "fire").

19. Thomas Hobbes, *De Cive*, XV., 18. The Latin text appeared in 1642, the English translation in 1651. One should note that the distinction between *latreia* and *douleia* is standard in Catholic-Protestant polemics: Calvin attacks this distinction in his *Institutes of the Christian Religion* (vol. I. 12), while Bellarmine defends it in his book on the saints.

20. "qui in Dei notitia educatus Veteri Testamento non fuit inassuetus, nec a Judaeorum conversatione alienus," *Historia religionis veterum Persarum*, 16.

21. This last theory will still be repeated in the article "Perses" in the *Encyclopédie, ou Dictionnaire raisonné des sciences, des arts et des métiers* (vol. 12, 421).

22. *Historia religionis veterum Persarum*, ch. 9, 159–168.

23. Ibid., ch. 4, 104.

24. Mithrae cultum, qui apud Persas erat tantum civilis . . . ad Graecos et Romanos . . . plane mutarunt et perverterunt et res falsas de Persis retulerunt. ibid., 109. Apud Persas non erat Mithrae cultus aliquis divinus, sed tantum civilis et caeremonialis, scil. Prostrationes et Salutationes, 118, cf. 122.

25. On the origins of this concept, see ch. II.2 above.

26. "Zoroastre," col. 3083, n. G. The first edition of Pierre Bayle's *Dictionnaire historique et critique* had been published in Rotterdam in 1697.

27. We shall return to the Chinese rituals in ch. VII.1 below. For a discussion of the nature of the Chinese rites quite contemporaneous with Hyde's book, see, for instance, Noel Alexandre, *Conformité des cérémonies chinoises avec l'idolatrie grecque et romaine* (Cologne, 1700), 41, n. 94: "Le culte que Confucius rendait aux Esprits était plutôt Religieux que civil." Hyde takes great trouble to show, precisely, the fundamental difference between Iranian and Greek and Roman religious practices.

28. Henry Lord, *A Display of Two Forraigne Sects in the East Indies, viz. the Sect of the Banians, the Ancient Natives of India, and the Sect of the Persees, the Ancient Inhabitants of Persia* (London, 1630), ch. 8. On this literature, see Joan Pau Rubiés, *Travel and Ethnology in the Renaissance: South India through European Eyes, 1250–1625* (Cambridge: Cambridge University Press, 2000).

29. Respectively, *Nouvelles de la République des Lettres* 1699, pp. 155–181 and 1701, pp. 243–268.

30. P. Bayle, *Dictionnaire historique et critique*, vol. 3, cols. 3077–3083.

31. Thomas Burnet, *Telluris Theoria Sacra* (London, 1681).

32. E. Pococke, *Specimen Historiae Arabum* (Oxford, 1806 [ed. S. de Sacy]), 152–153. The first edition was published in 1650.

33. For the English usage, see the *Oxford English Dictionary* (Oxford: Oxford University Press, 1971), *s.v.* "dualism." "Dualism" is attested mainly in the nineteenth century. The entry "Dualisme" appears in the *Encyclopédie* in 1755. See further *Historisches Wörterbuch der Philosophie,* vol. 2, (Basel: Schwabe, 1972), 297–299. s. v. Dualismus.

34. *Encyclopédie* vol. 5, (Amsterdam 1755), cols. 151–152. Isaac de Beausobre's study of Manichaeism is also referred to; cf. entry for "Perses" in *Encyclopédie*, vol. 12, col. 420ff.

35. See below, pt. 2, in this chapter.

36. See Duchesne-Guillemin, "The Pre-History of Iranian Studies," 12–13.

37. "Les savantes recherches de Hyde allumèrent, il y a peu d'années, dans le coeur d'un jeune Français, le désir de s'instruire par lui-même des dogmes des guèbres." I quote according to 1789 edition, 392.

38. On travelers literature dealing with Iranian religion, see Nora Kathleen Firby, *European Travellers and Their Perceptions of Zoroastrians in the Seventeenth and Eighteenth Centuries* (Berlin: D. Reimer, 1988). Firby mentions that Jean-Baptiste Tavernier, whose *Travels in India* was originally published in 1676, probably saw a copy of *Arda Viraz Nameh* (42–46).

39. T. Maurice, *Indian Antiquities* (London, 1800), 8.

40. See Johann Gottfried Herder, *Werke, V, Schriften Zum Alten Testament* ed. V. R. Smand (Frankfurt: Deutscher Klassiker Verlag, 1993), 429–457.

41. Shaul Shaked, "Some Notes on Ahreman, the Evil Spirit, and His Creation," in *Studies in Mysticism and Religion Presented to Gershom G. Scholem,* eds. Ephraim Elimelech Urbach, Raphael Jehuda Zwi Werblowsky, and Chaim Wirszubski (Jerusalem: Magnes Press, 1967), 227–234.

42. See Shaul Shaked, ed., *Irano-Judaica: Studies Relating to Jewish Contacts with Persian Culture through the Ages* (Jerusalem: Ben Zvi, 1982). Shaked has also edited various sequels to this volume.

43. For a classical statement, see, for instance, Thomas S. Kuhn, *The Structure of Scientific Revolutions* (Chicago: University of Chicago Press, 1962).

44. See Arno Borst, *Die Katharer* (Freiburg: Herder, 1991), 34–38, on Protestant and Catholic attitudes toward the Medieval Cathars. Jacques Benigne Bossuet, in his *Histoire des variations des Eglises protestantes* (1685), bk. 10, dealt extensively with the identification of the Protestants as inheritors of the medieval heretics. See, for instance, the following sentence: "Mais de tous les prédécesseurs que les Protestants se veulent donner, les Vaudois et les Albigeois sont les mieux traités, du moins par les Calvinistes." (Bossuet, *Oeuvres*, vol. 19 [Versailles: Lebel, 1816], 82). In the early eighteenth century, Jacques Basnage, and especially Gottfried Arnold, in his *Unpartheyischen Kirchen-und Ketzerhistorie* (first published in Frankfurt, 1699–1700), answered this accusation from the Reformed viewpoint.

45. See in particular Richard H.Popkin, "Manichaeism in the Enlightenment," in *The Critical Spirit: Essays in Honor of Herbert Marcuse*, eds. K. H. Wolff and B. Moore Jr. (Boston: Beacon, 1967), 31–54.

46. On Beausobre's biography, see F. Hartweg, "Le Grand Beausobre: Aspekte des intellektuellen und kirchlichen Lebens der ersten Generation des Berliner Refuge," in *Geschichte als Aufgabe: Festschrift für Otto Büsch zu seinem 60 Geburtstag*, ed. Wilhelm Treue (Berlin: Colloquium, 1988), 55–81. See also Bertram E. Schwarzbach, "Politics and Ethics in the Huguenot Diaspora: Isaac de Beausobre in Berlin," in *New Essays on the Political Thought of the Huguenots of the Refuge*, ed. John Christian Laursen (Brill's Studies in Intellectual History 60; Leiden; New York; Köln: Brill, 1995), 109–129. In his only mention of the *Histoire Critique de Manichée et du Manichéisme*, Schwarzbach writes: "Reading his occasionally obsessive *History of Manes and Manichaeism* led us to expect a rather silly scholar [*sic*!]" (113). See further Dominique Bourel, *Le dernier Moïse: Moses Mendelssohn: la fondation du judaïsme moderne* (Paris: Gallimard, 2004).

47. See Christian Velder, *300 Jahre Französisches Gymnasium Berlin* (Berlin: Nicolai, 1989), 37–42 ("Isaac de Beausobre: die theologische Schulaufsicht").

48. Isaac de Beausobre, *Histoire critique de Manichée et du Manichéisme* (*HCMM*), 2 vols. (Amsterdam: F. Bernard, 1734 and 1739). On Beausobre's life, see the biographical sketch (signed F.M.D.S.E.) prefacing *HCMM*, vol. 2. See further Schwarzbach, "Politics and Ethics in the Huguenot Diaspora," n. 1, 109, on the possible authorship of this sketch (Jean-Henry-Samuel Formay?), which apparently does not appear in all copies of the book.

49. On the origins as historiographical myth, see Giovanni Filoramo, *Figure del Sacro: Saggi di storia religiosa* (Brescia: Morcelliana, 1993), 10.

50. See Julien Ries, *Introduction aux études manichéennes*, vol. 1 (Ephemerides Theologiae Lovanienses 33, 35; Louvain, 1957–1959), 455. On the history of Manichaean studies, see already Henrik Samuel Nyberg, "Forschungen über den Manichäismus," *ZNTW* 34 (1935): 70–91; reprinted in Geo Widengren, ed., *Der Manichäismus* (Wege der Forschung; Darmstadt: Wissenschaftliche Buchgesellschaft, 1977), 3–28, see esp. 6. See further L. J. R. Ort, *Mani: A Religio-Historical Description of His Personality* (Supplements to *Numen*; Leiden: Brill, 1967), 1–4.

51. See Jean-Claude Picard, "L'apocryphe à l'étroit: notes historiographiques sur les corpus d'apocryphes bibliques," *Apocrypha* 1 (1990): 69–117, esp. 82–83.

The deist critique of Christian tradition is also intensely interested in biblical apocryphal literature; see Francis Schmidt, "John Toland: critique déiste de la littérature apocryphe," *Apocrypha* 1 (1990): 119–145. Toland endeavors to blur the traditional boundaries between canonical and apocryphal texts.

52. "Sans le savoir, Arnold suggère tout un programme à Isaac de Beausobre." Ries, "Introduction aux études manichéennes," vol. 1, 472. In *HCMM* (vol. 1, 239), Beausobre supports Arnold's new methods, against the opposition of Lutheran orthodoxy.

53. "Les doctrines des Manichéens sont si pitoyables qu'il suffit de les rapporter pour les réfuter."

54. *Histoire de la Réformation, ou origine et progrès du Luthéranisme dans l'Empire et les Etats de la Confession d'Augsburg, depuis 1517 jusqu'en 1530.* (Berlin: François de la Garde, 1785), 2 vols. That it was written before *HCMM* is stated in the editors' preface. For reasons not specified, it had been impossible to print it in Holland. The book is dedicated to the King of Prussia by Marthe Magdalène de Beausobre, granddaughter of the author, from Saint Petersburg. The preface states: "Déjà on n'attache plus à certaines opinions religieuses la même importance que dans les seixième et dix-septième siècles. En France, on est revenu de bien des préventions contre la doctrine des Réformés."

55. See the biographical sketch of Beausobre in *HCMM,* vol. 2.

56. Both works, again, were published posthumously. Isaac de Beausobre's *Examen* was published together with his *Supplément à l'histoire de la guerre des Hussites de l'Enfant* (Lausanne; Geneva: M.-M. Bousquet, 1745), 113–159. *Remarques historiques* was published by his daughter, Charlotte de Beausobre (Hague: P. de Hondt, 1742), 2 vols.

57. Beausobre knew Toland personally. According to Gesine Palmer there exists testimony about at least one conversation between the two, in presence of Princess Sophie-Charlotte (personal communication).

58. Mosheim "introduit un principe nouveau, désavoué par les savants de tous les siècles: In antiquis rebus, sine testimoniis scriptorum, nihil plane decerni potest, aut dirimi."

59. In the author's words, "on [y] trouve aussi l'histoire de Basilide, de Marcion, de Bardesanes, etc . . . et de leurs sentimens, et où l'on découvre l'origine de plusieurs cultes, cérémonies, etc . . . qui se sont introduits dans le Christianisme." *HCMM,* vol.1, p. XVII.

60. On "fable" as equivalent to "myth," see ch. II.2, above.

61. For an example of a monograph on Manichaeism written in Latin in the early eighteenth century, see J. C. Wolf, *Manichaeismus ante Manichaeos, et in Christianismo Redivivus* (Hamburg: Liebezeit, 1707).

62. "Ce nom de Gnostiques est fort vague: on l'a donné à plusieurs sectes très différentes," in vol. 1, 368–369.

63. Respectively, in vol. 1, 377 and 367. Incidentally, from Moses Gaster in the late nineteenth century to Gershom Scholem and his students in the twentieth century, modern studies of the earliest phases of Jewish mystical trends grant much attention to Gnostic parallels to the cosmic dimensions of the body of God, the *shiʿur qoma.*

64. On Zoroastrianism, see, for instance, Bruno Henning, *Zoroaster, Politician or Witch-Doctor?* (Oxford: Oxford University Press, 1951). On Manichaeism, see Shaked, "Some Notes on Ahreman, the Evil Spirit, and His Creation."

65. "Les Perses ne croyaient point à deux dieux," *Histoire de Manichée*, I. 172. Prideaux had dealt with Zoroaster's system in his *The Old and New Testament connected in the History of the Jews and neighbouring nations* (London, 1716) which de Beausobre knew in French translation: Humphrey Prideaux, *Histoire des juifs et des peuples voisins* (Amsterdam, 1722).

66. Cf. Beausobre, *HCMM*, vol. 1, 488: "Les Manichéens n'ont cru qu'un seul Dieu." In this, Mani was not alone among ancient heretics: none of them believed in many gods (I.497). See further Beausobre, *HCMM*, vol. 2, 582: "Les Manichéens n'ont adoré qu'un seul Dieu."

67. "L'anthropomorphisme fut une production de l'hérésie manichéenne et de la stupidité monacale," Beausobre, *HCMM*, vol. 1, 500.

68. Beausobre, *HCMM*, vol. 2, book 4, ch. 1, 7. Beausobre refers here to Menasseh Ben Israel, *de Creatione Problemata XII*.

69. Beausobre, *HCMM*, vol. 2, 179. On Huet and his *Demonstratio Evangelica*, see ch. IV.1 above.

70. See ch. IV.2 above.

71. Ries, *Introduction aux études manichéennes*, vol. 1, 475.

72. Ibid.

73. Pierre Cacciari published his tract in 1751. Mosheim's *De rebus Christianorum ante Constantinum Magnum commentarii* appeared in 1753. See Ries, *Introduction aux études manichéennes*, vol. 1, 477–478.

74. See Ries, *Introduction aux études manichéennes*, vol. 2, 388.

75. On the Jewish apocryphal traditions in the *Cologne Mani Codex*, see John C. Reeves, *Heralds of That Good Realm: Syro-Mesopotamian Gnosis and Jewish Traditions* (Nag Hammadi and Manichaean Studies 41; Leiden; New York; Köln: Brill, 1996). Cf. my review in *Journal of Theological Studies* 49 (1998): 320–322.

VI. FROM *MOHAMMEDIS IMPOSTURAE* TO THE *THREE IMPOSTORS*

1. Albert Hourani, *Islam in European Thought* (Cambridge: Cambridge University Press, 1991), 7. Cf. the title of a book written by the German orientalist Carsten Colpe, *Problem Islam* (Frankfurt: Athaeneum, 1989).

2. On false prophets in the Bible and in the early Jewish and Christian background of early Islam, see Guy G. Stroumsa, "False Prophet, False Messiah, and the Religious Scene in Seventh-Century Jerusalem," in *Redemption and Resistance: The Messianic Hopes of Jews and Christians in Antiquity*, eds. James Carlton-Paget and Markus Bockmuehl (Edinburgh: T. & T. Clark, 2007), 278–289.

3. See Norman Daniel, *Islam and the West: The Making of an Image* (Edinburgh: Edinburgh University Press, 1960), 295–301

4. See James T. Monroe, *Islam and the Arabs in Spanish Scholarship (Sixteenth Century to the Present)* (Medieval Iberian Peninsula Texts and Studies, vol. 3;

Leiden: Brill, 1970), 3. On Arabic studies in the Renaissance, in England and France, see respectively Samuel Chew, *The Crescent and the Rose: Islam and England during the Renaissance* (New York: Oxford University Press, 1937), and Josée Balagna Coustou, *Arabe et humanisme dans la France des derniers Valois* (Paris: Maisonneuve Larose, 1989).

5. Quoted by Daniel J. Vitkus, "Early Modern Orientalism: Representations of Islam in Sixteenth and Seventeenth Century Europe," in *Western Views of Islam in Medieval and Early Modern Europe*, eds. David R. Blanks, Michael Frasetto (New York: St. Martin's Press, 1999), 207–230; see 226. For a rich study of early modern European iconography of Islam, see Thomas Kaufmann, *"Türkenbüchlein:" Zur christilichen Wahrnehmung "türkischen Religion"* in *Spätmittelalter und Reformation* (Forschungen zur Krichen- und Dogmengeschichte, 97; Göttingen: Vandenhoeck & Ruprecht, 2008).

6. I am referring in particular to the second volume of Jonathan Israel's comprehensive history, *Enlightenment Contested: Philosophy, Modernity, and the Emancipation of Man, 1670–1752* (Oxford: Oxford University Press, 2006), esp. ch. 24: "Rethinking Islam: Philosophy and the 'Other'," 615–639. Israel is more interested in the treatment of Islamic philosophy, particularly in the critique of revealed religion in medieval Islamic philosophy and heretical thought.

7. For summary presentations of the prehistory and origins of the modern study of Arabic and Islam, see, for instance, Philip K. Hitti, *Islam and the West* (New York; Toronto; London: Van Nostrand, 1962), 48–63, and Maxime Rodinson, *La fascination de l'islam* (Paris: Maspero, 1980), 68–70. See further George Toomer, *Eastern Wisedome and Learning: the Study of Arabic in Seventeeenth-Century England* (Oxford: Clarendon Press, 1996), 7–13.

8. *Viaggi di Pietro della Valle il Pellegrino descritti da lui medesimo in lettere familiari all'erudito su amico Mario Schipano* (Rome: Vitale Mascarde, 1650–1663).

9. On European encounters with Persia in our period, see in particular Ahmad Gunny, *Images of Islam in Eighteenth-Century Writings* (London: Grey Seal, 1996)

10. Paul Rycault, *The Present State of the Ottoman Empire, Containing the Maxims of the Turkish Politie, the Most Material Points of the Mahometan Religion, Their Sects and Heresies, Their Convents and Religious Votaries, Their Military Discipline* (London, 1670). In the 1686 edition of the work, bk. 2 ("Of the Turkish Religion,") runs from p. 184 to p. 320. New edition Frankfurt: Institute for the History of Arabic-Islamic Science, 1995. Note that Rycaut also published (anonymously) a book on the Jewish false messiah Sabbatai Zevi: *The Counterfeit Messiah; or False Christ, of the Jews at Smyrna, in the year 1666*. He also translated to English the *Comentarios reales* of Garcilaso de la Vega (in 1688).

11. Joseph Pitts, *A True and Faithful Account of the Religion and Manners of the Mohammedans* (Exeter, 1704). Cf. Aziz al-Azmeh, *Islamic Studies and the European Imagination* (Inaugural Lecture, University of Exeter, 17 March 1986). Al-Azmeh notes that Pitts's book was very successful and was reprinted four times, as late as 1774. The lecture is reprinted in A. Al-Azmeh, *Islam and Modernities* (Third ed., London; New York: Verso, 2009), 174–195.

12. Michel Baudier, *Histoire générale de la religion des Turcs, avec la naissance, la vie, et la mort de leur Prophète et les actions des quatre premiers califes qui l'ont suivi* (Paris, 1626).

13. See Geoffroy Atkinson, *Les relations de voyages du XVIIe siècle et l'évolution des idées: contribution à l'étude de la formation de l'esprit du XVIIIe siècle* (Paris: Champion, 1926), 42.

14. Chalcondyle Laonicus, *Histoire générale des turcs, contenant l'Histoire de Chalcondyle*, traduite par Blaise de Vigenaire (Paris, 1662), 158.

15. Laonicus, *Histoire générale des turcs*, 161–167. And see Maimonides, *Guide of the Perplexed* (transl. Shlomo Pines [Chicago: Chicago University Press, 1963]) III. 46. Maimonides, of course, thought that Christianity, not Islam, was to some extent tainted with idolatry.

16. See, for instance, Alastair Hamilton, "The English Interest in the Arabic-Speaking Christians," in *The 'Arabick' Interest of the Natural Philosophers in Seventeenth-Century England*, ed. G. A. Russell (Brill's Studies in Intellectual History, vol. 47; Leiden; New York; Köln: Brill, 1994), 30–53.

17. Michel Le Quien, *Oriens christianus in quatuor patriarchatus digestus, in quo exhibentur Ecclesiae patriarchae caeterique praesules totius Orientis*, published posthumously (3 vols., Paris, 1740).

18. See Bernard Heyberger, *Les chrétiens du Proche-Orient au temps de la réforme catholique: Syrie, Liban, Palestine, XVIIIe siècles* (Bibliothèque des Ecoles françaises d'Athènes et de Rome 284; Rome: Ecole française de Rome, 1994).

19. See, for instance, Alastair Hamilton, "Eastern Churches and Western Scholarship," in *Rome Reborn: The Vatican Library and Renaissance Culture*, ed. Anthony Grafton (New Haven; Vatican; Washington, D.C.: Yale University Press; Bibliotheca Apostolica Vaticana; Library of Congress, 1993), 225–249.

20. The Maronite College was established in Rome in 1584.

21. See Antoine Galand's preface to Barthélemy d'Herbelot's *Bibliothèque Orientale* (Paris, 1697), xv ("la Religion Musulmane").

22. Guillaume Postel, *De la République des Turcs, et là où l'occasion s'offrera, des moeurs et loy de tous Muhamedistes* (Poitiers, 1560). William J. Bouwsma, *Concordia Mundi: The Career and Thought of Guillaume Postel (1510–1581)* (Cambridge, Mass.: Harvard University Press, 1957), does not dwell on Postel's Islamic interests.

23. See Alastair Hamilton, *William Bedwell the Arabist, 1563–1632* (Leiden: Brill, 1985), 69. In 1623, Samuel Bochart went to study with Bedwell (ibid., 52). See further Toomer, *Eastern Wisedome and Learning*, 56–64. *see* p. 192, n. 11,

24. See for instance Grotius, *De veritate religionis Christianae* (originally published in 1627), VI. 1, comparing Mahomet with Christ. (Incidentally, this book was translated to Arabic by Edward Pococke.)

25. Toomer, *Eastern Wisedome and Learning*, 43. Casaubon was quick to recognize Erpenius's outstanding gifts. Erpenius met Buxtorf in Basle, and Bedwell in Britain, through Scaliger's recommendation (Toomer, ibid., 58.) When he died, he was preparing an edition of the Koran, with Latin translation and commentary. On Erpenius's role in Leiden, see further J. Brugman, "Arabic Scholarship," in *Leiden University in the Seventeenth Century: An Exchange of Learning*, eds.

T. H. Lunsingh Scheurleer and G.H.M. Posthumus Meyjes (Leiden: Brill, 1975), 203–215, and J. Brugman and F. Schroeder, *Arabic Studies in the Netherlands* (Netherlands Institute of Archaeology and Arabic Studies, Cairo, vol. 3; Leiden: Brill, 1979), 3–21.

26. As noted by Alastair Hamilton, Joseph Scaliger deplored that the treatment of Arabic was done mainly by scholars uninterested in Arabic culture. See Hamilton, *Europe and the Arab World: Five Centuries of Books by European Scholars and Travellers from the Libraries of the Arcadian Group* (Oxford: Oxford University Press and Azimuth Editions, 1994), 20.

27. Johann-Heinrich Hottinger, *Historia Orientalis, ex variis Orientalium monumentis collecta* (Zurich: Bodmer, 1651). Hottinger, who had studied in Geneva, Groningen, and Leiden, taught Church History in Zurich since 1642, whence he moved to Heidelberg in 1655, to teach oriental languages and biblical criticism. He was then invited to teach in Leiden, but drowned crossing the Limmat, together with three of his sons. *(1667)*

28. By Sabians, early modern authors, relying on Maimonides, also mean the pagan pre-Islamic Arabs. For further discussion, see ch. IV above.

29. The figure of Pococke dominates Toomer's *Eastern Wisedome and Learning*. The same year, 1634, that Pococke had been appointed to the chair of Arabic at Oxford, saw the publication of the first reasonably accurate translation of the Koran, by George Sale.

30. E. Pococke, *Specimen Historiae Arabum* (Oxford, 1650). See Toomer, *Eastern Wisedome and Learning*, 224 and n. 661. In this work, Pococke also deals with the religion of pre-Islamic Arabia.

31. Simon Ockley (1678–1720), who taught Arabic in Cambridge, held a similar view of Muhammad.

32. E. Pococke, *Philosophus Autodidactus, sive Epistola Abi Jaafar Ebn Tophail De Hai Ebn Yokdhan* (Oxford, 1671). In 1660, Edward Pococke the Younger, with his father's help, had already translated Ibn Tufail's text to English. See Toomer, *Eastern Wisedome and Learning*, 218–220, 222. The English version appeared as *The History of* Hai Eb'n Yockdan, *an Indian Prince, or Self-Taught Philosopher* (London, 1686).

33. See, for instance, Lawrence I. Conrad, ed., *The World of Ibn Tufayl: Interdisciplinary Perspectives on* Hayy Ibn Yaczan (Leiden; New York: Brill, 1996).

34. See G. A. Russell, "The Impact of the *Philosophus Autodidactus*," in *The 'Arabick' Interest of the Natural Philosophers in Seventeenth-Century England*, ed. G. A. Russell (Leiden: Brill, 1994), 224–65. See further Israel, *The Enlightenment Contested*, 628–631.

35. Simon Ockley, *The Improvement of Human Reason: Exhibited in the Life of Hai ebn Yokdhan, Written in Arabick above 500 Years Ago, by Abu Jaafar ebn Tophail. In which Is Demonstrated, by What Methods One May, by the Meer Light of Nature, Attain the Knowledg of Things Natural and Supernatural; More Particularly the Knowledg of God, and the Affairs of Another Life* (London, 1708).

36. Toomer describes Pococke's attitude toward Islam as "enigmatic" (*Eastern Wisedome and Learning*, 223). See further, ibid., 223–226.

37. See Henry Laurens, *Aux sources de l'orientalisme. La Bibliothèque orientale de Barthélemi d'Herbelot* (Paris: Maisonneuve Larose, 1978). D'Herbelot also prepared an anthology of texts to fit the *Bibliothèque,* as well as an Arabic, Persian, and Turkish dictionary. These two unfinished works have remained unpublished.

38. "C'est le fameux Imposteur Mahomet, Auteur et Fondateur d'une hérésie, qui a pris le nom de Religion, que nous appellons Mahométane" (D'Herbelot, *Bibliothèque orientale,* 648); "Ce nom et ce surnom du faux prophète Mahomet"(ibid., 659)

39. On Galland, see Mohamed Abdel-Halim, *Antoine Galland—sa vie et son oeuvre* (Paris: Nizet, 1964).

40. See Laurens, *Aux sources de l'orientalisme,* 28. Laurens refers to the "close links" between the *Bibliothèque orientale* and the *Mille et une nuits* (2). He emphasizes the importance of religion for d'Herbelot and mentions that the text includes 685 entries (out of 8,204) that deal with Islam.

41. Discours pour servir de Préface à la *Bibliothèque Orientale,* p. VI.

42. "Ceux qui auront la curiosité de s'instruire des sentiments des Mahométans," ibid., p. IX.

43. H. Prideaux, *The True Nature of Imposture, fully display'd in the Life of Mahomet, with a discourse annexed for the vindicating of Christianity from this charge – offered to the consideration of the Deists of the present age* (London, 1697). In his introductory address "to the reader" (p. III), Prideaux claims to offer in the book arguments against the deists who "take upon themselves to call Christianity a Cheat, and an Imposture." The work was translated almost immediately to French: *La vie de Mahomet, où l'on découvre amplement la vérité de l'imposture* (Amesterdam, 1698). It appeared the next year in Paris under a slightly different title: *La vie de l'imposteur Mahomet, recueillie des auteurs arabes, persans etc . . .* (Paris, 1699). On the impact of this translation, see R. Tobin, "The Sources of Voltaire's 'Mahomet'," *The French Review* 34 (1961): 372–378. A German version appeared in Leipzig in 1699 and a Dutch one in Amsterdam in 1723.

44. See Toomer, *Eastern Wisedome and Learning,* 289–292, who adds that Prideaux's main service to the study of Arabic was his recommending to Ockley to take it up. Prideaux's book would influence Voltaire, who could speak in his ambitious *Essai sur les moeurs,* first published in 1756, of Muhammad's "enthusiasm."

45. See the full title of the longer version published in London in 1712: *Four Treatises Concerning the Doctrine, Discipline and Worship of the Mahometans, vis. 1. An Abridgment of the Mahometan Religion, Translated Out of Arabick into Latin by H. Reland, and from Thence into English. 2. A Defence of the Mahometans from Several Charges Falsly Laid against Them by Christians, Written in Latin by H. Reland, and Translated into English. 3. A Treatise of Bobivius (Sometime First Interpreter to Mahomet) Concerning the Liturgy of the Turks, Their Pilgrimage to Mecca, Their Circumcision, Visitation of the Sick, etc, Translated from the Latin. 4. Reflections on Mahometanism and Socinianism, Translated from the French, to which Is Prefix'd the Life and Actions of Mahomet, Extracted Chiefly*

from Mahometan Authors. Like George Sale, Reland seeks to rehabilitate Islam also to refute Catholic accusations about similarities between Islam and Protestantism. See Henri Laurens, *Les origines intellectuelles de l'expédition d'Egypte: l'orientalisme islamisant en France (1698–1798)* (Istanbul; Paris: Isis, 1987), 85.

46. Israel, *Enlightenment Contested,* 627.

47. Toomer, *Eastern Wisedome and Learning,* 313–314.

48. Hazard, *La crise de la conscience européenne,* quoted by Abdel-Halim, *Antoine Galland,* 153.

49. Alastair Hamilton, "The Study of Islam in Early Modern Europe," *Archiv für Religionsgeschichte* 3 (2001): 169–182. Hamilton refers to Pierre Chaunu's pithy characterization of the seventeenth, eighteenth, and nineteenth centuries: "Le dix-septième et le dix-neuvième inventent, le dix-huitième illustre, accumule, et prépare."

50. Pierre Bayle (1647–1706), a Huguenot who spent most of his adult life in Rotterdam, published a second edition of the *Dictionnaire historique et critique* in 1702. I use Elisabeth Labrousse's reprint of the 1740 edition (Hildesheim; New York: Olms, 1982). Bishop Berkeley, using a neologism, called Bayle a freethinker.

51. Bayle, *Dictionnaire,* vol. 2, 675. (The entry goes up to 691.)

52. Ibid., 258, 277.

53. Ibid., 684, n. AA and 685, n. DD.

54. "Sa vie ne réfutait-elle pas fortement cette imposture?" Ibid., 268 II.

55. "Voila comment la moitié du monde se moque de l'autre," Ibid., 691, n. QQ.

56. See in particular John Toland, *Nazarenus; or, Jewish, Gentile, and Mahometan Christianity* (first published in 1718), ed. Justin Champion (Oxford: Voltaire Foundation, 1999), letter 1, 135. See also, in the same volume, Toland's *Christianisme Judaïque et Mahométan,* an interesting text never published by its author, esp. ch. 15, 281: "Vous scavez, monsieur, a quell degré prodigieux l'imposture et la crédulité agissoient de concert dans les premiers temps de l'Eglise chrétienne."

57. Comte de Boulainvilliers, *La vie de Mahomet, avec des réflexions sur la religion musulmane et les coutumes des mahométans* (London and Amsterdam: Paul Hubert, 1730). The book was probably written in the early 1720s.

58. Boulainvilliers had studied with Richard Simon and was a reader of Bayle.

59. Boulainvilliers, *La vie de Mahomet,* 248–249, quoted by Israel, *Enlightenment Contested,* 616.

60. Laurens, *Origines intellectuelles,* 28, argues that Boulainvilliers was probably the first to see Muhammad as the Arabs' lawgiver. He notes that the expression would become more common after 1750 and refers to François Henri Turpin, *Histoire de la vie de Mahomet, législateur de l'Arabie* (1773).

61. In this context, Jonathan Israel refers in particular to Voltaire. J. Israel, *Enlightenment Contested,* 617. See further F. O. Nolte, "Voltaire's *Mahomet* as a Source of Lessing's *Nathan der Weise* and *Emilia Galotti,*" *Modern Language Notes* (1933): 152–156. On Boulainvilliers's influence on Voltaire's image of Muhammad, see Djavad Hadidi, *Voltaire et l'Islam* (Paris: Publications orientalistes de France, 1974), 33–40.

62. Jean Gagnier, *La vie de Mahomet, traduite et compilée de l'Alcoran, des traditions authentiques, de la Sonna* (Amsterdam, 1732): "le plus scélerat de tous les hommes et le plus mortel ennemi de Dieu." Gagnier had already published, in 1723, a Latin translation of a Medieval Arabic text: *Ismail Abu'l Feda, de vita et rebus gestis Mohammedis.*

63. Israel, *Enlightenment Contested,* 626. I quote according to the edition of Winfried Schroeder, *Anonymus, Traktat über die drei Betrüger, Traité des trois imposteurs (L'esprit de Mr. Benoit de Spinosa)* (Philosophische Bibliothek 452; Hamburg: Felix Meiner, 1992).

64. See Gerhard Bartsch, ed., trans., *De Tribus Impostoribus Anno MDIIC, Von den Drei Betrügern 1598* (Berlin: Akademie-Verlag, 1960).

65. "Un livre chimérique, dont tout le monde parle, et que personne n'a vu." P. Marchand's *Dictionnaire historique* was published in The Hague, 1758–1759. See now Georges Minois, *Le traité des trois imposteurs: histoire d'un livre blasphématoire qui n'existait pas* (Paris: Albin Michel, 2009).

66. Fontenelle had already identified fear as being at the origin of religion in *De l'origine des fables* (published only in 1724, but written before the end of the seventeenth century).

67. *Traité des trois imposteurs,* ch. 3, 8.

68. Ibid., ch. 3, 9.

69. "Chaque République, chaque Etat, chaque Ville et chaque particulier avait ses rites propres et pensait de la Divinité à sa fantaisie." Ibid., ch3, 9, 56.

70. Ibid. ch. 3, 9, 56, n. 123; see further 72, n. 142.

71. Ibid. 56–57.

72. Silvia Berti, "Unmasking the Truth: The Theme of Imposture in Early Modern European Culture, 1660–1730," in *Everything Connects: Essays in Honor of Richard H. Popkin,* eds. James E. Force and David Katz (New York: Brill, 1998), 19–36, 23. See further Margaret C. Jacob and Winhand W. Mijnhard, eds., *The Dutch Republic in the Eighteenth Century: Decline, Enlightenment, and Revolution* (Ithaca; London: Cornell University Press, 1992), 11–12.

73. Justin Champion, "Legislators, Impostors, and the Politic Origins of Religions: English Theories of Imposture from Stubbe to Toland," in *Heterodoxy, Spinozism, and Free Thought,* eds. S. Berti, F. Charles-Dambert and R. Popkin (Dordrecht, 1996), 333–356. In his *Lettres Provinciales,* published in 1656, Blaise Pascal addresses the Jesuits in the following terms: "Mes Révérends Pères, vos impostures croissent tous les jours . . ."(15th letter, quoted by Berti, *Unmasking the Truth,* 25).

74. See *Oxford English Dictionary* online, entry for "impostor." The impostor can be a magician or a priest.

75. Following an accusation to that effect by Pope Gregory IX, in 1239.

76. ("The Law of Moses is for children, that of Christ cannot be practiced, that of Muhammad is for swine"). Ernest Renan, *Averroès et l'Averroïsme: essai historique* (Paris: Calmann-Levy, 1882 [1852]), 278–300. "Ainsi, le XIIIe siècle arrivait par toutes les voies à l'idée de religions comparées, c'est-à-dire à l'indifférence et au naturalisme." (Renan, *Averroès,* 282). From the medieval thinkers, the concept would have circulated up to the Renaissance, through various heretics such as Simon of

Tournaix, Boccaccio, Pomponazzi, and Giordano Bruno. Cf. Mario Esposito, "Una manifestazione d'incredulita religiosa nel medioevo: Il ditto dei "Tre Impostori" e la sua trasmissione da Federico II a Pomponazzi," *Archivio Storico Italiano* 16 (1931): 3–48

77. Louis Massigon, "La légende *"de tribus impostoribus"* et ses origines is-lamiques," *Revue de l'Histoire des Religions* 41 (1920): 74–78.

78. See Sarah Stroumsa, *Freethinkers of Medieval Islam: Ibn Al-Rawandi, Abu Bakr al-Razi, and Their Impact on Islamic Thought* (Leiden; Boston: Brill, 1999), 214–219.

79. Charles Blount, *Life of Apollonius* (London, 1680). Jonathan Israel notes that Blount was the first to incorporate ancient polytheism into radical thought (*Enlightenment Contested,* 362). One of the best-known cases of religious impos-ture in the Greco-Roman world was that of Alexander, a false priest of Asclepius from Abonoteichus, a small city in remote Paphlagonia, on the southern shore of the Black Sea, (fl. 150–170 C.E.). His tricks were related and laid bare by Lucian of Samosata.

80. Sir T. Browne, *Tracts* (1684), 3: "The Impostour Barchochebas." Indeed, Bar Kochba, Apollonius, and Sabbatai Zevi came to be seen, together, as three im-postors, for instance, in J. C. Poncelin de la Roche Tilbiac, *Superstitions orientales* (1785).

81. *Apologie pour tous les grands hommes qui ont été accusés de magie* (Paris, 1653), 34–37. Chapters are devoted, inter alia, to Zoroaster, Orpheus, Pythagoras, Numa Pompilius, Democrites, Empedocles, and Apollonius.

82. On Selden, see ch. II.1 above.

83. See Friedrich Niewöhner, *Veritas sive Varietas: Lessings Toleranzparabel und das Buch Von den drei Betrügern* (Heidelberg: Lampert Schneider, 1988), 179–187. See further F. Niewöhner, "Terror in die Herzen aller Könige!" Der Mes-sias und das Ende der Weltlichen Welt im Jahre 1210 nach Maimonides," in *Der Brief in den Jemen, Texte zum Messias,* ed. Sylvia Powels-Miani (Düsseldorf: Par-erga, 2002), 9–26. Maimonides does not use a single term, bur rather a series of different terms, to denote imposture.

84. See Herbert of Cherbury, *De religione gentilium: eorumque apud eos causis* (Amsterdam, 1663).

85. Thomas Hobbes, *Leviathan,* ch. 1, 12.

86. "Mahomet qui s'occupa avec tant d'ardeur à civiliser ses compatriotes," *Superstitions de tous les peuples du monde.* (Amsterdam, 1789), 84. On the same page, the Hottentots and the inhabitants of Madagascar are said to be in great need of "quelque législateur." See further the radical thinker Edward Elwall (1676–1744), who defends both the strict monotheism of the Muslims and their (as well as the Jews') willingness to suffer martyrdom for their faith at the hands of so-called Christians (*Idolatry Discovered and Detested . . .* (London, 1744 [1st ed. 1725]), 23–24.

87. Mark Silk, "Numa Pompilius and the Idea of Civil Religion in the West," in *Teologie politiche: Modelli a confronto,* ed. Giovanni Filoramo (Brescia: Morcel-liana, 2005), 335–356. See further G. G. Stroumsa, "Moses the Lawgiver and the Idea of Civil Religion in Patristic Thought," ibid., 135–148.

88. Josephus, *Against Apion,* II. 170–171. On this comparison, see further ch. VII.2 below.

89. Clement of Alexandria, *Stromateis* I.15. 71.1. Cf. ibid., I.15.69. 6–70.1 for Pythagoras and Zoroaster. See further Stroumsa, "Moses the Lawgiver,", 135–148. For Numa as a Pythagorean philosopher in ancient literature, see A. Willi, "Numa's Dangerous Books: The Exegetic History of a Roman Forgery," *Museum Helveticum 55* (1998): 139–172, esp. 144–145.

90. Clement, *Stromateis* I.15.71.1; Eusebius, *Praeparatio Evangelica,* IX.6.

91. Note that Voltaire's *Dictionnaire philosophique* refers to Numa under the entry "charlatan."

92. For the Syriac edition of this text, see *The Apology of Timothy the Patriarch before the Caliph Mahdi.*(Aarhus: Gabriel George, 1999). See further I. Shagrir, "The Parable of the Three Rings: A Revision of Its History," *Journal of Medieval History* 23 (1997): 163–177.

93. Friedrich Niewöhner has argued that Lessing's choice of the legend of the three rings was meant to counter the *Traité des trois imposteurs.* In his complex and fascinating book, Niewöhner suggests that the two traditions were intermingled in the Middle Ages and that the author of the original *De tribus impostoribus* was a second- or third-generation Marrano; see Friedrich Niewöhner, *Veritas sive varietas,* 399–403. Cf. Shagrir, "The Parable of the Three Rings," 175, n. 28.

94. There is a vast literature on the contemporary debate on orientalism; for a *mise au point,* see, for instance, Alec L. Macfie, *Orientalism* (London: Longman, 2002). For a rather different perception of orientalism from that of Said on the part of a Muslim scholar, see Hichem Djait, *L'Europe et l'islam* (Paris: Seuil, 1978). For a balanced history of Arabic and Islamic European scholarship, as well as a critical discussion of Said's book, see Robert Irwin, *For Lust of Knowing: The Orientalists and their Enemies* (London: Penguin, 2006).

VII. FROM CHINA TO ROME

1. On Matteo Ricci, see, for instance, Jonathan D. Spence, *The Memory Palace of Matteo Ricci* (New York: Viking, 1984). On the perception of China in early modern Western Europe, see J. D. Spence, *The Chan's Great Continent: China in Western Minds* (New York: Norton, 1998). On the early history of the Jesuit mission, see Liam Matthew Brockey, *Journey to the East: The Jesuit Mission to China, 1579–1724* (Cambridge, Mass.: Harvard University Press, 2007). See also Nicolas Standaert, ed., *Handbook of Christianity in China,* vol. 1 (Leiden: Brill, 2001).

2. On accommodation, see in particular David E. Mungello, *Curious Land: Jesuit Accommodation and the Origins of Sinology* (Honolulu: University of Hawai Press, 1989). See further Johannes Bettray, S.V.D., *Die Akkommodationsmethode des P. Matteo Ricci, S. J. in China* (Analecta Gregoriana 76; Rome: Aedes Universitatis Gregorianae, 1955).

3. See Louis Le Comte, S. J., *Nouveaux Mémoires sur l'Etat Présent de la Chine* (Paris, 1696), vol. I, 30: "les jésuites s'appliquèrent avec un zèle que nos ennemis ne peuvent s'empêcher de louer, à l'étude de la langue et des sciences du Païs." See

further Paul Rule, *K'ung-Tzu or Confucius? The Jesuit Interpretation of Confucianism* (Sidney; Boston: Allen & Unwin, 1986).

4. "De tous les peuples d'Orient, les plus polis et les plus spirituels sont les chinois." Charles Le Gobien, S. J., *Histoire de l'Edit de l'Empereur de la Chine en faveur de la Religion Chrestienne, avec un éclaircissement sur les honneurs que les chinois rendent à Confucius et aux morts* (Paris, 1698). For the comparative analysis of India, China, and Japan by the sixteenth-century Jesuit Alessandro Valignano, see Michael Lackner, "The Other as Manifold: A Jesuit's Comparative Approach to China, Japan, and India," (forthcoming). I wish to thank Professor Lackner for sending his article ahead of publication.

5. For instance, in Louis Le Comte, *Des Cérémonies de la Chine* (Paris, 1700), vol. 1, 148.

6. See, for instance, Athanasius Kircher, *China Monumentis qua sacris, qua profanis* (Amsterdam, 1667).

7. See, for instance, Le Comte, *Des cérémonies de la Chine*, 55, where he writes, referring to various prostrations and offerings to the dead and to Confucius: "nous crions d'abord anathème, idolâtrie, abomination. Quoyque assurément les chinois ne pensent à rien moins, qu'à un culte religieux." On the formation of the Western image of Confucius and Confucianism, see Lionel M. Jensen, *Manufacturing Confucianism: Christian Traditions and Universal Civilization* (Durham, N.C.: Duke University Press, 1997).

8. On Varro's *theologia tripertita,* and on *theologia civilis* in particular, see, for instance, Jörg Rüpke, *Die Religion der Römer* (Munich: Beck, 2001), 121–136. For more details, see further Burkhart Cardauns, "Varro und die römische Religion. Zur Theologie, Wirkungsgeschichte und Leistung der 'Antiquitates Rerum Divinarum,'" *Aufstieg und Niedergang der römischen Welt* II. 16.1 (Berlin: de Gruyter, 1978), 80–103. For further discussion, see ch. II.1 above.

9. Philippe Couplet, S. J., published a translation of Confucius's *Analects* (made in collaboration with three other Jesuits) under the title: *Confucius Sinarum Philosophus, sive Scientia Sinensis latine exposita* (Paris: Daniel Horthemels, 1687).

10. Joachim Bouvet, S. J., *Histoire de l'Empereur de Chine présentée au roi,* (The Hague: Meyendert Uytwerf, 1699), Dedicatory Epistle, 8.

11. Bouvet, *Histoire de l'Empereur de Chine,* 147–149: "le Christianisme, qui est la perfection de la Loy naturelle . . . La Religion [chinoise], si on la considère dans sa véritable origine, et selon ses légitimes principes établis par les anciens Sages de la Chine, et non selon l'idée qu'en ont à présent la plupart de leurs Docteurs modernes, ne diffère guère, ou même point du tout, de la Loy naturelle." In a sense, Matteo Ricci was trying to establish and "ethical theism" which could offer a common ground to Confucianism and Christianity. See C. Spalatin, "Matteo Ricci's Use of Epictetus' *Encheiridion,*" *Gregorianum* 56 (1975): 551–557. For a different kind of attempt at seeking parallels to Chinese doctrines in better-known religious literatures, see Theophilius Spitzelius, *De Re Literario Sinensium Commentarius* (Leiden: Petrus Hackius, 1660).

12. Nicoló Longobardi, *Recentissima de amplissimo regno Chinae item De Statu Rei Christianae apud Magum regem Mogor, et de morte Taicosamae Iaponionorum Monarchae* (Moguntia, 1601), "tum quod Chinenses maximum par-

tem sint athei, qui uti non credunt Pagodis, id est, bonzorum idolis, sic nihili quoque pendunt eorumdem ministros."

13. N. Longobardi, *Traité sur quelques points de la religion des Chinois* (Paris: Guérin, 1701). I quote according to the critical edition by Wenchao Li and Hans Poser in Gottfried Wilhelm Leibniz, *Discours sur la théologie naturelle des chinois* (Frankfurt: Klostermann, 2002), 113–156. See especially sect. 3, 121–122. Cf. Michel Tardieu, *Annuaire du Collège de France,* 2004–2005, 404. There is a huge bibliography on Leibniz's views on China. See, for instance, Olivier Roy, *Leibniz et la Chine* (Paris: Vrin, 1972).

14. Longobardi, *Traité,* sect. 14, 139.

15. Ibid., sect. 16, 141.

16. "le peuple le moins payen"; N. Trigault, S. J., *Histoire de l'Expédition chrestienne en la Chine* (Paris: Pierre Le Mur, 1618 [originally published in Latin, Rome: Christoph. Mangius, 1615]), ch. 10, 157: "De toutes les sectes des Payens, au moins qui sont venues à la connaissance de notre Europe, je n'en ay cy devant lu aucune, qui soit tombée en moins d'erreurs, qu'on lit le peuple de la Chine estre tombé les premiers siècles de son antiquité. Car je ly dedans leurs Livres, que dès le commencement les Chinois ont adoré une suprême déité, qu'ils appellent Roy du Ciel, ou d'un autre nom, Ciel et Terre." From this, Trigault concludes that the religion of the ancient Chinese was natural religion (ibid., 158). Later on in his work (ch. 11, 179–184 [116–126 in the Latin edition], he describes the fascinating dealings of Matteo Ricci with Chinese Jews. The latter, having heard of the Jesuits' presence and thinking they were some kind of "Reform Jews" sought to cultivate relations with them (hoping they would provide suitable matches for their daughters) and offered Ricci the title of Master of the Synagogue, on the condition that he gave up eating pork, removed the "portraits of a woman" from the Jesuit "synagogues" and stopped believing that the Messiah had already come.

On the place of natural religion in the Jesuits' understanding of Confucianism and its echoes in contemporary debates, see Daniel P. Walker, "The Survival of the Ancient Theology in Late Seventeenth-Century France and French Jesuit Missionaries in China," in his *The Ancient Theology: Studies in Christian Platonism from the Fifteenth to the Eighteenth Century* (London: Duckworth, 1972), 194–230.

17. Noël Alexandre, *Conformité des cérémonies chinoises avec l'idolâtrie grecque et romaine. Pour servir de confirmation à l'Apologie des Dominicains Missionaires de la Chine* (Cologne: Héritiers de Corneille d'Egmont, 1700), 84.

18. Ibid., Avant-Propos.

19. Ibid., 93.

20. A similar accusation of imposture against the Jesuits was made by the Reformed theologian Pierre Jurieu. See Th. Le Tellier, *Défense des nouveaux Chrestiens et des missionnaires de la Chine, du Japon, et des Indes, contre deux livres intitulez La morale pratique des Jésuites, et l'Esprit de M. Arnauld* (Paris: Estienne Michallet, 1687), 13. See further *La bonne foy des anciens Jésuites missionniares de la Chine, sur l'idolatrie des Chinois dans le culte qu'ils rendent à Confucius et aux Morts, Démontrée par des extraits fidèles des Livres des RR Pères Athanase Kirchere, Nicolas Trigault, Alexandre de Rhodes et autres* (Cologne, 1700).

21. On the "Querelle des rites," see, for instance, H. Bernard-Maître, S. J., "Chinois (rites)," in *Dictionnaire d'Histoire et de Géographie Ecclésiastiques*, vol. 12, 731–741 (1953). For a significant collection of polemical texts, see *Recueil des Pièces des differens de Messieurs des missions étrangères et des religieux de l'Ordre de S. Dominique touchant le culte qu'on rend à la Chine au philosophe Confucius* (Cologne: Jean Le Sincère, 1700). See further a pamphlet by Thomas Gage, *A Duell between a Iesuite and a Dominican* (London, 1651), which starts with the phrase: "*odia religionum sunt acerbissima.*"

22. The infatuation with things Chinese in the eighteenth century has given birth to a huge literature. For a good bibliography, see Bruno Neveu, "La Chine en Europe," *Dix-huitième siècle* 28 (1996): 135–140.

23. See, for instance, John Scheid, "L'impossible polythéisme: les raisons d'un vide dans l'histoire de la religion romaine," in *L'impossible polythéisme: Etudes d'historiographie religieuse*, ed. Francis Schmidt (Paris: Archives contemporaines, 1983), 425–457. Richard Pfeiffer, *History of Classical Scholarship* (Oxford: Oxford University Press, 1970; 2 vols.), lacks a serious discussion of the early modern study of Roman religion. Similarly, I found few significant remarks on our specific topic in Otto Gruppe, *Geschichte der klassischen Mythologie und Religionsgeschichte* (Leipzig: Teubner, 1921), and in the respective introductions of Georg Wissowa, *Religion und Kultus der Römer* (Munich: Beck, 1902) and Kurt Latte, *Römische Religionsgeschichte* (Munich: Beck, 1960). Rüpke's excellent synthetic work on Roman religion, *Die Religion der Römer,* does not discuss the history of scholarship.

24. On Renaissance mythographies, see Jean Seznec, *The Survival of the Pagan Gods: The Mythological Tradition and Its Place in Renaissance Humanism and Art* (New York: Pantheon, 1953), 219–256 [originally published as *La survivance des dieux antiques* (London: Warburg Institute, 1940)].

25. See also Barnabé Brisson, *De formulis et solemnibus populi Romani, verbis libri VIII* (1583). This book is mentioned by Wissowa in the introduction to his *Religion und Kultus der Römer*, 8–11.

26. See Francis Haskell, *History and Its Images: Art and the Interpretation of the Past* (New Haven; London: Yale University Press, 1993), 16–17. I have been able to consult Du Choul's book in the Italian translation: *Discorso della religione antica de Romani* (Lyon, 1659).

27. If Numa can be compared with Solomon, one could have expected a parallel between Romulus and David. I have not encountered such a parallel anywhere, however.

28. See, for instance, Sabine MacCormack, "Limits of Understanding: Perceptions of Greco-Roman and Amerindian Paganism in Early Modern Europe," in *America in European Consciousness* (1493–1750), ed. K. Ordahl Kupperman (Chapel Hill: University of North Carolina Press, 1995), 79–127.

29. "E come la osssservanza del culto divino e cagione della grandezza delle republiche . . ." (*Discorsi sopra la prima deca di Tito Livio*, I. XI. 18). I have used the following edition: Niccolo Machiavelli, *Discorsi sopra la prima deca di Tito Livio* (Milan: Rizzoli, 1984), 91–94. The text was first published in 1517.

30. See John G. A. Pocock, *The Machiavellian Moment: Florentine Political Thought and the Atlantic Republican Tradition* (Princeton: Princeton University Press, 1975); on Machiavelli's views of Roman and Christian religion, see esp. 191–218.

31. See ch. II.1 above.

32. See, for instance, Justus Lipsius, *De Vesta et Vestalibus Syntagma* (Antwerp, 1603); *non vidi.*

33. The work was in gestation for a long time; it appeared, in ten volumes, in 1719. J. S. Semler's Latin translation, *Antiquitates Graecae et Romanae,* was published in Nuremberg in 1757. On Montfaucon's work, see A. Schnapp, *La conquête du passé: aux origines de l'archéologie* (Paris: Carré, 1993), 287–292.

34. As far as I can see, it was first published in London, 1699. It would be republished as late as 1768 in Dublin (11th ed.).

35. Peter Gay, in his *The Enlightenment: An Interpretation: The Rise of Modern Paganism* (New York: Knopf, 1966), 479, notes this interest on the part of the *philosophes,* but does not really discuss it. Together with Montesquieu, he mentions, of course, Gibbon, as a major figure having seriously reflected on Roman religion. I do not deal with Gibbon's views here as they are well known.

36. "Comme la religion et les lois civiles doivent tendre principalement à rendre les hommes bons citoyens" (*De l'Esprit des lois,* XXIV, 14).

37. "Je trouve cette différence entre les législateurs romains et ceux des autres peuples, que les premiers firent la religion pour l'Etat, et les autres l'Etat pour la religion." Referring to the *Politique des Romains dans la religion,* Mark Silk, "Numa Pompilius and the Idea of Civil Religion in the West," in *Teologie politiche: Modelli a confronto,* ed. Giovanni Filoramo (Brescia: Morcelliana, 2005), 335–356, describes how Montesquieu transformed Numa into an Erastian (ibid., 349).

38. Josephus Flavius, *Contra Apionem,* II, 170–171.

39. On *theokrateia* in this text, see Hubert Cancik, "Theokratie und Priesterschaft: die mosaische Verfassung bei Flavius Josephus, c. Apionem 2, 157–198," in *Religionstheorie und Politische Theologie, III: Theokratie,* ed. Jacob Taubes (Munich: Fink and Paderborn: Schoningh, 1987), 65–77, and Yehoshua Amir, "*Theokrateia* as a Concept of Political Philosophy: Josephus' Presentation of Moses' *Politeia,*" in *Studia Classica Isarelica* 8–9 (1985–86): 83–105. Much has been written on the concept. See, for instance, Bernhard Lang, "*theokrateia,*" in *Handbuch religionswissenschafticher Grundbegriffe,* vol. 5, eds. Hubert Cancik, Burkhard Gladigow, Karl-Heinz Kohl (Stuttgart: Kohlhammer, 2001), 178–189.

40. *Politique des Romains dans la religion,* in Montesquieu, *Oeuvres complètes,* ed. Roger Caillois (La Pléiade; Paris: Gallimard, 1949), 90.

41. "divinité suprême, dont les divinités du peuple n'étaient qu'une participation": *Politique des Romains dans la religion,* 87. The concept of *Etre suprême,* which would have such a future during the French Revolution, already appears in Bayle's *Dictionnaire historique et critique,* first published in 1696. See there, for instance, *s.v.* "Caïnites," (IV, 307a).

42. "esprit de tolérance et de douceur qui régnait dans le monde païen."

43. "une charge civile," *Politique des Romains dans la religion,* 89.

44. "Les rois de Rome avaient une espèce de sacerdoce," ibid., 91.

45. "Rome se soumit elle-même aux divinités étrangères, elle les reçut dans son sein; et, par ce lien, elle s'attacha des peuples qui la regardèrent plutôt comme le sanctuaire de la religion que comme la maîtresse du monde," ibid., 91.

46. "pour ne pas multiplier les êtres," ibid., 92.

47. "Les Romains, qui n'avaient proprement d'autre divinité que le génie de la République," ibid., 92.

48. See what Montesquieu has to say about Japanese festivals: "[Je remarque] que les fêtes du Japon sont plutôt civiles que sacrées, plus employées à la joie et à se visiter qu'aux exercices religieux: car ils ont une idée, qui me plaît beaucoup, que les Dieux se plaisent à voir les hommes gais dans leurs jours de fêtes." *Mes pensées*, in Montesquieu, *Oeuvres complètes*, 1553.

49. See *Grande Encyclopédie*, I.14, 86.

50. *Superstitions de tous les peuples du monde, ou tableau philosophique des erreurs et des faiblesses dans lesquelles les superstitions tant anciennes que modernes, ont précipités les hommes de la plupart des nations de la terre* (Nouvelle éd., t. IV,; Amsterdam, 1789), 19.

51. Nicolas-Antoine Boulanger, *L'antiquité dévoilée par ses usages: examen critique des principales opinions, cérémonies, et institutions religieuses et politiques des différents peuples de la terre*, vol. 3 (Amsterdam, 1766), bk. 5, ch. 1, 97–152. Diderot wrote the introduction to the book. On Boulanger, see Frank E. Manuel, *The Eighteenth Century Confronts the Gods*, (New York: Atheneum, 1967), 210–227: "Nicolas-Antoine Boulanger: the Trauma of the Flood."

52. Charles De Brosses's *Du Culte des Dieux Fétiches ou parallèle de l'ancienne Religion de l'Egypte avec la religion actuelle de Nigritie* had been published anonymously in 1760, without indication of a place (new ed., Paris, 1988); see also the Italian translation and commentary, with a rich introduction by Alessandra Ciattini and Stefano Garroni, *Sul culto degli dei feticci* (Rome: Bulzoni, 2000). I was unable to consult Jean Lévesque de Burigny, *Mémoire sur le respect que les Romains avaient pour la Religion*. In his *Histoire de la philosophie payenne, ou sentimens des philosophes et des peuples payens les plus célèbres sur Dieu, sur l'âme, et sur les devoirs de l'homme* (2 vols., Hague, 1724), this author sought to emulate the Christian apologists of the first centuries. In a later edition (Paris, 1754), *Histoire de la philosophie payenne* has become *Théologie payenne*. On Montesquieu on China, see Jonathan I. Israel, *Enlightenment Contested: Philosophy, Modernity and the Emancipation of Man, 1670–1752* (Oxford: Oxford University Press, 2006), 660.

53. On Constant's opus, see Pierre Deguise, *Benjamin Constant méconnu: Le Livre De la Religion* (Geneva: Droz, 1966). The chapter specifically dedicated to Rome is "*De la Religion,*" vol. 4, pt. 11, ch. 7, 294–343.

EPILOGUE

1. In Anna Maria Jones, ed., *The Works of Sir William Jones*, vol. 1 (London, 1799), 229–231. On "Oriental Jones" and his pioneering work, see Alexander Murray, ed., *Sir William Jones, 1746–1794: A Commemoration* (Oxford; New

York: Oxford University Press, 1998). Cf. Wilhelm Halbfass, who writes in his *India and Europe: An Essay in Understanding* (Albany: State University of New York Press, 1988), 22–23: "The study of Indian religion and philosophy, in particular, continued to follow the Greek patterns . . . Even such pioneers of modern Indian studies such as W. Jones, Anquetil Duperron and Chr. Lassen still combined the retrospective study of the Greek and Roman materials with the direct, future-oriented exploration of the Indian sources."

2. See Francois Bernier, *Voyages, contenant la description des états du Grand Mogol* (Paris: 1670), vol. 2, *Lettre à Monsieur Champlain, touchant les superstitions, estranges façons de faire, et doctrines des Indous ou gentils de l'Hindoustan*, 140. On Nobili, see Ines G. Županov, *Disputed Mission: Jesuit Experiments and Brahmanical Knowledge in Seventeenth-century India* (New Delhi: Oxford University Press, 1999).

3. I quote from Gruzinski, *Les quatre parties du monde*, 246. Cf. ibid., n. 131, 486.

4. Bernier, *Voyages*, 101–106.

5. Ibid., 135–140.

6. M. de la Créquinière, *Conformités des coutumes des Indiens orientaux avec celles des Juifs et des autres peuples de l'antiquité* (Bruxelles: de Bacher, 1704). The book was immediately translated by John Toland and published under the title: *The Agreement of the Customs of the East Indians with Those of the Jews Being the First Essay of This Kind, towards the Explaining of Several Difficult Passage in Scripture and Some of the Most Ancient Writers by the Present Oriental Customs* (London: W. Davis, 1705). On La Créquinière's book, see Prosper Alphandéry's [untitled] detailed review in *Revue de l'Histoire des Religions* 87 (1923): 295–305. Alphandéry's text is particularly interesting from our perspective, as it shows that historians of religions of a previous generation could show excellent knowledge of the early stages in the history of scholarship, referring, for instance, to Spencer, or to Fontenelle (Salomon Reinach, quoted by Alphandéry, 294).

7. Ibid., p. IV.

8. The full title reads: *A Comparison of the Institutions of Moses with Those of the Hindoos and Other Ancient Nations, with Remarks on Mr. Dupuis's Origin of All Religions, the Laws and Institutions of Moses Methodized, and an Adress to the Jews on the Present State of the World and the Prophecies Relating to It* (Northumberland: A. Kennedy, 1799). In his *Adress to the Jews*, Priestley announces the future glorious restoration of the Jews (who "are destined, in the wise councils of God, to be the first of nations," 195) in Palestine, following "the breaking up of the present European monarchies, the extinction of the papal power, and the overthrow of the Turkish Empire." See there, 407.

9. Priestley, ibid., 33–48.

10. For the persistent importance of Bochart among eighteenth-century theologians, see, for instance, Johannes David Michaelis, *Spicilegium geographiae Hebraeorum exterae post Bochartum* (Göttingen, 1769), which also presents itself as a commentary on Gen 10.

11. On the role of the sons of Noah in this transformation, see Bruce Lincoln, "Isaac Newton and Oriental Jones on Myth, Ancient History, and the Relative Prestige of Peoples," *History of Religions* 41 (2002): 1–18.

12. See ch. 5, 1, and Bruce Lincoln, "Isaac Newton and Oriental Jones."

13. Charles de Brosses, *Du culte des dieux fétiches, ou parallèle de l'ancienne religion de l'Egypte avec la religion actuelle de Nigritie* (Paris, 1760). On the context of the book and its influence, see Alessandra Ciattini's and Stefano Garroni's introduction to their annotated translation: Charles de Brosses, *Sul culto degli dei feticci*, 9–92. (Cf. ch. VII, n. 52 above).

14. Boulanger's *L'Antiquité dévoilée* was published posthumously in 1766 in Amsterdam (publisher: Marc Michel Rey). The idea of "revealing antiquity" seems to have been rather popular at the time. See, for instance, Le citoyen d'Yervale [Jean Sylvestre Bailly], *L'antiquité dévoilée par les principes de la magie naturelle, ou Théorie des anciens législateurs, qui a donné l'idée des Jardins des Hespérides et du Paradis terrrestre* (Paris[?]: an VIII [1799–1800]).

15. See Frank E. Manuel, *The Eighteenth Century Confronts the Gods* (New York: Atheneum, 1967), 221, who refers to Nicolas-Antoine Boulanger's *Essai sur le gouvernement, où l'on prouve l'influence de la religion sur la politique* (1788).

16. "Nous avons d'abord examiné les fêtes séculaires des Mexicains: elles ont servi à expliquer les usages que les Romains et les Juifs pratiquaient en pareille occasion sans en connaître la raison." Nicolas-Antoine Boulanger, *L'antiquité dévoilée*, III, 417 (bk. 6, ch. 2).

17. On Dupuis and his work, see Manuel, *The Eighteenth Century Confronts the Gods*, 259–270.

18. See in particular Jean Starobinski, "Fable et mythologie aux dix-septième et dix-huitième siècles dans la littérature et la réflexion theorique," in *Dictionnaire des Mythologies*, Yves Bonnefoy, ed. (Paris: Flammarion, 1981), 390–400.

19. Nicolas Fréret, "Mythologie," *Encyclopédie, ou Dictionnaire raisonné des sciences, des arts et des métiers,* vol. 10 (Paris, 1765), 924a-926a.

20. "Mais l'Encyclopédie considère encore, sous ce nom ["Mythologie"] tout ce qui a quelque rapport à la religion payenne, c'est-à-dire, les divers systèmes et dogmes de Théologie, qui se sont établis successivement dans les différens ages du paganisme; les mystères et les cérémonies du culte dont étaient honorées ces prétendues divinités, les oracles," ibid., 924a.

21. "La Mythologie, envisagée de cette manière, constitue la branche la plus grande de l'étude des Belles-Lettres," ibid.

22. Eusebius, *Praeparatio Evangelica*, I. 10. On Sankhuniaton and Philo of Byblos, see. Albert I. Baumgarten, *The Phoenician History of Philo of Byblos: A Commentary* (EPROER 89; Leiden: Brill, 1981). On early modern scholarship on Sanchuniaton, see Corrine Bonnet, "*Errata, absurditates, deliria et hallucinationes* (J. Scaliger). Le cheminement de la critique face à la mythologie phénicienne de Philon de Byblos: un cas problématique et exemplaire de *testis unus*," *Anabases* 11 (2010), forthcoming.

23. Gregorio Garcia, O. P. *Orígen de los Indios del Nuevo Mundo (Valencia 1607)*, IV, 22, in particular 237. See further Georgius Hornius, *De originis Americanis libri quatuor* (1652), for whom the Phoenicians came to America from the West, the Chinese from the East, and the Scythians from the North. Cf. Don Cameron Allen, *The Legend of Noah: Renaissance rationalism in art, science and letters* (Urbana: University of Illinois Press, 1949), 128. See chs. I.1 and IV. 1 above.

24. See Peter G. Bientenholz, *Historia and Fabula: Myths and Legends from Antiquity to the Modern Age* (Leiden: Brill, 1994), 232 ff.

25. Etienne Fourmont, *Réflexions sur l'origine, l'histoire et la succession des anciens peuples: Chaldéens, Hébreux, Phéniciens, Egyptiens, Grecs, etc. jusqu'au tems de Cyrus* (Paris, 1747). See further the developments on the "philosophia Phoenicarum" in Jacob Brucker, *Historia critica philosophiae* (Augsburg, 1742), I.

26. See Bruce Lincoln, "The History of Myth from the Renaissance to the Second World War," in his *Theorizing Myth: Narrative, Ideology, and Scholarship* (Chicago and London: University of Chicago Press, 1999), 47–75; see esp. 47.

27. August Christian Wolf, *Prolegomena ad Homerum* (Göttingen, 1795). Translation by Anthony Grafton, Glenn W. Most, James E. G. Zetzel (Princeton: Princeton University Press, 1985).

28. On the development of anti-Semitic categories and habitus in nineteenth-century classical scholarship, see in particular Martin Bernal, *Black Athena: The Afro-Asiatic roots of classical civilization* (London: Free Association Books, 1987).

29. See Marc Cluet, ed., *La fascination de l'Inde en Allemagne, 1800–1933* (Rennes: Presses Universitaires de Rennes, 2004). Note that in the age of colonialism, nineteenth-century ethnographic scholarship too-often exhibits not only anti-Semitic tendencies but also clear indications of racist attitudes. See, for instance, David Chidester, *Savage Systems: Colonialism and Comparative Religion in Southern Africa* (Charlottesville: University Press of Virginia, 1996). See further Christopher Herbert, *Culture and Anomie: Ethnographic Imagination in the Nineteenth Century* (Chicago; London: Chicago University Press, 1991).

30. See, for instance, Michel Despland, *L'émergence des sciences de la religion: la monarchie de Juillet: un moment fondateur* (Paris: L'Harmattan, 1999). See further Tomoko Masuzawa, *The Invention of World Religions; or, How European Universalism Was Preserved in the Language of Pluralism* (Chicago and London: University of Chicago Press, 2005). As David Chidester has shown in *Savage Systems: Colonialism and Comparative Religion in Southern Africa*, the act of comparison itself gave rise to the notion of the purportedly distinct and concrete identities.

31. "Nous sommes encore loin de pouvoir souder solidement tous les anneaux de cette longue chaîne; les orientalistes et les philologues classiques ne peuvent encore se tendre la main par-dessus la Méditerranée." F. Cumont, *Les religions orientales dans le paganisme romain* (4e. ed.; Paris: Geuthner, 1929), 16. On Cumont's conception of religion, see Corinne Bonnet, "'L'histoire séculière et profane des religions' (F. Cumont): Observations sur l'articulation entre rite et croyance dans l'historiographie des religions de la fin du XIXe siècle et de la première moitié du XXe siècle," in *Rites et croyances dans les religions du monde romain (Entretiens Hardt sur l'antiquité classique, LIII)*, ed. John Scheid (Vandoeuvres-Geneva: Fondation Hardt, 2006).

32. R. Schwab, *La renaissance orientale* (Paris: Payot, 1950).

33. F. F. Ellinwood, *Oriental Religions and Christianity* (New York: C. Scribner's Sons, 1892).

34. "L'élément barbare ne se glisse qu'en prenant l'apparence et la couleur du mythe grec. Plus tard, les cultes étrangers ne se donneront plus la peine de changer

de vêtement. Isis, Serapis, Mithra viendront trôner en pleine Grèce, sous leur accoutrement exotique, comme pour préluder a ces monstrueux amalgames où les superstitions de l'Orient et celles de l'Occident, les excès du sentiment religieux et ceux de la pensée philosophique, l'astrologie et la magie, la théurgie et l'extase néo-platonicienne semblent se donner la main." Ernest Renan, *Etudes d'histoire religieuse* (3rd ed.; Paris: Michel Lévy Frères, 1858), 48. On Cumont and nineteenth-century orientalists, and in particular Renan, see Corinne Bonnet and Françoise Van Haeperen *Introduction historiographique* to their new edition of Cumont's *Religions orientales dans le paganisme romain* (Turin: Aragno, 2006), xxx–xliv.

35. "Elles prenaient l'homme tout entier." Cumont, *Religions orientales,* 40.

36. "L'unité de la race indo-européenne, en son opposition avec la race sémitique, reconnue dans les religions comme dans les langues, servira désormais de base à l'histoire des religions de l'antiquité." Renan, *Etudes d'histoire religieuse,* préface, v.

ACKNOWLEDGMENTS

Most chapters in this book are based on the following articles, which have been significantly revised and expanded for inclusion here. They are listed in chronological order.

"Jewish Myth and Ritual and the Beginnings of Comparative Religion: The Case of Richard Simon," *Journal of Jewish Thought and Philosophy* 6 (1997): 19–35.

"Comparatisme et philologie: Richard Simon et les origines de l'orientalisme," in *Le comparatisme dans l'histoire des religions*, eds. François Boespflug and Françoise Dunand (Paris: Cerf, 1997), 47–62.

"The Birth of Manichaean Studies: Isaac de Beausobre Revisited," in *Studia Manichaica*, eds. Ronald E. Emmerick, Werner Sundermann, and Peter Zieme (Berlin: Akademie Verlag, 2000), 601–612.

"*Homeros Hebraios:* Homère et la Bible aux origines de la culture européenne (17e-18e siècles)," in *L'Orient dans l'histoire religieuse de l'Europe*, eds. Mohammed Ali Amir-Moezzi and John Scheid (Turnhout: Brepols, 2000), 87–100.

"John Spencer and the Roots of Idolatry," *History of Religions* 40 (2001): 1–23.

"Richard Simon: From Philology to Comparativism," *Archiv für Religionsgeschichte* 3 (2001): 89–107.

"Thomas Hyde and the Birth of Zoroastrian Studies," *Jerusalem Studies in Arabic and Islam (JSAI)* 26 (2002): 216–230.

"Enlightenment Perceptions of Roman Religion," in *Epitome tes oikoumenes: Studien zur römischen Religion in Antike und Neuzeit*, eds. Jörg Rüpke et al. (Potsdam: Steiner, 2002), 193–202.

"*Antiquitates Judaicae:* Some Precursors of the Modern Study of Israelite Religion," in *Jews, Antiquity, and the Nineteenth Century Imagination*, eds. Hayim Lapin and Dale B. Martin (Bethesda: University Press of Maryland, 2003), 17–32.

"Noah's Sons and the Religious Conquest of the Earth: Samuel Bochart and His Followers," in *Sintflut und Gedächtnis*, eds. Martin Mulsow and Jan Assmann (Munich: Fink, 2006), 307–318.